VIRTUAL TEAMS

Books by Jessica Lipnack and Jeffrey Stamps

Virtual Teams: Reaching Across Space, Time, and Organizations with Technology (1997)

The Age of the Network: Organizing Principles for the 21st Century (1994)

The TeamNet Factor: Bringing the Power of Boundary Crossing Into the Heart of Your Business (1993)

The Networking Book: People Connecting with People (1986)

Networking: The First Report and Directory (1982)

Holonomy: A Human Systems Theory (1980, *by Jeffrey Stamps*)

VIRTUAL TEAMS

*People Working Across Boundaries
with Technology*
Second Edition

JESSICA LIPNACK AND JEFFREY STAMPS

JOHN WILEY & SONS, INC.

New York • Chichester • Weinheim • Brisbane • Singapore • Toronto

This publication is designed to provide accurate and authoritative
information in regard to the subject matter covered. It is sold with
the understanding that the publisher is not engaged in rendering
legal, accounting, or other professional services. If legal advice or
other expert assistance is required, the services of a competent
professional person should be sought.

ISBN 0-471-38825-4

Printed in the United States of America.

10 9 8 7 6 5 4 3 2 1

To
Miranda Shoket Stamps
and
Eliza Lipnack Stamps

ACKNOWLEDGMENTS TO THE
SECOND EDITION

Many people helped to bring out this second edition very quickly. For those who also helped on the first edition, your **names** appear in bold type.

First our interviewees who squeezed us into impossibly busy schedules: Robin Abrams, Ventro; David Anderson, SETI; Keoki Andrus, The Launch Group; Tom Botts, Shell U.K.; Russ Baird, General Electric; Joe Bonito, Pfizer Pharmaceuticals; **Harry Brown,** EBC Industries; Phil Carroll, Fluor Corporation; Russ Conser, Shell Technology Ventures; David Gensler, Gensler; Steve Glovinsky, UNDP; Meta Greenberg; **Al Gilman; Loree Goffigon,** Gensler; Terry Heng, Motorola; Mike Howland, Applied Knowledge Group, Inc.; Hank McKinnell, Pfizer, Inc., Bart Piepers, Concept-international; Linda Pierce, recently of Shell Oil Company; **Howard Rheingold; Dennis Roberson,** Motorola; David Sibbett, Grove Associates; Tom Steffens, U.S. Special Operations Command; Bob Stone, Public Strategies Group; Marcel Storm, Concept-international; John Whyte, Ernst & Young International; **Gary Wheeler,** Perkins & Will; and Carol Willett, Applied Knowledge Group, Inc.

Sun Microsystems receives its own paragraph for offering "graceful" virtual responses in Internet time: Sandy Belknap, Suzie Grace, Ed Hoff, Scott Johnson, **Jim Lynch,** John McEvoy, Al Ormiston, Peter Pazmany, Daniel Poon, Terry Sheridan, Linda Short, and Adrienne Whitmore, and Lynda Kaye of Ketchum Thomas.

Likewise Buckman Labs, where **Bob Buckman,** Steve Buckman, Sheldon Ellis, Dean Didato, Mark Koskienemi, Tim Meek, Drew Mohler, Edsen Peredo, and **Alison Tucker** all participated in interviews that **Barbara McConville** arranged.

Three of our clients have given us opportunities to test these ideas in real time: Shell, where we have had the privilege of working with the "gifted class," led by Tom Botts and Linda Pierce, along with Carolyn Yapp and Tom Kunz; at Pfizer Central Research Group, where Jim McCarthy introduced us to Linda Benner, Glenn Gross, Eric Erickson, and Simon Rhodes; and General Electric, where Russ Baird and our colleague Steve Schoonover of Schoonover Associates have worked side by side with us to adapt the work to that culture.

Thanks to the miracle of e-mail, a number of fast typers answered questions almost immediately: Jay Albany, Kozmo.com; **Peter Buesseler, Brian Stenquist** and **Terri Yearwood** of Minnesota Department of Natural Resources; John Kamensky, National Performance Review; Stewart Brand; **Sture Karlsson,** TetraPak; **John Lawrence,** UNDP; **Will Hutsell** and **Nancy Ledford,** Eastman Chemical Company; **Robert Gilman,** Context Institute; Allegra Fuller Snyder and Jaime Snyder, Buckminster Fuller Institute; **Frank Starmer; Timm Esque;** Steve Kelman; William A. Himmelsbach, VHA Metro; Richard Huntington and Ralf Maurer, Results Management Services; Diane Lesner and Mohan Kumar, Motorola; Oonagh Butler; Pfizer; Diane Wright, Ernst & Young International; and Darren Roberts, Gensler. We also appreciate the help of Henrik Bendix, **Doug Engelbart,** Leon Navickas of Centra, and **AnnaLee Saxenian.**

Steve Teicher, with whom we explored these ideas at Apple, and **Bernie DeKoven,** a pioneer in virtual work, get special awards for interviewing themselves online.

Lisa Kimball, Caucus Systems, receives a paragraph of *her* own. An old friend and colleague whom two of our interviewees name as the "greatest networker" they know, Lisa's ability to connect people and ideas is brilliant.

Peter Wiley opened doors once again, introducing us to key interviewees. **Reuben Harris,** Naval Postgraduate School, remains a trusted adviser.

Patricia Nelson and Ike Williams, our agents at Palmer and Dodge, with help from Hope Denekamp, make the book contracting process easy. **Jeanne Glasser** is our editor again, guiding us through the work ways of our venerable publisher, **John Wiley & Sons.**

Christine Furry, North Market Street Graphics, made book production easy. Thank you, Chris.

Anthony Antonuccio; Dan Bathon; Scott Benson; Bob Buckman; Adam Crescenzi; Jon Fleischmann, Frank Andryauskas, and BagelNet; David Haber; Tim Kilcoyne; Eric Lipnack; Jack and Mary Merselis; Mike Schield; Jay Riley; Ross Whiting; and, particularly, Bruce Bedford, said yes to our company at exactly the right moments for this book.

Our friends and family, Rosalind and Jake Joffe; Emily LaMont and Jean Nichols of The Jane Gang; Sylvia Nasar; Linda Russell; Judy Smith; Susan Stamps; Ron and Cathy Cordes; and Kate and Ben Taylor all have done their parts, too.

We are blessed with our colleagues at NetAge: Don Arnoudse, who cofounded NetAge with us, Jennifer Chambers, Keith Ehrlich, Kate Harper, Dan Kaplan, Carrie Kuempel, Jeff Schriesheim, and **Annie Marascia,** whose name not only belongs in bold but in bright lights for the many hours she has put in bringing this book to a close. This is the fourth time Annie's been part of a book with us, and the first that she's led support. Impeccable work, Annie. Karl Grossner, Lisa Schiffman, and Celia Wiley all contributed to NetAge in ways that made writing this book much easier. And **Bill** and **Pam Johnson,** early and longtime supporters of our work, remain in our lives, making connections.

Finally, bows to our daughters, **Eliza** and **Miranda,** yet again, now completely grown. This book's publication marks Miranda's graduation from college and Eliza's entrance into her senior year. The Acknowledgments of our books record your life progressions that bring inexpressable joy and love from your very proud parents.

JESSICA LIPNACK
JEFFREY STAMPS

West Newton, Massachusetts
July 2000

ACKNOWLEDGMENTS TO THE
FIRST EDITION

A book is a complex project. We have been blessed with the help of many people who are our colleagues in trying to understand the new organizational phenomenon of virtual teams.

Jim Childs, our editor and publisher on our last two books and our publisher once again on this one, was the first to express interest in the book. This long collaboration continues to inspire us. Jeanne Glasser, our editor, has been an enthusiastic source of energy and encouragement. Publishing with the nearly two-centuries-old John Wiley & Sons is an honor.

Reuben Harris, chair of the Department of Systems Management at the Naval Postgraduate School and a dear friend, gave us early and invaluable guidance on how to approach this topic. Bob Buckman of Buckman Laboratories calls Reuben "America's best-kept business secret." Perhaps we can help put an end to that secret.

A group of devoted people took the time to line edit the manuscript for no reason other than that the topic interests them. They are the kinds of friends everyone wants. Their hard-hitting queries caused us to write a better book: Kathi Albertini, Frank Alla, Rick Berenson, Don Brown, Curt Crosby, Bernie DeKoven, David Paeper, Pete Rogers, Caryn Siegel, Gary Wheeler, and Peter Wiley. This was the second time Kathi and Frank provided this service to us. And Frank did triple duty—we also interviewed him for the book, as we did Curt, Bernie, and Gary. David and Caryn generously volunteered from afar. Pete, a member of our extended family, did such an extraordinary job as an editor that he may have yet another career in his future. Peter went far beyond the call of duty. Abiding thanks to all of you.

Cathy and Ron Cordes, colleagues and dear friends, were unwavering in one commitment. Weekend after weekend during the book's writing, they made sure that we ate at least one very delicious meal. They also made us laugh. We use their wonderful product TeamFlow in all our projects. Judy Smith, another extended family member, called innumerable times to ask how it was going, as she has on all our books. For nearly 20 years, she has housed us when we visit our publisher.

As part of our research for this book, we interviewed 75 people. We thank them for the time they took to carefully consider the complex questions that face organizations when people work across boundaries:

Rebecca Adamson, First Nations Development Institute
Frank Alla, Management Insight Technologies
Haluk Ariturk, The Acacia Group
Fern Bachman, Jr., Apple Computer
Victor Baillargeon
Larry Banks, Hewlett-Packard
Erik Boe, Apple Computer
Antonia Bowring, Women's World Banking
C. Marlin Brown, Sun Microsystems Computer Company
Don Brown, NASA/Johnson Space Center
Harry Brown, EBC Industries, Inc.
Bob Buckman, Buckman Laboratories
Peter Buesseler, Minnesota Department of Natural Resources
Rita Cleary, The Learning Circle
Camen Criswell
Curt Crosby, Sun Microsystems Computer Company
Bill Crowley, SunExpress
Richard Dale
Earnest W. Deavenport, Eastman Chemical Company
Bernie DeKoven, Mattel Media
Timm Esque, Intel Corporation
Susen Fagrelius, Susen Fagrelius & Associates
Mike Fraser, National Oceanographic and Aeronautics Administration
George Gates, Core-R.O.I.

David Gibson, SunService
Al Gilman
Diane Gilman, Context Institute
Loree Goffigon, Gensler
Rogier Gregoire
Georgene Hanson-Witmer, Boise Cascade
Nadia Hijab, United Nations Development Programme
Will Hutsell, Eastman Chemical Company
Jean Ichbiah, Textware Solutions
Sture Karlsson, Tetra Pak Converting Technologies
Rob Lau, Steelcase, Inc.
John E. S. Lawrence, United Nations Development Programme
Celestine Lee, SunService
Ed Lynch, Identity Clark County
Jim Lynch, Sun Microsystems
Kathleen Shaver Madden, Foundation for International Nonlinear
    Dynamics
Pamela Martin, Apple Computer
Ginger Metcalf, Identity Clark County
Arch Miller, Executive Forum
Jeff Morgan, *Men's Health*
Charles T. Nason, The Acacia Group
Ike Nassi
Dan Nielsen, Voluntary Hospitals of America
Aron Oglesby, Dance New England
Lynda Popwell, Eastman Chemical Company
Leslie Rae, Science Applications International Corporation
Frank Reece, US TeleCenters
Dennis Roberson, NCR Corporation
Charlie Robertson, Red Spider
Judi Rosen, CSC Index
Rustum Roy, Pennsylvania State University
Harry Saal, Smart Valley, Inc.
Scott Simmerman, Performance Management Company
Nova Spivack, EarthWeb
John Steele, Eastman Chemical Company

Brian Stenquist, Minnesota Department of Natural Resources
Evelyne Steward, The Calvert Group
Cane Strahorn, Boise Cascade
W. R. Sutherland, Sun Microsystems
Steve Teicher, Apple Computer
Steve Tromp, First Community Bank/BankBoston
Alison Tucker, Buckman Laboratories
Valerie Veterie, Pfizer, Inc.
Jim Vezina, Carnegie Group, Inc.
Art Wagner, Blue Sky Advertising/Marketing, Inc.
Irvenia Waters, APM, Inc.
Linda J. Welsh, Sun Microsystems
Clay Wescott, United Nations Development Programme
Gary Wheeler, Perkins & Will/Wheeler
Scott Woods, SunService
Yurij Wowczuk, Wheeling Jesuit University
Tern Yearwood, Minnesota Department of Natural Resources
Tom Young, SunService

Another group provided help in connecting us with our interviewees: Calvin Colbert, Voluntary Hospitals of America; Rod Cox and Lynn Swartzlander, Executive Forum; George Brennan, Bob Farkas, Debbie Moore, and Lola Signom, NCR Corporation; Patricia Fiske, Worldwide Partners; Alex Kleinman, The Advisory Board Company; Bahman Kia and Jose Cruz-Osorio, United Nations Development Programme; Barbara McConuville, Buckman Laboratories; Tony Pribyl, *Men's Health;* and Patricia Sutton and Nancy Ledford, Eastman Chemical Company.

Annie Marascia, who has lived through three books with us, has been tireless—a sophomore in high school when she started with us, she is now a sophomore in college. Lorienne Schwenk has been a talented research assistant.

Nancy Marcus Land at Publications Development Company of Texas has made this book's production a virtual team dream.

Marion Metcalf and Lisa Kimball provided key insights as they both did on our last book. Thank you, sisters. Al Gilman was an early and perceptive contributor to the ideas.

Our clients and their organizations are where we learn the most. We are especially grateful to Steve Teicher and Pam Martin at Apple for many hours spent on various continents exploring virtual teams in practice. Gail Snowden of First Community Bank/BankBoston and Heather Stoneback of Rodale Press have taught us things we could only know by learning about their organizations. We are also grateful to our many friends at Steelcase, including Bill Miller, Doug Parker, and Kyle Williams. Steelcase makes it possible for virtual teams to work together. Our 15-year connection with The Calvert Group has taught us how values sustain virtual teams. Our colleagues with whom we organized "MassNet: Collaboration for the CommonWealth" showed our local community what can happen when diverse organizations decide to cooperate.

Finally, as has been the case with all our books, our daughters, Liza and Miranda, are the point of it all. Having lived with these ideas since they were born, they know more than anyone.

JESSICA LIPNACK
JEFFREY STAMPS

West Newton, Massachusetts
February 1997

CONTENTS

LIST OF ILLUSTRATIONS

INTRODUCTION

You're in a start-up or a dorm, an old brick-and-mortar or a high-flying tech company, your own attic or a garage; working your e-business with people here, there, and everywhere, on the phone, in e-mail, trading URLs like Pokémon cards.

We know that the people you work with often are more than 50 feet away, which means distance causes you problems. You work with people in other organizations all the time. These boundaries pose problems, too: Who decides what and when?

> *With these problems come new possibilities—and a chance to change the world.*

Change

Imagine radically improving your ability to team. Improve our collective capabilities and we improve everyone's ability to solve their own problems. With better virtual teams, we can accept challenges with others that are impossible alone. This is true for all of us, regardless of where we sit in our own little worlds. Executive teams guiding multinationals, IPO-bound kids, or product development teams working for customers. It's true whether you are only a few entrepreneurs in a virtual network or a participant in a multicountry NGO working on sustainability.

This book is about people like you who work across boundaries of all kinds everywhere. You do so with the help of and in response to technology. In the years since we began our research, writing, and practice of networked organizations, the technologies to connect them have become ubiquitous. Evidence is plain in the new address that exists nowhere in physical space:

www.virtualteams.com

Technology extends our capabilities, but organizing to do things together is only human. The most profound change of the new millennium is in the way we're organized. Trends thousands of years old suddenly shift as a literal new universe with its own civilization materializes in thin air right in front of us.

Society established the bigger-is-better trend in organizational design long ago. At the dawn of the agricultural era, the average size of human groups suddenly grew from a multimillion-year-old pattern of 20-person camps to farming towns of hundreds and cities of thousands. "Bigger" has had a largely uninterrupted run for 12,000 years—until right now. In a comparative nanosecond of evolutionary time, centralization and hierarchy have slammed into global limits. We've decentralized our work, distributing into perpetually re-forming groups.

Communication technologies and computer networks underwrite this pregnant moment. The Internet and the web, astonishingly enough, are bringing individuals, small groups, and chosen communities back to center stage.

As more people interconnect online, we increase our capacity for both independence and interdependence. Competition and cooperation both thrive in our new culture. The global Internet fosters numberless combinations of groups of every size, sponsoring mass individuality and massive participation. Cyberspace is a vast new civilization, containing both places of commerce and an already deep social life mirrored in countless conversations.

In time, virtual teams will become the natural way to work, nothing special. Virtual teams and networks—effective, value-based, swiftly reconfiguring, high-performing, cost-sensitive, and decentralized—will profoundly reshape our shared world. As members of many virtual groups, we will all contribute to these ephemeral webs of relationships that together weave our future.

The twenty-first-century trend is "smarter together." Smarter teams are the cells of larger intelligently networked organizations. Ignite intelligence and we change the world.

The dictionary reminds us what this word actually means. *Change,* likely Celtic in origin, derives from the Latin *cambiare,* meaning "to exchange, barter."[1] "Give and take reciprocally," the word *change* implies.

From the Source

Since the days of the acoustic-coupler, 300-baud modem, we've been talking to and working with the people who've literally developed the Internet and to those who are developing the capacity to use it organizationally. The subject of our conversations? Organizations of the future, "networked communities,"[2] virtual teams.

As writers, researchers, consultants, speakers, and software designers, we have known and been part of many different organizations. From engagements that lasted only a few hours, to projects of a few days, to multiyear programs, we have acted as "drop-in" outside experts, involved facilitators, core members, and leaders of customer teams. We have worn corporate badges, received passwords to internal computer systems, and occupied offices within our clients' buildings. We have even worn the badges of our customers' customers.

We've been at this a long time, so long that our babies are now the age of the dot-commers.

Indeed, we've been writing this book for 21 years.

In 1979, we began to contact people and gather information for our first book. *Networking* (Doubleday, 1982) was condensed, rewritten, and published in England as *The Networking Book* in 1986.[3] Grassroots, nonprofit, and intergovernment organizations are the database for that work. Since then, we've received vast amounts of material from all around the world, heard from people in most of the world's countries, and visited with networkers from every continent, including Antarctica.

We've had to keep our "kook-a-lator" handy, as Lisa Kimball, founder of Caucus Systems (and the person whom Howard Rheingold, author of *The Virtual Community,* calls "The greatest networker I know"), names it. When you're looking at the future, errant life forms appear. People have told us about their plans to solve the global bandwidth problem by bouncing signals off the millions of meteors orbiting the earth; we have for a dozen years received occasional snail mail from someone in California who signs notes only with a J; and then there is the "mail art" network from Japan.

The shift is everywhere. Soon after the release of our 1982 study of 1,600 grassroots networks, we found that the leading edge of change to networked organizations was ironically shifting to big business as the impact of technology on teaming accelerated. Our consulting practice has grown there ever since.[4] In 1992, we began a trilogy of new books drawing primarily on our research and experiences in business: *The TeamNet Factor* in 1993, *The Age of the Network* in 1994, and *Virtual Teams* in 1997.

With *Virtual Teams,* we come close to the heart of our personal experience. We have always worked in small groups across distances and organizational boundaries. We ourselves are a core group: a married twosome who are also parents, friends, coauthors, and business partners.

Our experience as a team of two began long ago at the dawn of our relationship in 1968. We met as students at Oxford University—Jessica, an undergraduate from Antioch College (and Pottstown, Pennsylvania), and Jeff, a Fulbright Scholar (from Gilford, New Hampshire).

In 1972 we married and moved with our first "personal computer"[5] into the house we're still living in. We began working life as independent entrepreneurs with a consulting business based on software, in the process writing a book to help states and municipalities assess the viability of cable television systems in their communities.[6]

Working in networks and virtual teams has always been a way of life for us. We've partnered with thousands of people on a wide range of projects for clients in every sector—from Shell Oil to the Presbyterian Church

(U.S.A.) to the United Nations. Working on the Internet has been a way of life since 1980 when we joined Murray Turoff, Starr Roxanne Hiltz, and others online as part of Electronic Information Exchange System (EIES), an early ARPANET experiment in virtual communities.

Networks have also been a way of thought for us. Since our first book, we've worked to link our evolving conceptual framework to general systems theory. Systems theory is about principles and patterns of organization that apply across disciplines—notoriously difficult boundaries to cross. Jeff's 1980 book (and doctoral dissertation), *Holonomy: A Human Systems Theory,*[7] came out the day we received our very first networking-book contract.

Systems principles have helped us recognize common patterns in the awesome variety of the newly emerging forms of human organizations. They underlie a powerful conceptual model of networks: people, purpose, links, and time. We've been testing variations on this model ever since we got started.

Good theory is very practical. It enables quick adaptation of shared learning to always-unique circumstances. Theory also provides a consistent, shareable, knowledge-based approach to develop and manage virtual teams. This is a way to test ideas and improve practical applications for collaborative work.

With the net and the web, practice explodes and now drives theory toward a new science of human interaction.

Failure

Everything that goes wrong with in-the-same-place teams also plagues virtual teams—only worse.

Egos, power plays, backstabbing, hurt feelings, low confidence, poor self-esteem, leaderlessness, and lack of trust all harass virtual teams. When communication breaks down, people must take measures to repair it. It is just that much more difficult to communicate across distance and organizations using tenuous electronic links.

Virtual teams are not a panacea for teams that do not work. We are not cheerleading for this gee-whiz-it's-a-new-and-better-way-to-do-things approach. Rather, our goal is to understand networks and help people succeed in virtual teams. Virtual teams are already prevalent and will be only more so in the years ahead.

> *Teams that do not recognize they are virtual are likely to fail.*

Many of the problems that virtual teams face are ancient in nature. Millennia of face-to-face exchanges inform most of our collective experience, tools, techniques, and lore. Methods that work to correct problems that arise in face-to-face teams are only the starting points for virtual teams.

We address the problems of *virtual* teams as directly as possible and recount what people we know are doing to solve them. We encourage you to draw on what you already know about working in groups. What do you do if a virtual team member is not participating? The same thing you do if a face-to-face team member is not participating. Communicate with that person by any and every means possible, find out what is preventing participation, and solve the problem. A body of detailed knowledge and techniques is accumulating rapidly in virtual organizational development (virtual OD).

We do not go into detail about *why* companies and other kinds of organizations form virtual teams. So far as we can tell, people create distributed groups for myriad reasons—such as when things go wrong, when the people required to do a project are spread out, and when networking is just the most effective, flexible, or only way to get things done in a particular instance.

Our purpose here is to present excellent examples of virtual teams and our thinking about how these new types of groups *can* excel. Thus, this is a book that shares best practices, not one that critically examines corporate behavior. In time, as the body of information grows, critical analysis will be essential to secure the foundations of network knowledge.

Reader Options

This book has five sections:

- Here and in Chapter 1 we discuss introductory material and the need for virtual teams.
- Chapters 2 to 5 put networks and virtual teams into larger contexts of organizational evolution, discussing trust, and the importance of place.
- Chapters 6 to 9 expand on each of the four parts of the model—time, purpose, people, and links.
- Chapters 10 to 12 offer practice and theory.
- Chapters 13 and 14 stretch our thinking ahead.

But people do not necessarily read books sequentially by chapter.

People have different ways of learning. Some prefer stories based on experience, some theory, others need practical ideas, and most of us need some vision. Readers of our previous books will recognize how we develop material for these four cognitive styles[8]:

- Vision (insight)
- Stories (experience)
- Principles (theory)
- How-to (practice)

While we have written a traditional book crafted with loving care to flow from beginning to end, we also offer choices. Some of you will begin at the end, some in the middle, still others will skim.

Key ideas in the book are in pullout quotes that look like this.

- See Chapter 1, "Why?," for an introduction to virtual teams, a definition, some examples, a sense of the big picture, and a taste of the principles.

- For those who wish to begin with the "Future," go straight to Chapter 14 at the end. Skim your way there for a quick overview of the book. Read the headings, look at the illustrations, and note the pullout quotes.
- If you prefer stories, turn to the opening sections of the chapters. There you will find case studies of Sun, Shell Oil, Buckman Labs, Motorola, Eastman Chemical, and Pfizer, among others, with impressive and sometimes astonishing virtual teams, some historical stories, and one scenario of team life on the web.
- Do you prefer concepts and models? Read the ends of the chapters. There you will find an integrated framework to understand and manage this new form of organization. We include important contributions from other writers and researchers. For deep divers, go to Chapters 11, "Navigate," 12, "Theory," and 13, "Think."
- Want to apply ideas immediately and practically? Get going in Chapter 10, "Launch," with a seven-step process for starting and launching virtual teams.

More? Click Here

We are still amazed it happened so fast. Need more information than we can possibly include between the covers of this book? Care to practice some of the things we write about? Check out our web site at www .virtualteams.com. That short script is all you need. And if you're reading this while connected to the net, that link and all the others are hot, so just click and go.

This book fits together with our own virtual team space on the web. On our site you will find information about the following:

- How to launch and sustain virtual teams
- How to design networked organizations
- Where to find the community of virtual team practitioners
- Our network of partner organizations, who, with us, provide the "people operating system™" for twenty-first-century work

As in our previous books, we provide extensive endnotes so that you can go directly to our sources and learn more for yourself. The abundance of material available through the web makes it easy for us to track down many facts and locate specific sources. We include the web addresses in the book references, old style. Online, new style, these references are only a click away.

Online web books will rapidly become a common complement to printed ones. To join this vanguard, just point your browser to our site—and connect.

---

www.virtualteams.com reflects our vision of a world that works collaboratively.

CHAPTER 1

WHY

The Way to Work

"Nothing is ever changed except by making it obsolete."
—Attributed to Bucky Fuller[1]

In a "whisper of time,"[2] the predictions of futurists have become front-page news. Work as we have known it for centuries is obsolete. If you participate in teleconferences, communicate via e-mail, or share information with colleagues on web sites, you work virtually.

What is driving this new way to work?

Continuous, wild change at breakneck speed; new, newer, and newest technology; globalization *and* localization; and a demand for social as well as financial performance all typify business in the Internet Age.

"We can't solve twenty-first-century problems with nineteenth-century organizations."[3]

Shapeshifters

Like Odo, the Star Trek shapeshifter on *Deep Space Nine,* work is dematerializing and rematerializing right in front of us. For centuries we've worked primarily face-to-face for the same boss. Now we work virtually across distance and reporting lines.

Neighborhood

The global communications web that makes everyone on the planet neighbors—long imagined in science fiction—is in place. Nearly every country in the world has Internet connections (Figure 1.1).[4] Coupled with such connectivity is the sheer complexity of markets and customers. Nothing is simple anymore.

Figure 1.1   Global Internet Map

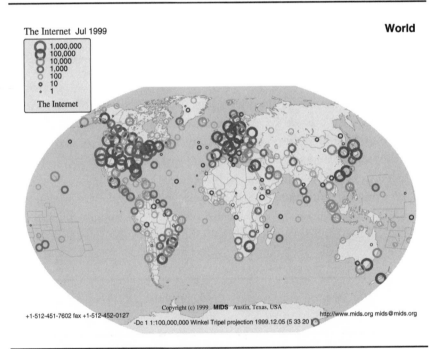

The Internet Jul 1999

1,000,000
100,000
10,000
1,000
100
10
1

The Internet

World

+1-512-451-7602 fax +1-512-452-0127

Copyright (c) 1999 **MIDS** Austin, Texas, USA

http://www.mids.org mids@mids.org

-Dc 1 1:100,000,000 Winkel Tripel projection 1999.12.05 (5 33 20

It is now *rare* that individual companies carry out projects completely by themselves. Our own Internet start-up at its seed stage involves a core group of 10 people surrounded, linked to, and intersecting with 10 times that many more, each of whom has his or her own tens and hundreds of connections. Our project, like yours, crosses internal and external boundaries, drawing together members situated anywhere and everywhere.

Consider Valent Software, the emblem of twenty-first-century business. Its 10 employees *never* really colocate, yet within three years they turn a $700,000 investment into a $45 million sale to a major web portal. They provide Lycos Clubs, a community-building facility critical to Lycos's success.

Both J. Scott Benson, the CEO, and the company's chief technology officer, Chris Williams, lived in Massachusetts. "[T]he president [Anthony Antonuccio] was parked in Utah, the engineering team [led by Leigh Turner] was based in [Columbus,] Ohio and a handful of other employees worked out of their dining rooms and basements," writes Julie Flaherty in a large feature in the *New York Times*.[5]

"The 'workplace' consisted largely of cell-phone calls, e-mail correspondence and meetings in hotel lobbies. Except for a small office in Woburn, Mass., that it rented primarily as a place to receive mail, Valent did not have a brick of property to its name."

Or consider the Dutch company that Bart Piepers[6] writes about: "Right now I (Bart) am sitting in [sic] the train. Marcel [Storm, his colleague and coauthor] and I live about 20 miles apart. All the people (about 10) that work for Concept-international in different projects live within a radius of about 150 miles in three different countries. Our goal is to become as international and virtual as possible."[7]

Allegiance to our projects is as strong as it is to our companies. "Who's the boss?" is a good question—if you even have one, or perhaps you have two. You may be part of a small team that sees something that needs to be done—then does it. All of you are leaders in your own domains. Perhaps you all work for different people who themselves cross in ever wider circles of connections. Before long, you may find yourself like the Time Based Notification team at Sun Microsystems, where 60 percent of the members move on to its successor project, the Glass House Gang (see Chapter 5, "Place"). They do their first project on a shoestring and the next with strong corporate investment.

Move in Sun's case is a relative concept. People don't "move" anywhere physically. Instead, trust binds them, as they can live primarily online. This is where the team works. To work on Sun's Time Based Notification team means to go online. Face-to-face meetings become ever more precious and increasingly rare.

The nine-to-five office as we have known it is more often than not—not. Fully one-third of the 25,000 dwellings in our city, Newton, Massachusetts, house white-collar businesses. "White-collar" itself is on the express train to antiquity. What with casual Fridays having crept backward through the workweek, even suit manufacturers are called upon to update their lines. You attend meetings in your pajamas, talk with people halfway around the globe, use insomnia to catch up online, worry about headset not car-seat comfort, and partner with people you have never—and may never—meet face-to-face. An MCI commercial got it right: the woman with "bed head" and in her slippers on a con call dreading the advent of videoconferencing.

Human beings have always worked and socialized in face-to-face groups. Now people no longer must be in the same building—never mind on the same continent—to work together. They belong to *virtual teams* that transcend distance, time zones, and organizational boundaries.

Ernst & Young International's chief information officer, John Whyte, "cut travel by 35 to 40 percent" with virtual teams. "We were spending well over a million a year." He compensates by breaking up his 100-person, three-continent, globe-circling organization into 10 teams of 10 people each. This unleashed what Whyte calls "lots of cross projects that are much closer to real events." Each team chooses its own ways to work virtually—weekly conference calls (the tried-and-true default communication technology for virtual teams), face-to-face, instant messaging on the Internet, videoconferencing, online whiteboarding.[8]

The use of teams is on the rise, and with a quarter of a billion people on the planet already online,[9] the face-to-face aspect of normal working relationships is changing dramatically.

Until the advent of the web, such ways of working were simply impractical. A few thousand lines of computer code written in Switzerland in

1989 to help out a network of particle physicists[10]—coupled with unprece-dented advances in technology—have transformed the world.

The web gives people the unprecedented ability to work together independent of place. Consider the implications of these numbers:

- In four years, the number of adult Americans online went from 9 percent to 56 percent.[11] They have access to a billion pages of content worldwide.[12]
- By 2005, there will be a PC and a wireless device in use for nearly every half-dozen people on the planet.[13]
- Internet growth itself—defined as the number of new host computers that comes online daily—is finally slowing.[14] Meanwhile, connections among people and computers are staggering and uncountable, "perhaps on the order of 100 percent annually," according to Matrix Information and Directory Services.[15]

At last, the planet is wired—though "wired" is not entirely accurate either. Much of our interconnection is wire*less*. Connected, linked, matrixed. We are the future now.

Distance-defying communication opens up vast new territory, un-bounded by space or time, for "working together apart."[16] For the first time since nomads moved into towns, work is diffusing rather than concentrating. Officially, we have moved from the Industrial to the Information Age.

Smart Work

New business models give rise to new organizational con-figurations that belie the classical competitive market.

Working across boundaries—in partnership over corporate lines with vendors and customers, in alliances with complementary enterprises, and in deals with direct competitors—is the norm.

To test this, play "Name the Competitors" in a big deal or new alliance. Shell and Texaco stations across the street from each other are owned by Motiva (retail East), Equilon (retail West), and Equiva Services, which the otherwise competing majors own together. Bank of America and Robertson Stephens comanage deals, such as the IPO for Internet Capital Group, in which Merrill Lynch is the lead underwriter. GM, Ford, and Daimler-Chrysler set up a joint venture for web-based supply chain management.[17]

There, on the web, business boundaries blur. "Name the Collaborators" is the new game. Lycos, the portal that goes public 10 months after it is founded,[18] is itself a network of 13 other sites. Ask Jeeves a question (you don't need the "http://," the ".com," or even the Jeeves—the three letters *ask* alone will get you there) and you go to a WebCrawler site with banner ads for AT&T's online billing and Barnes & Noble, each just a finger flex away. Click and you're on a site in Tasmania or Toledo (Ohio) or Toledo (Spain). Place itself has dissolved, a current reality declared in *The Death of Distance*,[19] the 1997 book by *Economist* writer Frances Cairncross.

"We don't have all the good ideas in the world," says Hank McKinnell, president and chief operating officer of Pfizer, the pharmaceutical company.[20] So his company has scores of cross-company collaborations with its competitors and promotes intracompany networking. "No matter how effective any one person is," McKinnell says,

"All of us are smarter than any of us."

When is the last time you worked on a project with only people whose offices or desks are near yours? Boundaries that separate functions and divisions within companies have become porous. People rarely work only by themselves. Even solo, independent contractors spend most of their time working in teams.

The boundary-crossing, virtual team is the new way to work.

When General Electric does a late-1990s assessment of critical capabilities for the future, it finds that "the skill of leading virtual teams is the new requirement," according to Russ Baird, head of GE's Six Sigma Quality Training at the corporate Leadership Development Facility at Crotonville,

New York. "We zeroed in on the skills for continued success and it became obvious that teams are more virtual than they've ever been and are rapidly becoming more so. Projects are becoming larger with multiple subteams crossing lots of functional as well as geographic boundaries. We have and need very diverse teams to address projects of this scope."[21] Since 1998, GE has been training its famous "Black Belts" in virtual teaming.

Jack Welsh, the company's chairman and chief executive officer, who all but brought the word "boundaryless" into the business lexicon, has made e-commerce the top priority for all the companies in the portfolio before he retires in 2001. His organizational-networking imperative is paying off—GE is the first company in history to report $10 billion in earnings.

Virtual Gap, Virtual Edge

With the technology and connections finally in place, we now face the truly difficult part of the virtual equation—the people element. Real groups are notoriously complicated. Anything that goes wrong face-to-face also goes wrong online, only faster and less gracefully. Going virtual[22] is for most people a wrenching experience, both in adapting to new technologies and in adopting new behaviors and working relationships.

Take a typical team, make it virtual, expect trouble. Working across organizational boundaries introduces communications and motivational problems. You immediately need to compensate just to bring the team up to the level of performance of a colocated team—to bridge the virtual gap (Figure 1.2).

There is good news. The steps that teams take to cope with their network nature—using collaborative technologies and designing flexible organizations—not only compensate for capabilities lost, but also establish the basis for extraordinary performance. By solving today's problem of poor performance among virtual teams, we prepare ground for tomorrow's dramatically smarter teams with a virtual edge.

Virtual teams are the people-operating systems for the twenty-first century.

Figure 1.2   The Virtual Edge

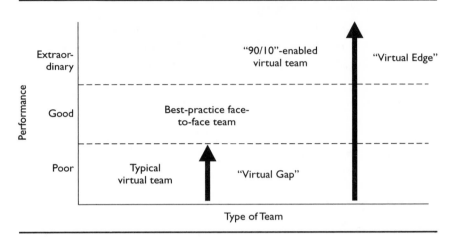

Like GE, many companies—large and small, old-line and broadband-new—are experimenting with different ecologies of people, organization, and technology. Of considerable consequence is how those who had access to collaborative technology from the beginning use it today. A stop on this journey is a company that always has lived by the technology it makes.

eSun

Sun Microsystems has been betting on cyberspace since its 1982 inception. The first computer it ever shipped had the basic protocols for Internet communication built into it.[23]

Sun maintains an extraordinary information infrastructure to support its 37,000-person company. What other companies manage with more people, Sun tries to achieve with better and faster communication. Some Sun people say they no longer use paper at all.

When web technology exploded in the mid-1990s, Sun embraced it immediately everywhere. Several thousands of web servers went up in a matter of months all across the company. CEO Scott McNealy's 1995 corporate-wide injunction "to operate on Internet time without compromising quality" set a daunting new standard. The company also launched a multiyear initiative to solve customer problems with cross-company teams, SunTeams (see Chapter 5, "Place").

Dot-comming Ourselves

Looking to the new millennium, the company decides to up the ante for itself again in 1999. Sun will become eSun. All customers will come to one Sun front door on the web: www.sun.com. Everything else will flow from there—from online purchasing for all products to MySun.com, where customers and employees will customize their own ways to work with, through, and at Sun.

The job of "dot-comming ourselves" falls to a Sun vice president and general manager from the field. Al Ormiston is just wrapping up his last special assignment—reintegrating Sun's aftermarket business into another Sun group. SunExpress had been spun off and now the company has brought it back inside. "There was lots of emotion," Ormiston recalls. "Then the world exploded and everything was 'portal this' and 'portal that.' " The reintegration unwittingly but opportunistically gives birth to the next major change in the way Sun does business.

eSun, now a corporate-wide initiative "to transform the way we do business,"[24] begins as an aftermarket online catalog for the System System Products group, following the SunExpress reabsorption. Then Sun's president and chief operating officer Ed Zander asks Ormiston to "take what you've learned and roll it out across the whole company."

The company that promises to "dot-com" everyone else faces a very big challenge. It has to break new ground faster than its customers and its competitors. That means the entrepreneurial models in each of Sun's groups have to be pulled into one set of best practices across Sun. Ormiston leads that charge.

Ormiston describes the early eSun meetings: "Imagine 30 to 40 people in the room with their arms crossed saying, 'I'm here but I don't want to be here.' " Providing "one face of Sun" to customers means consistency across areas that always have been autonomous in the groups—inventory, purchasing, pricing, terms, and conditions, not to mention back-end technology choices that are extremely important to engineers. "They could all do their own thing in the past. It was a real tangled web," but after a few years, Ormiston says, "the web forced everyone to take the same approach. We needed a single web-buying environment." Instead, Sun then had four major divisions, each with its own sales organization and business rules. With eSun, customers come in through the same front end and are guided to the store, the communities, and other Sun services.

Communication

To avoid setting up a "central group with a mandate-like structure," Ormiston instead sets up a virtual organization. First he works with each Sun group to name its own eSun vice president, who reports both to the division and to eSun, along with eSun Program Management Offices that have the staffs to maintain them.

"Half the battle is being understood," Ormiston says, so he also asks each division to name a person to the eSun Communications Council. About 15 people from across the company (including public relations, advertising, marketing communications, and human relations) convene. "The idea is 'from our mouth to their ears.' Their whole job is to be sure that our messaging is consistent," he says. "Every time we have 10 new slides explaining what eSun is, they go out through the council."

The Communications Council owns the eSun site. "We post everything there," he says, "Notes, meetings, road maps. It's the first time that we've publicly put up everything we do and it causes heartburn. We agreed up front to publish a monthly online eBook with the good, the bad, and the ugly so that we can maintain a nonparochial point of view. Collaborative teaming is just beginning to work with all the products."

Communication is intense. The eSun program management officers have two or three conference calls a *week*. The same group comes together face-to-face for a day twice a month. And the directors from each division meet face-to-face for a day once a month.

How many people does it take to add the *e* before the company's name? Ormiston estimates that a little more than 1 percent of the company is involved in eSun, 400 in total, with 100 on the business side and three times that many on the information technology side.

"When I came in from the field to do eSun, I assumed that everything would change because the president said so. No. It doesn't work that way when people understand that everything they've been doing for years is going to change or go away."

Even for a company like Sun that's lived by the net since Day One, transitioning to the new world is a challenge. Ormiston calls eSun "a mixed conversation. Some people feel very strongly aligned and some people feel like they're getting run over. There's lots of culture and psychology that goes on. We haven't solved it completely yet, but we're trying."

It's refreshing to talk to people at Sun. They admit that life is difficult in the Network Age and earnestly use their own behavior and technology to improve.

"eSun is the new Sun, and when we're done," he pauses, then continues, "I guess we'll never be done."

Internet speed, indeed.

How It Feels

In a word, it feels different. It's a blurry, messy world and everyone is scrambling to catch up.

New Leaders

The younger generation may have a natural advantage in the new world, but leadership in the morphing business environment remains complex.

"In a networked organization leaders have to use influence and powers of persuasion, which is much more complex and much more challenging than giving orders," says Phil Carroll, chairman and chief executive officer at Fluor Corporation. (Carroll was president and CEO at Shell Oil Company in the 1990s—see Chapter 2, "Networks"). "Young leaders have the ability to operate in this new environment. They recognize that they're not working on the authoritarian model."

Leaders must think differently about themselves, Carroll says. "You are not the source of all wisdom." He calls it an emotional challenge "if you are predisposed to want to exercise leadership from the more authoritarian model. If that's what you want to be, you'll find this other kind of leadership difficult and very frustrating because at times it's slower and not as efficient and you don't get your way. And for some people that is a problem."

Tom Botts, who worked for Carroll at Shell and is now head of Shell U.K.'s Gas Directorate, talks about "unleashing leadership capacity." When he took over as treasurer of Shell Oil Company, he tore down the walls on two floors of Shell's headquarters in Houston, redesigning the space for flow and communication. He did the same thing at Shell U.K.'s headquarters in London nine months after he took on his post there, including removing the walls around his own office. "Doing away with the trappings of power like a big office helps dispel the notion that leadership only rolls down from top," Botts says. "Leadership capacity is buried in the organization and it needs to be unleashed. When you do that, people step to the front with ideas and actions that are pretty imaginative and that others might not have thought them capable of in the past."

Two generations of leaders, old-line company, new thinking.

Pace

Robin Abrams, a self-described "gray-hair," has grown up with the Internet, switching courses and careers with the times. Originally a banker, Abrams came to Chemdex as chief operating officer from the presidency of Palm Computing (makers of those handheld devices that people stare and poke at during meetings). Before Palm, she was president of Hewlett-Packard's VeriFone, one of the original virtual companies. (Its product is entirely virtual—the electronic banking system for credit card purchases—and they have created a culture to match.) Prior to Palm, she ran sales on various continents for Apple. Never mind that she has a law degree and a bachelor's in science.

We first met Abrams in 1995 at the launch meeting of Apple's international engineering group in Tokyo. She headed Apple's sales and marketing in Asia and stopped by the meeting on her way from Hong Kong (where she, her husband, and two young daughters then lived) to Apple's Research and Development campus in Cupertino, California. Even though Abrams was riding the crest of Apple's wave in Asia with market share above 20 percent, she dragged her own suitcase behind her through Tokyo's subway maze and jumped into the conversation within moments of entering the meeting.

Eight months after she came to Chemdex in June 1999, Abrams changed jobs again, to the same position in Ventro Corporation, of which Chemdex is just a part. Ventro is one of the new breed of "business-to-business vertical marketing companies."[25] Chemdex is one of the verticals.

Chemdex is a nifty business idea that would be simply unthinkable without the Internet, web-friendly databases, and a sufficient population of people online. It is the ultimate food co-op for the life sciences industry. It allows enterprises, researchers, and suppliers to network in an industry whose supply chain has been classically inefficient. It's hard for suppliers to find their customers; it's even more difficult for the customers to place their orders. Enter Chemdex, which

- Digitizes more than a million SKUs spread across the suppliers' numerous 5-pound paper catalogs.
- Equips customers to easily access them by placing icons on their PC desktops.
- Builds the business rules of each participating company into their online use.

"Researchers should be inventing, not paging through catalogs," Abrams remarks. By ephemeralizing the process, Chemdex dramatically reduces expenses from an average of "$80 to $120 down to $40 to $60 for a purchase order."

Abrams is using videoconferencing more than ever before for interviewing, customer meetings, and negotiating contracts. "I've never done that before, but the customer's time is more precious than mine. You just don't have to do everything face-to-face."

Until Chemdex, Abrams had never negotiated a single contract without meeting her partners face-to-face. "Momentum is so important now," she says. "You don't have six weeks to build bridges." Abrams demonstrates this urgency even in her speech. Equipped with a headphone and typing at top speed using electronic shorthand, it's hard to take down her words as rapidly as she fires them out.

"You have to be sure to hire people who are pretty savvy with people skills," she says. "Interviewing now is painting an opportunity and giving the candidate tools to make the assessment. It's a 50/50 deal. They're interviewing you as much as you're interviewing them."

Success in this world requires new business sensibilities. "Gross margin is a rule to be broken," she explains. "In the old mainframe days, we expected gross margins to be 60 points, 15 points in PC days. Our model is 5 points of operating profit. How does that work? By delivering a high volume of transactions."

The business pace "creates a phenomenal level of energy," she says, with people putting in six days a week. And it requires trust. "Visibility, visibility, visibility," she suggests, extolling the value of face-to-face. "People need to see you."

Ventro, like many similar companies, has a great cultural challenge: "To blend the talent between young bright minds and the gray-hairs," she says. "The management team has to be ready, willing, and able to learn. The pioneer is always tweaking the model, so you have to hire people willing to learn and course-correct on the fly.

"There's no looking back over your shoulder after making a decision. You have to be adept and speedy at conflict resolution because momentum is such an asset. You're with a bunch of 32- to 35-year-olds, bright and willing to break all the rules and ask all the right questions. But you still have to surround them with a sufficient level of experience in channel strategy, brand building, and product management while keeping this momentum going. If you had all bright 32-year-olds or all bright gray-hairs, it wouldn't work."

Bridging the Virtual Generation Gap

The need for adult supervision is a new organizational requirement in the twenty-first century. Before we know it, 10-year-olds will be running the world. Perhaps they already are.

Since the 1990s, a new generation has come into business positions previously reserved for people two or three times their ages. Why? Because the new entrepreneurs have the ideas and the skills to work in the new way—but not yet the business experience to apply them. There's room for both generations.

Rear Admiral Tom Steffens, director of the Center for Intelligence and Information Operations at the U.S. Special Operations Command in Tampa, Florida, has his own experience of the generation gap: "I always find that I am about two thoughts behind in any 'chat session' I have with my son, who is a sophomore at Virginia Tech.

"The under-30-somethings are more likely to be more computer-facile than their more senior leaders, who may not even have the simple skill of rapidly pointing and clicking (and perhaps even typing). Of course, no leader wants to look incapable of anything, much less using a computer, which every third grader can do, so if the collaboration tool requires you to master Windows or whiteboarding or Internet chat while dealing with the time lag that is inherent in much of it (compared to a telephone) . . . well then, just forget it and call everyone to your office or HQ for a conference, even if it takes a few days or weeks before everyone can fit it into their schedule."[26]

The gap goes even deeper for Steffens. It's conceptual as well. In his view, the older generation thinks linearly, whereas "two generations behind ours think differently . . . they look at things as whole concepts and visualize the picture (still worth a thousand words, or is it a thousand terabytes?). So the whole collaboration concept works faster with them."

From the perspective of the younger generation, it's equally complex. "We have 26-year-olds who've only ever had one job before managing large groups of very smart grads just a few years younger," says Jay Albany, who is 23, and works in a dot-com.

It's not uncommon for people in Albany's position in start-ups to work 16-hour days. This is fast work but it's not necessarily smart, which is where the voice of experience makes its contribution in the Internet economy.

The Virtue of Virtual

The word *virtual* has made it into everyday language. Virtual has the same Latin root as *virtue*, an intimately personal quality of goodness and power. Its archaic meaning is an apt definition for successful virtual teams: "effective because of certain inherent virtues or powers."

Here are three contemporary meanings for *virtual:*

- "Not real" but "appears to exist," something "that appears real to the senses" but is not in fact
- "Not the same in actual fact" but "in essence," "almost like"
- Virtual as in "virtual reality," a recent meaning invented for an emerging capability

When we use the term *virtual,* we do *not* mean it in the first sense, the way an old American TV commercial for audiotape did: "Is it live or is it Memorex? With Memorex, you can hardly tell." With a virtual team, you can tell: Virtual teams are living, not Memorex. They are most definitely *real* teams, not electronic representations of the real thing.

The "almost like" definition, as in "they act virtually like a team," is on target. There are similarities, but also critical differences. A virtual team conjures up a different picture from that of people in the same organization working together in the same place. People also use *virtual* to connote the same-but-different nature of a "virtual corporation," "virtual organization," and "virtual office."

The third and newest meaning of *virtual* attests to forces that have moved teams into an altogether different realm of existence—virtual reality—or, more precisely, *digital* reality. Electronic media together with computers enable the creation of new kinds of spaces. They are real to the groups that inhabit them, yet are not the same as physical locations.

Virtual teams go digital.

Cyber Real

With electronic technology, virtual teams provoke entirely new ways of working and organizing. To physically travel across distances faster than the speed a person can walk requires technologies and authorities—captains of ships that sail across oceans to new worlds, engineers guiding trains that chug over mountain ranges to new frontiers, aircraft pilots for safe takeoffs and landings.

In cyberspace, you are captain; you steer.

The word *cyberspace* is telling. Although the term *cybernetics*, meaning "steersman" in Greek, was first coined by Norbert Weiner and his colleagues in the early 1940s to describe the "science of control and communication in both animals and machines,"[27] no "cyber" words appeared in the 1955 *Oxford Unabridged Dictionary*. Four decades later, *The New Shorter Oxford* defines *cyberspace:* "space perceived as such by an observer but computer generated and having no real existence; the space of virtual reality."

Virtual? Yes. Having no real existence? No.

In 1989, Tim Berners-Lee, working at CERN (Conseil Européen pour la Recherche Nucleaire)[28] in Geneva, Switzerland, started to develop protocols that would give the particle physicists there a powerful new way to interconnect their global research community using the Internet.

The essential technologies and agreements that make the web possible are very simple and come from humble beginnings. The astonishingly easy-to-use computer language for designing web pages is called HyperText Markup Language (HTML), and the communication that connects web sites follows the now-famous standard, HyperText Transfer Protocol (HTTP).

By 1993, the required protocols were in place, and in the fall of that year, students at the University of Illinois (including Marc Andreessen, who went on to found Netscape) created the NCSA Mosaic browser. With an easy way to steer through cyberspace, the World Wide Web took off and never looked back.

In a few short years, the web has become the communication *phenome extraordinaire*. Suddenly, anyone with Internet access can explore a billion postings around the world on nearly every conceivable topic, gliding from continent to continent in click-of-a-mouse time.

Ted Nelson and Doug Engelbart are among the earliest seers in the 1960s to envision the possibilities of hypertext and the resulting global web of networked knowledge. The word *hypertext* is self-descriptive: It is text that is hyperactive. Anything written in hypertext (or any data element) can become what amounts to a computer button of its own, representing simple but profound linking capability. Click your mouse and off you go to that destination. This means that everything on the web can be interrelated—linked.

Companies, libraries, universities, governments, hobbyists, nonprofits, politicians, social activists, families, and just plain folks all have jumped onto the web. For virtual teams, the use of password-protected sites brings a singular value.

For the first time, teams can virtually colocate all the information and interactions they need to work together in context.

That does not mean that all the team's information is on the site, but it does mean that the site can point you to wherever you need to go. Pointers are embedded in text, outlines, graphics, maps, and other media. Virtual reality for virtual teams is already digital and rapidly becoming conceptual.

The eruption of the web allows virtual teams to create private digital places. These interactive sites—protected, members-only islands within the global Internet ocean—signal a sharp uptick in the human capability to group.

Definition

What, exactly, is a virtual team?

A virtual team is a group of people who work interdependently with a shared purpose across space, time, and organization boundaries using technology.

Face-to-face interactions among people from the same organization typify old models of teamwork. What sets virtual teams apart is that they routinely *cross boundaries*. What makes virtual teams historically new is the awesome array of interactive technologies at their disposal.

Webs of technology and trust link virtual teams.

Regular meetings, encounters in the hallway, getting together for lunch, dropping into one another's offices—these paint our conventional portrait of getting things done.

People do not routinely see one another when they are in different places, spread out around the world, or even housed in different parts of the same city. Motorola, for example, has some 20 locations just in the northwest Chicago area, each of which has multiple buildings. Many teams today *never* meet face-to-face, but work together only online. Such is the case with the 1,250 employees of Buckman Laboratories in Memphis, Tennessee, who form and disband numerous situation-specific virtual teams on a daily basis—even though the people in them are spread all around the globe.

One major reason why many virtual teams fail is because they over-look the implications of the obvious differences in their working environments. People do not make accommodation for how *different* it really is when they and their colleagues no longer work face-to-face. Teams fail when they do not adjust to this new reality by closing the virtual gap.

Proximity

What first comes to mind when you think of a team? A group of people working side by side or in close proximity to one another—a basketball or soccer team, perhaps?

From a personal perspective, the important distances are the very short ones. How close people prefer to be for interpersonal interactions varies by culture—from inches to feet.[29]

How far away do people have to be before they need to worry about compensating for distance? Or put another way, how close do you have to be to get the advantage of being in the same place? That is, what is the "radius of collaborative colocation?"

Based on proximity, people are not likely to collaborate very often if they are more than 50 feet apart.[30]

The startling data that MIT professor Tom Allen has been compiling for the past several decades show that the radius is very small. The probability of communicating or collaborating more than once a week drops off dramatically if people are more than the width of a basketball court apart. To get the benefit of working in the same place, people need to be quite close together.

To put this in perspective, think of the people you regularly work with. Are they all within 50 feet of you? Or are some of your coworkers a bit more spread out—down the hall, on another floor, in another building, or perhaps in another city or country? Increasingly, the people we work with are no longer within shouting distance. Any team of more than about 10 or 15 people is, due to sheer physical mass, probably more than 50 feet apart (Figure 1.3).

Globally, the farther apart people are physically, the more time zones they must cross to communicate. Thus, time becomes a problem when people who are not in the same place need some of their activities to be in sync. The window for routine same-time (synchronous) work shrinks as more time zones are crossed, closing to effectively zero when people are on opposite sides of the globe. But even people who work together in the same place can have problems being in the same place at the same time, like those in sales or consulting who rarely occupy their offices at the same time. Even apparently colocated teams often cross time boundaries and need to think virtually.

MyOrganization.com

Do all the people you rely upon to get your job done work for you or your boss? Probably not.

Figure 1.3   Colocated to Virtual Distance

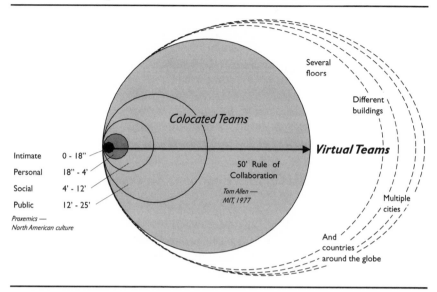

Most core business processes require that people regularly work across organizational boundaries. Supply chain management, marketing, product development, sales, quality improvement, and change management are just a few activities that require virtual teams to work over walls and across borders.

Large-scale-systems change invariably requires teamwork across organizational borders. To reinvent its administration and information management system, the U.S. Department of Commerce involves hundreds of people in teams from five major bureaus and dozens of smaller organizations. Usually numbering 8 to 10 people each, these virtual teams also comprise scores of contractors who provide everything from consultation on change management to software programming.

Alliances, joint ventures, and partnerships all require companies to establish cross-boundary teams.

Benefits

Doing together what we can't do alone.

So why put up with the burden of working across boundaries? Because, when successful, virtual teams dramatically improve business performance. For Shell Oil Company, virtual teams[31]:

- *Reduce costs* by cutting travel costs and time, creating new "e-economies" of scale, and designing better digitally enhanced processes.
- *Shorten cycle time* by moving from serial to parallel processes, establishing better communications, and generating more widespread trust.
- *Increase innovation* by permitting more diverse participation, stimulating product and process creativity, and encouraging new business development synergies.
- *Leverage learning* by capturing knowledge in the natural course of doing the work, gaining wider access to expertise, and sharing best practices.

Growth

Virtual teams are not just a great way to organize and make use of cutting-edge technology. Whether consciously or not, many companies are betting their future on virtual teams as their strategic differentiator. By employing virtual teams, they can do things that are impossible within the prevailing model of side-by-side, nine-to-five work.

Virtual teams are a strategy for success.

If they cannot accomplish their goals within their own four walls, net-savvy companies climb over them and partner with someone or several someones with whom they can make it happen. If their competition suddenly overpowers them, twenty-first-century organizations see virtual teams as the way to become smarter, more flexible, adaptive, and more competitive.

The way is not easy. Virtual teams are microcosms of the organizations and environments that spawn them. Today's teams are complex and reflect all the stresses and strains induced by the extraordinary shift in human civilization now completed. As the Industrial Age recedes and the zenith of the Network Age looms ahead, we and our groups are stretched betwixt and between. We are born into the old-age past, yet must navigate in the new-age present.

Virtuous Loop

Old management molds that funnel information up and send orders down are cracking apart. More information is more omnipresent to more people. Competitive pressures to constantly improve cost and quality drive radical redesign of business models and work processes. All the while, information seeks its natural path, defying gravity, flowing with its own simple process physics and mindless of boundaries drawn in the physical world.

There is a *virtuous feedback loop*[32] building in the development of virtual teams that promises an exponential rise in performance. Virtual teams are not a fad. They are here to stay and soon to be ubiquitous.

This virtuous loop story begins with yesterday's assumption that people must colocate to work together. Shoulder to shoulder, the traditional team works together, handing off their work to the next team in chains of larger processes, the bucket brigade of working groups, organizational building blocks of closely spaced bodies stacked in command-and-control pyramids. This is the idealized machine organization of the Industrial Age.

Today, however, technology, speed, globalization, and complexity are rearranging this root premise of work design. Two things happen: Distance and time become problems to solve, and organizational issues develop within rigid hierarchy-bureaucracies. To deal with the demands of competition that force cross-boundary work, organizations create virtual teams.

Electronic, particularly digital, media that people typically use to compensate for distance eventually create new possibilities. Entirely new ways for people to work interactively lead to new networked forms of organization. As the shift to information work accelerates, new energy is pumped into the system as increasingly more work is devoted to digital products and services.

As the technologies and processes of virtual work improve, more work is designed to gain virtual benefits. This only fuels the accumulating trend toward virtual teams, making it easier for them to come together and work interdependently. More virtual teams mean more networked organizations replacing or transforming traditional hierarchy-bureaucracies.

More virtual teams in the newly fertile digital environment also mean we have the possibility of regularly reaching heights of performance and group intelligence only rarely experienced by traditional teams.

Looking Forward and Back

A good virtual team is, at its heart, a good team. Since many virtual teams do meet periodically, or a few times, or at least once, they also find themselves in the conventional face-to-face setting.

We are untrained for life and work in the fluid, instantaneous global village. Thus, we need new models for teams that also incorporate the timeless features of working together.

Four words capture the essence of virtual teams: people, purpose, links, *and* time.

- *People* populate and lead small groups and teams of every kind at every level—from the executive suite to the subcommittees of the local school's parent association.
- *Purpose* holds groups together, which for teams means a focus on tasks—work progressing from goals to results.
- *Links* are the channels, interactions, and relationships that weave the living fabric of a group unfolding over time. The greatest difference between in-the-same-place teams and virtual ones lies in the nature and variety of their links.

- *Time* is a dimension common to all life and one that dominates virtual teams—schedules, milestones, calendars, processes, and life cycles.

Work in a world where the sun never sets is very complex. There are few maps and lots of complaints. People are trying to feel their way, uncertain that they are making the right decisions.

For virtual teams and networks to be truly transformational, they must include what is timeless and enduring in human groups. They also need to reflect the features that are really new in the turbulent years following the turn of the millennium. The organizing challenge of our time is to learn to work in virtual teams and networks while retaining the benefits of earlier forms.

CHAPTER 2

NETWORKS

From Tribes to Networks

For the past 20 years, while living and working with computers, we've been talking and writing about a time in the future when the transforming trends of the Information Age finally would overcome the Industrial Age ones. Once, our refrain was that the network is the natural form of human organization for the twenty-first century. That time has come. We've been swirled through this epochal portal as a global society, like millions of butterflies caught in the same net.

It's Official

In the big picture, this is humanity's *fourth* great socioeconomic-technological threshold. We're now zooming up the steep climb of an accelerating paradigm shift completing its transformation, a moment that has been a century in the coming.

The seeds of the newest age are planted in the scientific revolution initiated at the turn of the twentieth century. Relativity and quantum theory challenge the prevailing reductionist and materialist view of Newton, laying the foundation for new perspectives on reality.

Gestating for a half century, the birth of the new age literally explodes into public view in 1945. In six short months, the world witnessed activation of the first digital computer, ENIAC, the dropping of atomic bombs on Hiroshima and Nagasaki, and the signing of the United Nations charter in San Francisco, California. But the Industrial Age hierarchical-bureaucratic world held sway nearly to century's end—even as the powerful forces of change ripened and grew.

Now we are fully moved into the Information Age. It's showdown time for us in learning these new ways to work. We each personally have no choice but to grapple with the difficult issues raised by the radical restructuring of human reality as a whole.

Virtual teaming is a twenty-first-century survival skill.

Each age produces a new variation on the ancient theme of teams (see Chapter 3). At a basic daily level, we all live in small groups that are teams when the purpose is task-oriented. *Virtual* teams cross boundaries of space, time, and organization using technology to extend human capabilities, which gives them uniquely new features.

Successful collaborative work requires 90 percent people and 10 percent technology. What works can be boiled down to one word: *trust* (the topic of Chapter 4). One story we tell there shows how real and enduring this quality is: It begins a thousand years ago. Today, the long-term benefits of great teamwork accumulate as social capital.

The Networked Community

The oil industry is simply a network of enterprise- and government-level virtual teams. There is likely not an exploration under way anywhere in the world that doesn't involve more than one company negotiating with at least one, if not several, governments and whose product is moved, refined, and distributed by at least a dozen more firms. Royal Dutch/ Shell Group, of which the Houston, Texas, Shell of this story is just a part, maintains more than 1,000 joint ventures.

In 1991, Shell Oil Company saw the worst performance in its nearly century-long existence. Suddenly, while Shell was looking backward, the world around it soared ahead. Showing just $21 million in net profits against its more than $22 billion in assets, Shell got its wake-up call that year, says Linda Pierce, a 33-year Shell employee who rose to the senior ranks of the company. "We realized that our failure actually began much earlier, when large investment decisions were being made at the very top of the company without a system, structure, or process for tapping into the knowledge of the organization."

For a century, the "majors"—Shell, Exxon, Texaco, and the like—have dominated the industry. In a few years' time during the 1980s, upstart companies, some with only a handful of employees, began to exploit cracks in the majors' business models. The singular world that Shell once ruled with only a few other competitors abruptly crowded with unlikely opponents. The competitive sky was turning colors that Shell could not even name.

First dozens and then hundreds of companies offered products and services along the whole value chain—exploration, production, chemicals, distribution, and retail. In the new oil business, services proved more profitable than the natural resource itself. Consider Landmark Graphics, now owned by Halliburton. It grew its 1984 computer-aided exploration software to fill 90 percent of the oil-exploration information technology market in just a few years.[1]

Shell's initial response was predictable: workforce reductions of one-third, from 33,000 to 22,000, along with the elimination of significant layers of middle management. "We looked very hard at cost cutting, which got us in touch with what our competition was doing. Much to our surprise, we learned that we were not competitive in producing a barrel of oil," Pierce says.

The Transformation

In 1993, Shell's then-vice president of administration and finance, Phil Carroll, took over as CEO. Within a few months, Carroll and a coterie of talented people, including Pierce, initiated what came to be known as "The Transformation," a radical redesign of the way the company operated. Their new vision was quite simple: to become "the premier company in the United States." Soon, imagined covers of *Fortune* appeared around the company, with pictures of Shell executives captioned by that phrase.

The changes to come would be profound. Carroll reorganized the company's top executives into a Leadership Council that replaced the existing three-person General Executive Office. This seemingly simple modification heralded a dramatic break with Shell's organizational history. Shell had been the classic hierarchy with decisions made privately at the top, then imposed downward through a slow-moving, inflexible, not-very-street-smart bureaucracy.

"We knew that an engaged workforce more fully involved in the business of the company would require a different kind of leadership," Pierce says. "We had technical leadership but not business leadership." The idea was that in the new Shell, no single place in the organization would make business decisions; *many* would.

Each principal business (exploration and production, chemicals, oil products) would be run by a chief executive officer responsible for delivering strategy and fulfilling financial commitments. Each also would have its own board of directors with seats held by executives from other internal businesses and corporate functions.

Soon thereafter, the 200 most senior leaders from across Shell convened as the Corporate Leadership group, threading still more connections across the company. Their charge was to protect both the welfare of the whole company and their own businesses simultaneously.

This new business model sent profit and loss to the major businesses, which in turn spawned a rich network of relationships among the company's financial officers. At one point, the chief financial officer of Shell Oil Company, the corporate "holding company" center of all the businesses, sat on 17 boards.

The Transformation also opened Shell's doors to the outside. Scores of creative people—authors, consultants, thinkers, musicians, graphic facilitators,[2] and industry experts—came through the Shell Learning Center. Carroll built the facility as an adjunct to the famous conference center at The Woodlands, the planned community outside Houston. The Learning Center was booked all the time, but no desks were in sight (except in the offices of the people running the place). Abundant instead were chairs on rolling casters, comfortable enough for daylong meetings, walls that you could pin anything to, flipcharts, projectors, computers for logging on to the company's network—and buffets of excellent food. It was a superb environment for learning and building trust.

The Learning Center also served as the meeting place for the company's many initiatives. Each initiative involved posing a set of questions to a cross section of Shell employees. Typically, these people would devote mixtures of full- and part-time effort to the initiative for as long as six months. By its conclusion, Shell would have a new approach to diversity, recognition, and strategic cost leadership.

In October 1997, Shell's planners, a small group of future-attuned strategists, many of whom had firsthand experience producing oil, presented a startling statistic to the Leadership Council at its annual retreat in Galveston. As recently as three years earlier, Shell had owned nearly 100 percent of the companies in which its assets were deployed. By the time of the October meeting, that number had sunk to 34 percent. Everything else was or soon would be in joint ventures with competitors (including its retail business with Texaco and Saudi Aramco) or in global alliances with its parent (Figure 2.1). The planners predicted that the number would plummet even lower when Royal Dutch/Shell turned all of its businesses into global ones. The conclusion was that Shell no longer stood alone; it was deeply enmeshed in a networked community whose rules, assumptions, and guiding principles diverged markedly from its previous architecture.

> *Shell moved from "control through ownership to influence through relationships."*[3]

Strategic Initiative Teams

A month later the Leadership Council convened 38 people to join them as part of a new group of Strategic Initiative Teams (SITs). A broad cross section of employees—from Chet Servance, a boilermaker at the company's Deer Park Refinery, to the company's then-treasurer Tom Botts— were invited. Their mission was to answer four fundamental questions

Figure 2.1   The Networked Community

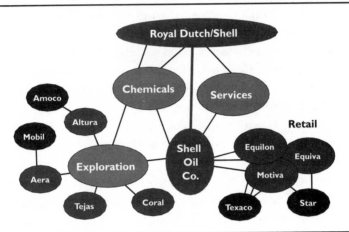

about the new Shell and to make recommendations that the company could act on immediately:

> How will we learn?
> What will it mean to be part of the Shell family?
> How will we develop our people?
> How will we govern?

They divided into four teams, with the Leadership Council addressing the fourth question on governance. Pierce calls it the best project she ever worked on. "They started as four teams and ended as one," she says. "It began with the Leadership Council's desires, but ultimately what drove the team was what they came to believe was important. That happened in a workshop [at the Learning Center], where the team became one and took over the design of the workshop, much to delight of the facilitators who had designed it!" Pierce is referring to Bill McQuillen and Jim Tebbe, the head facilitators for the SIT. "They get credit for creating the conditions that allowed it to happen," Pierce believes.

It ultimately was a very large virtual team. Around the 38 core members were an additional 90 on the Employee Panel, a review team recruited as being representative of the broader community in which Shell lives. Panel members, nicknamed "the spoons" because of their role in "stirring the pot" in support of the networked community, included a school superintendent, a local minister, the president of a local trucking company, and several spouses of Shell employees. This design ensured that the SIT would not act in isolation. Regular reviews took place with the spoons, who in turn spoke with their constituencies about the meaning of the new Shell.

The SIT provides a striking example of shared leadership at the highest strategy levels. Botts led the initiative as principal coordinator of the effort, working closely with Pierce in her role as the liaison to the Leadership Council. The four subteams, including the Leadership Council itself, were responsible for answering one of the four questions; each had its own leaders and facilitators. McQuillen and Tebbe shared responsibility for designing the meetings that convened the whole SIT group.[4] Ed Kahn, another senior facilitator at Shell, designed and led meetings with the spoons. The Leadership Council members also wove more strands—each belonged to the governance team and also served as cosponsor to one of the three other teams. As outside consultants, we contributed leadership and content expertise on networked organizations.

"Networks are leaderful. Any virtual team that attempts to operate with one formal leader is not going to make it," Pierce says. She points to Botts's style of leadership as required in new organizations. He's a learner, she says. "In the networked world, things are continuously changing, so the leader with the answers has no answers. Tom continuously holds the questions, not the answers." Pierce refers to this quality as "hearing the music," meaning that there is a new background coherence for people in networked organizations. To hear it, you have to part with the traditional trapping of power—having the single right answer. Otherwise, you only hear noise. Create questions, not simple answers, and you will excel, she believes.

In a few short months, with people continuing to work their day jobs, the SIT turned out a "Networked Community Fieldbook,"[5] that included seven "enabling recommendations" to propel the new Shell to a higher level of performance:

1. Executive Sponsorship of the process
2. Network Leadership Group comprising leaders throughout the community
3. Network Learning and Support Center to help build new competencies
4. People Movement, meaning that job postings are fluid throughout the community
5. Information technology infrastructures for communication and sharing
6. After Action Review, an institutionalized learning process
7. Communities of Practice in pursuit of improved business performance

The Leadership Council endorsed and approved the recommendations upon the fieldbook's presentation, demonstrating how well the team had managed the expectations of its stakeholders. Within a few weeks, the following occurred:

- The Network Learning and Support Center set up shop.
- The company made investments in developing communities of practice[6] across the larger network.
- The U.S. Army's practice of After Action Reviews to evaluate all meetings was instituted.
- The building of the information infrastructure to accommodate cross-boundary work was accelerated.

Even larger changes in Shell's operating model came to pass that following summer that were served well by the work of the SIT. Royal Dutch/Shell Group, the parent company, "globalized" all the U.S. businesses, meaning that they became accountable directly to their global organizations. For example, Exploration and Production, long based in Houston and New Orleans and the heart of the Shell Oil Company's revenue stream, became part of Royal Dutch/Shell's global "Exploration Production" organization. Similar changes were made in the Houston-based chemical and services organizations.[7]

Pierce and others believe that the work of the SIT, educating people about the power of working across more porous boundaries, is helping to ease the transition to the global Shell organization, which itself is grappling with the next level of planetary complexity.

"The global leaders have taken on huge accountability," she says. "'Think globally, act locally'[8] is a snappy little phrase, but what does it mean to operationalize it? Does the global team trust the local team? Is the local team able to operate with the whole in mind? It's a very hard decision to close a local plant."

There is no insurance policy for companies like Shell that are moving from the Industrial Age to the Information Age. But the investment it has made in preparing for the future is instructive for other brick-and-mortar companies. Technology and resources alone do not enable success; people do.

What's Old, What's New?

Alvin and Heidi Toffler's 1980 book, *The Third Wave*, became the popular herald of a transition from the Industrial Age to the Information Age. It caught the crest of an idea almost four decades in the making. Now the transition is conventional wisdom. Three transformations divide human history into four great ages characterized by nomadic, agricultural, industrial, and information-based cultures (Figure 2.2).

Each age has its signature form of organization.

- People first honed their *small group* skills as hunter-gatherers. The nomadic era, beginning between 2 and 3 million years ago, was the source of our cultural DNA, when our very early ancestors acquired the ability to speak, make tools, and configure organizations. Populations were small,[9] as were families.
- *Hierarchy* grew up with agriculture. The agricultural era began 10,000 to 12,000 years ago and marked a dramatic shift from the

Figure 2.2 Four Ages of Organization

Small Groups	Hierarchy	Bureaucracy	Networks

Nomadic	Agricultural	Industrial	Information
3 million... 10,000 B.C.	10,000 B.C... 18th century	18th century... 20th century	1945... 21st century
Members	Levels	Purpose	Links

nomadic era. Farming and herding eventually replaced hunting and gathering. Populations grew larger, cities and towns developed, and family size increased as people settled down.

- The Industrial Age gave birth to *bureaucracy*. Beginning with ideas and technologies in the fifteenth century, this age became prominent in the eighteenth century, dominant in the nineteenth, and mature in the twentieth. It saw factories replace farms as the economic engine. Populations exploded and urbanized, while families grew smaller. This age spawned the new digital civilization.

- The Information Age brought us *networks*. For the last half of the century, we have been riding the turbulence of this transition as great paradigms struggle for control. The torch now has been passed. The world's economies are information-based, electronically connected, and globally interdependent. Population is still rising, families are diversifying, and the planet has grown very small indeed.

The new virtual organizations are at once very old and very new, very small and very large. The small-group virtual team is rooted in the very old and draws on skills accumulated over millennia. Networks are the very new, meeting the need for greater scope, speed, and flexibility. They grow together at the creative leading edge of epic change.

Groups Forever

We have always—and will always—live and work in small groups. Small groups permeate every kind of organization, from microcompanies and start-ups to small teams in big firms to executive committees of boards of directors.

> *The high-performance, information-enabled,* virtual team *is the Network Age version of the small group.*

Each age adds its special characteristics to the previous one. Small groups have personalities and identities and may carry the seeds of later larger organizations. As people gain status in new roles and perform tasks, they expand the vertical and horizontal dimensions of organization over the ages.

Hierarchy Structures

Jim is in Robin's group. Robin is on the executive team and reports to David, the CEO, who is accountable to the board. In hierarchy, there are many status bands of low, middle, and high ranks, with even more grades within them. Interestingly, this example comes from Ventro, a dot-com company, not an old-line one.

> *Hierarchy dramatically steepens the who's-on-top status dimension in small groups.*

As the source of legitimacy in business, owners, who have capital, also bring hierarchy. They officially crown an authority structure of executives and workers.

Hierarchy has helped people build societies among strangers throughout history. As a business grows beyond the point where everyone knows one another, hierarchy is inevitable.

Frank Reece, the founder of US TeleCenters (now View Tech), explains how quickly his company became compartmentalized. "I started with a handful of people and before we knew it, we were 350 employees, thousands of customers, and dozens of suppliers. I could see the bureaucracy growing, and I was afraid I would create a company I would hate."

Every successful entrepreneur bemoans the loss of the "family feeling" as greater size demands structure and formality.

The Egyptian pyramids are the great organizational achievement of the agricultural era, the literal eternal symbol for successive ranks culminating in a pinnacle of power. A traditional organization chart brings the pyramid to mind.

Hierarchies alone are not enough. Success brings change, and simple hierarchies are notoriously unstable in the face of the unexpected. Ancient empires rose and fell as populations expanded and capacity became overextended. Boom-bust cycles eventually gave rise to bureaucracies.

Bring On the Boxes

Science ushered in the Industrial Age. Behind logic and the laws of motion chugged the steam engine. Its cargo? Another organizational revolution: rational bureaucracy.

Bureaucracy bulges out sideways with specialized functions, tasks, and roles.

For 300 years, corporations, nations, and organizations of all kinds became more efficient with the organizing prowess of bureaucracy. Bureaucracy, while specializing horizontally, embraces hierarchy, which controls vertically. Together they manage much greater social and economic complexity than either could do alone. The Industrial Age became much more complicated than the agricultural era.

But the beat of change continues, faster still. Unfortunately, when faced with continuous uncertainty and change, bureaucracy is like kudzu, the vinelike weed that spreads until it overruns everything, choking out other forms of life instead of simply connecting people in existing organizations who probably have the answer. Then the "problem" turns into a department.

So a bureaucracy grows, ever bigger, ever slower, until it just sits there, failing to innovate or change, placing drag on everything else. Finally, complexity outruns bureaucracy's ability to organize it.

"Only Connect"

The Internet, with its extraordinary spread of new connections, is in a class by itself. This technological innovation has come to affect human life on a global scale in the space of a proverbial instant.

A parallel growth in connections is happening in organizations: Alliances, joint ventures, and partnerships are forming at an accelerating rate among firms of all sizes. Services are today's economic growth sector, taking advantage of the combination of people and process. Manufacturing is shrinking, as agriculture did in the Industrial Age, even as productivity grows.

Connect! It's the organizing imperative of the Network Age.

In the Information Age, relationships are fundamental. Links are displacing the focus on matter, which lay inert at the center of the Industrial Age worldview.

Today we are challenged to cope with continuous global change that constantly presents us with more opportunities. Relationships—technological and human—drive the reorganization of work. Bureaucracy begins the horizontal expansion of organizations; networks take the expansion to mach speed.

Network the Ages

What to save? What to change? Where to stay the course? When to leap ahead?

The complexity that faces twenty-first-century business outstrips the capacity of the accumulated wisdom of earlier ages. So we have collectively invented something new: *networks.* In the big picture, the overall pace of change drives the next form of organization. With new technology eventually comes the ability to manage in an increasingly larger and deeper context.

Each age of organization builds upon and includes the past. Networks in particular are inclusive by nature. Breadth gives them resilience; diversity gives them insight; independent members keep them vibrant and learning.

In the Network Age, we still have hierarchies and bureaucracies, just as we continue to have farms and factories. Fire departments, typically regarded as among the least innovative of organizations, turn out to be among the most adaptive for the twenty-first century.[10]

Fire

American fire departments incorporate all forms of organization—small groups, hierarchies, bureaucracies, and networks of all sizes.

Fire fighting captures the headlines and provides riveting visuals for local TV news. The fire department springs into action as a hierarchy when battling blazes. It prepares for the crisis with command-and-control systems, practice, and training. If your home erupts in flames, you don't want a group standing around outside trying to reach consensus on how to approach the problem. You want someone calling the shots for a highly skilled group of professionals who understand how to deal with heat, chemicals, and combustion gone out of control.

While fire fighting gets public attention, departments spend only a small part of their time putting out fires (in Boston, for example, only 5 percent). When not fighting fires, the department stays busy as a classic bureaucracy: It enforces codes, ensures pressure in water lines, updates its training, and maintains its apparatus. A chief shouting orders is of very little use if the hydrant isn't delivering water. You need experts who understand pumps, pressure, and the mechanics of the city water system. Uniform codes fight fires, too.

Firefighters are also very local. They often use networking for fire prevention, which requires education, persuasion, role models, and working directly with people in the community. Schoolchildren have no patience for—or need to know about—sprinkler requirements. Their parents need to get the message about the importance of smoke detectors, fire extinguishers, a second exit from bedrooms, and "stop, drop, and roll" advice. The glamour of a visit to the local firehouse and a ride on an engine leave indelible memories in children's minds, but they don't make children fire safe. Commitment to ongoing education does, a distinct and suitable role for networks of people working together in small groups.

Modern fire departments also forge large, interorganizational networks for mutual aid. A group of communities agrees to act as a virtual fire department and back up one another in a particularly bad fire. Each community gains protection and reduces costs. Here local hierarchies use networks to achieve something together that they cannot accomplish alone. In this field, as in many others, people also use formal networks (e.g., trade associations) to pass legislation, share information, take on large-scale education efforts, and promote professionalism.

All kinds of organizations can learn from the local fire department. In emergencies, clear lines of authority prevail. For routine situations and environments, rules and regulations provide standards. Networks educate, innovate, motivate, and provide backup when a hierarchy-bureaucracy reaches its limits.

Fire departments—among the oldest of America's institutions and found throughout the world—may be role models for the twenty-first-century organization.

A Slice of Time

A fire department provides a cumulative "geologic slice" of the evolution of organizations (Figure 2.3).

Figure 2.3   Layers of Organization

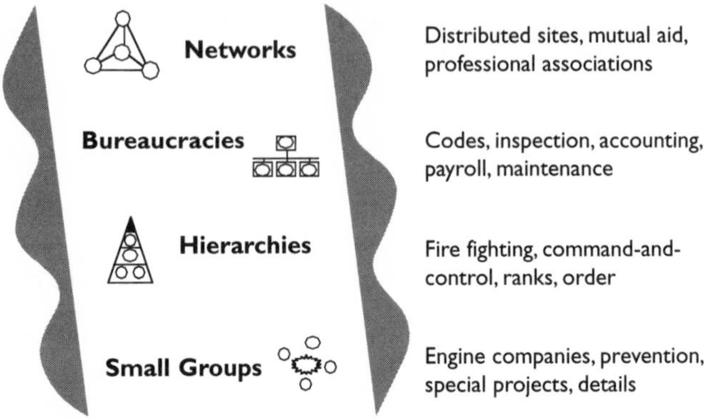

Networks	Distributed sites, mutual aid, professional associations
Bureaucracies	Codes, inspection, accounting, payroll, maintenance
Hierarchies	Fire fighting, command-and-control, ranks, order
Small Groups	Engine companies, prevention, special projects, details

Small groups comprise the deepest layers. Hierarchy, with its chiefs and sergeants, is the next layer, imposing vertical control. Bureaucracy appears in more recent layers, bringing horizontal specialties. Finally, at the top, in the verdant, living topsoil, we see intensely linked, warp-speed networks. Like the fire department, most organizations today mix the forms.

Even in today's Internet start-ups, traditional face-to-face small groups continue to be the basic work unit. At the same time, information-enabled virtual teams cross functions, deliver results to customers, and undertake special projects. All the while, the old (or even new) hierarchy continues to set strategy, maintain authority, and cope with crises, with senior employees upholding the bureaucracy.

Although most people complain bitterly about them, bureaucracies, when appropriate and enabling, can be elegantly functional, high-performance entities. They standardize contractual agreements and develop common methods by which work gets done and paid for. In networks, people forge links as they cross internal functions, geographic boundaries, and even corporate lines with remarkable speed. The people in the network come from the bureaucracy and the hierarchy. Their new relationships to one another create the networks.

The most literal way that networks include earlier forms is by linking all types of organizations.

> *Members of a network do not themselves have to be networks.*

The U.S. Intelligence Community, comprising the 14 intelligence agencies of the U.S. government—Central Intelligence Agency, National Security Agency, Defense Intelligence Agency, and the like—is a network. It really has no one boss, though for administrative reasons, it reports to the director of the CIA. Each of its constituent parts, however, is a strict hierarchy. At the global level of scientific projects, the International Gemini Project, which points the world's two largest optical and infrared telescopes outward to pick up the "most faint and distant galaxies,"[11] is a multinational collaboration of seven governments: Argentina, Australia, Brazil, Canada, Chile, the United Kingdom, and the United States.

This diversity in the parts also pertains inside an enterprise. Departments in the same company often use different organizational forms—quite effectively if they are appropriately tuned to the environment and technology. For example, typically, marketing and product development groups are more agile in their styles than accounting and maintenance.

To repeat: *All the parts of the network do not have to be the same.* The twenty-first-century organization comprises all types: small groups, hierarchies, bureaucracies, and networks.

Managing

Today, regardless of size, most businesses exist in a global context. Asea Brown Boveri, the Swiss-based $25 billion "multidomestic," operates across more than 100 national borders. "We're facing a new world where speed, flexibility, and brain power are the keys," says Göran Lindahl, ABB's president and CEO.[12]

"The world is getting smaller," says Harry Brown, whose company, EBC Industries, has pioneered partnering with competitors. Brown's company has just picked up a project in South America to produce discontinued parts for surplus vehicles bought in the United States. The customers find Brown's firm through what Brown calls "the chain of knowledge." Another company in their network already is supplying transmission parts. The project has caused EBC to consider a new line of business, making repair parts for old Jeeps. "Every time you open one of those doors, another one opens up," Brown says.[13] Perhaps unnecessary to say is the obvious: Neither Brown nor his partner firm travel anywhere to carry out this project.

The wave of revolutionary changes catches every organization scrambling to survive and position itself to prosper as the fundamental rules of the game change—from our own Internet company to a behemoth the size of General Electric to your company to nonprofits, government agencies, schools, denominations, and political parties. We all are unavoidably in the storm-wracked passage to a new, expansive, information-based economy and culture.

All around us we see the future come alive as we push the frontiers of markets, technologies, and human performance. Trial and error underlie the rapidly accumulating knowledge of what works virtually.

The New

Fortunately, the old forms of organization as they currently exist will not mire us forever. We do not have to take all that is oppressive about hierarchy and bureaucracy with us as we speed into the Network Age.

We believe that some hierarchical structure is necessary for any complex, multilevel organization. Hierarchies represent ultimate ownership control and decision making and will continue to do so. However, in the Information Age, new forms of leadership that are more participatory and diverse also emerge to fulfill these needs.

Search on the keyword "Co-CEO" and you'll find thousands of links to companies where power is shared at the top—from Wit Capital, the first online investment bank, to Ameritrade Holding Company to Sony.[14]

As with Shell Oil Company, these companies push more decisions down and out, closer to the work and the customer. We must leave behind something to make this possible—in this case, the narrow, one-way channels of communication and decision making and the cultures of hoarding information for power. The nature of control changes with widespread communication and knowledge. Local decision making combines with centralized information sharing in the network-enabled hierarchy.

Bureaucracies continue to serve as our legal guardians, as specialization remains essential to cope with complexity in the Information Age. Micromanagement, fortunately, will go the way of the dinosaur.

Federal Express says that its information system is more valuable than its transportation system. Employees have the power to act at every point of customer contact, supported by a tracking system that is accessible to all. FedEx is among the earliest companies to allow customers to track their own transactions.

> *At FedEx, bureaucracy becomes an enabling infrastructure rather than a nightmare of bottlenecks.*

Some bureaucracies are being transformed rather than replaced. New relationships erupt spontaneously among the departmental boxes as connections multiply.

As an offshoot of the quality movement, the U.S. Department of Energy's Quality Panels convened for weeklong meetings several times a year during the 1990s. There, people in the field gave useful input on policy and regulations to headquarters. When government budget cuts hit in the late 1990s, quality panels were vulnerable. The panels were very expensive, entailing the high costs associated with face-to-face meetings. Travel, lodging, and meals became increasingly difficult to justify in budgets that involved personnel reductions.

So DOE has moved to "virtual quality panels," with the added benefit of increasing dialogue among the panel members. "The guy in Albuquerque never got to see what the guy in Rocky Flats had said," explains Carol Willett, whose company, Applied Knowledge Group, facilitates the virtual panels and provides web sites for their non-real-time continuation. "It turned a sequential coordination process that took months into a network collaboration process allowing more voices to be heard in a fraction of the time and cost."[15]

Personally Speaking

We all belong to many different groups simultaneously. Moving from group to group, we can travel through the ages.

A firefighter can stride through all four ages in a single workday.

Upstairs over the station house is a small world, with a kitchen, break room, and bunks where the informal small group sleeps. It's a very placid environment—until the alarm goes off. Then the group dons its firefighting gear, snaps into a military unit, and heads for the crisis. After the blaze is put out, the firefighter gets into an inspector uniform, wearing bureaucracy to assess the damage and investigate the cause. That night, the uniform comes off and a person with a mission to save lives joins with a network of teachers and other leaders working to prevent fires in the community.

Useful, timeless, basic human capabilities recur in each new age. Our life is a mosaic of past and future. Each of us, like the firefighter, exists simultaneously in all four ages.

The postindustrial model is *inclusive* of old models, not a *replacement* for them. The laws of motion in everyday life did not grind to a halt when quantum physics overwhelmed Newtonian absolutes at the dawn of the twentieth century. Gravity did not reverse itself when Einstein discovered relativity.

Connectivity is exploding, yet face-to-face encounters account for most of our small-group knowledge. Historically, hierarchy in particular has depended on the sensory power of personal characteristics (the person, the body, the booming voice, the physical displays) and of powerful settings to maintain control.

It's hard to bring physical bearing to bear when you're communicating by e-mail. All the CAPITAL LETTERS and !@*$* characters of indignation on the computer screen can't compare with someone on a power trip staring you down. Physical qualities and locations are less important in the ephemeral age. We are learning new, more horizontally connected, participatory ways of achieving higher levels of small-group performance.

So, alongside the old is the new. We are rediscovering ancient small-group, face-to-face knowledge. At the same time, we're inventing some brand-new skills for the geographically diffuse groups of the future.

CHAPTER 3

TEAMS

Toward the Twenty-Second Century

"Long Distance Operator.
This is Memphis, Tennessee."

—Chuck Berry, 1958

"90% people, 10% technology.
This is Memphis, Tennessee."

—Bob Buckman, 2000

The city famous for Elvis, Beale Street, and the blues is also home to a company now celebrated in virtual team circles. Buckman Labs is a long-time innovator with its problem-solving, customer-centric, globe-circling "knowledge transfer" network. After more than a decade of pioneering, Buckman has answered many questions that other companies are just starting to ask.

Our Company Never Closes

Buckman Laboratories International, Inc., with $310 million in revenues, provides specialty chemicals to the pulp and paper, water, and leather industries. Buckman products allow manufacture of paper products, swimming pools without algae, and leather for Toyota and Lexus car seats.

Bob Buckman, former chairman and CEO of Bulab Holdings, Inc., the holding company of Buckman Labs, takes a small note card and a pen from his breast pocket and draws a little picture to illustrate his vision. "The number of connections among people multiplies exponentially when all are linked point to point," he says, putting his pen to the midpoints where the connections *between* the people intersect. You need a company where everyone has access to the collective intelligence of the organization regardless of time or space, he believes.

Buckman inherited his company from his parents, Stanley and Mertie, who started Buckman Laboratories in 1945[1] with five associates in the small back office of a former lumberyard not far from Café Society, the popular Memphis eatery where we're having lunch. Their single customer, Whiting Paper Company, needed its product, a microbicide that three years later became the industry standard. The company continued its steady growth until 1978 when things changed suddenly: Bob's father died at the office of a heart attack.

Bob unexpectedly found himself chief executive. Buckman Labs is a different company from the one his parents started. When he took over, the company was well on its way to becoming the firm it is today. The enterprise comprises operations in 22 countries, employs 1,300 people speaking at least 15 languages, and produces more than a thousand products. Bob also has a different management style from his father. Twenty-six people reported directly to "Dr. Stanley," an unworkable structure in his son's estimation. So, from his earliest days, "Bob" worked to create a less bureaucratic, more responsive, and very intelligent organization.

In his speeches, Buckman refers to 1984 as the starting point for his company's "journey—it's not a project," he says.[2] That year he met author Tom Peters, whose 1983 best-seller, *In Search of Excellence,* coauthored with Robert Waterman, revolutionized how people look at their businesses (and broke open the business-book industry). Buckman was among the first to attend Peters's Skunkcamp—designed by Reuben Harris,[3] Peters's then-partner (the two had met as doctoral students at Stanford Graduate Business School)—an intensive week-long course on unconventional business ideas. Buckman eventually sent most of his senior management to the program.

Fate intervened again in the mid-1980s when Buckman ruptured a disk that left him flat on his back for several weeks. His mind had been churning since meeting Peters and Harris, (who joined the Buckman board of directors in 1999) and he began experimenting. But when he found himself unable even to sit up, he realized that if he couldn't get to his office, he would be completely cut off from work. He wondered: "Why do organizations spend huge sums of money on systems that function only when people are in the office?" He not only characterized the lives of his executives, managers, and people in sales but also anticipated changes ahead.

Buckman came up with the idea that fit his immediate need and would catalyze the redesign of the company.

He decided to put everyone online.

His experiment proved so successful that everyone from Peters himself to Fast Company to Harvard Business School has written about it. HBS's case study describes Buckman's mission this way: "If he could connect people through a network, he could 'replace the depth of knowledge offered in a multi-tier hierarchy with the breadth of knowledge that is the sum of the collective experience of employees.'"[4]

In 1992, before the general commercial availability of the Internet, K'Netix, the Buckman Knowledge Network, was born, an online system that allowed everyone in the company to talk to everyone else anywhere at any time. In a pre-web era, it was a major challenge to get thousands of people around the world comfortable with logging in every day to solicit and contribute advice to people they rarely if ever saw.

The impetus for K'Netix was the desire to share best practices for solving customer problems. "We couldn't run Ph.Ds around the world fast enough at the speed that we needed," Buckman recalls. How did he do it? Buckman offered these thoughts on successful implementation from his twenty-first-century hindsight:

- *Technology.* Everyone in the global Buckman network has access to PCs and laptops. When they travel, they can take "electronic first aid" kits with them, equipped with whatever they will need for where they're going (telephone connectors, adapters, and cables).
- *Free, unrestricted access to the Internet.* "We say, 'Go play, go learn.' People have to learn how to be comfortable with technology," he says.
- *Coaching and facilitation.* For the first several years, coaches regularly spent 12 hours a day online just helping people become comfortable. Today, every online discussion area has its own moderator, many of whom have gone on to invent their own ways of working online.
- *Culture change.* "It's 90 percent culture change and 10 percent technology," he says. "It's people who bring about the change in the way that they work."

Alison Tucker, now director of Global Media and Promotions for Buckman, is the company's original online coach and over the years has participated in each online innovation.

She says she spent "endless amounts of time online. I was learning to manage all these crazy discussions. When we started out, half the things going on were not business-related—people talking about their kids and their dogs. We've always been this global company, but people didn't have a chance to talk until this happened. We'd have chat sessions [realtime, online text exchanges] at 5:30 or 6:00 P.M. Memphis time with people saying, 'I have to go answer the phone or door.' People in Japan were telling jokes to people in Brazil.

"Our use was very high at the beginning while everyone was learning, and now it's leveled out," Tucker says. "The key thing is to be patient and advertise, advertise, advertise to your people. We didn't have anybody to learn from. And we still don't, but we're learning from each other."

The initial getting-to-know-one-another frenzy lasted for about three months before things began to settle down into scientific and business conversations.

To encourage company-wide participation, Buckman himself takes to the world circuit. He gives speeches on the role of knowledge transfer and his belief that the company's intelligence lies "between the ears of the people, not in some database." From the beginning, he has been an active daily participant. "It has to have unequivocal leadership at the top," he says.

For the first six months of K'Netix, the company ran weekly reports to see who was participating and who was not. Every Friday morning, everyone in the company received a report via e-mail that listed the people who had not logged in by the previous afternoon. Buckman himself sent messages to these people asking why they weren't online and whether they needed any help. The desire to be absent from the list was so strong that the reports were discontinued after only six months.

Soon, people were participating in dozens of knowledge-sharing meetings online. Customer problems that once took days to resolve could be answered in a few hours.

By today's stupefying technology standards, the Buckman global network was—and remains—fairly elementary. After its first five years using a cumbersome IBM network that required different codes for different countries, the company moved to CompuServe in 1992.

"We chose CompuServe because of ease of use," explains Tucker. It offers local dial-in numbers in all the countries where Buckman has operations. While other companies have developed complex groupware and knowledge management systems, Buckman chooses instead to outsource and buy retail. ("The only reason companies create their own systems today is ego!" Buckman says emphatically.)

CompuServe, now part of its former arch rival America Online, also offers simple software for online discussions, called *forums*. Each forum is on a separate topic, and any authorized person can read and post messages. Because it captures everything electronically, the system maintains its own ongoing discussion history that can track decision making and problem solving. Buckman has numerous forums on topics germane to its business, including everything from customers to strategy to new product development. The forums are portable; when Buckman switches platforms again to Internet newsgroups the forum topics continue.

From Drums to Advice

Steve Buckman (Bob's cousin), now the Buckman Labs' CEO, recalls how different customers are today from the past. "Fifteen years ago, they said, 'If you don't make it, why are we talking to you?' Now they say, 'We know you don't make it but go find it, buy it, and make it work.' We're really an intermediary."

Buckman Labs' customer, SAPPI, an Italian papermaker early to automate, is planning a new system to bring out a new grade of paper in South Africa. "They sent a simple e-mail with their query and they got back 10 articles on how to do it. They were just amazed we would do this for them. Customers want us as consultants on how to solve their problems, but they also want us to bring in the product. We don't want to have to go three different places to solve the problem, procure the chemicals, and implement it in their production system," Steve Buckman explains.

The company's business model is maturing. As products become commodities, a company like Buckman "just can't pump things out quickly enough. We're all selling the same kinds of chemistry," says Sheldon Ellis, vice president of the Bulab Learning Center. Today Buckman is also a service company where knowledge is the capital. "We actually can make more money solving problems and handling processes for customers than shipping drums [of chemicals] alone," Ellis says.[5]

In May 1997, Bob Buckman asked Ellis to pull together a plan for the Bulab Learning Center, where education and training can be delivered to the Associates anytime anywhere in the world on an as-needed basis. "Bob said he wanted the Learning Center operational in less than a month," Ellis recalls. "I went to two folks from the Knowledge Transfer Division [knowledge management and information technology groups] with business skills and said, 'I'm asking you to leave what you're doing and get on the ride of your life. This will be the coolest thing you've ever done.'

"We built the architecture then plugged in everything we could find. I was reading how to do [Lotus] Notes development on a tour bus in Mexico, and my modem burned out, so I had to have a new one FedExed. We worked day and night and threw a lot of things together very, very quickly."

Three-and-a-half weeks later, Bulab Learning Center is operational with 75 courses available online.

Today the Learning Center employs 10 people from Asia, South America, and the United States who speak 11 languages and come from a variety of specialties: a chemical engineer, an agronomist, a computer scientist, a papermaking scientist, a political scientist, and a Spanish linguist. Among their many ambitions is one to make the site fully accessible in the company's four principal tongues—English, Spanish, Portuguese, and German. "There aren't many others trying to do a multilingual, academic, technical, personal/professional, career-development, learning-center web site," Ellis says.

They offer "knowledge" in many media, including traditional face-to-face courses with hard copy (they call it "standup"). The Learning Center produces thousands of CDs, offers 500 online courses through partnerships with 20 universities, stores countless presentations and documents, and is developing new ideas by the day. "We're constantly taking things up and down," as Ellis puts it, regularly trying things out on the site.

"Philosophically we're going to more contextual learning," Ellis says. "Instead of long classes, we're developing just-in-the-nick-of-time learning nuggets around what people need to know." They're also setting up communities of practice that offer, for example, the group of microbiologists across the company "a voice and a platform and mechanism to be able to build" the tools they need. "We're creating virtual places for people to learn." By redefining the approach and radically lowering the cost of delivery, Buckman is now able to offer the courses free to the students.

The Culture Shop

Edson Peredo, the company's president and a Brazilian who ran operations there for many years, describes himself as "not a fancy user but a frequent user." Peredo believes that cultural barriers "will be there for years to come," preventing people from using technology to its greatest advantage. "Most of my people still prefer face-to-face or at least a phone call. Perhaps this is due to the degree of trust and sensitivity about information that goes across the table or phone line. But as far as transferring information, I wouldn't give that up for anything," he says citing how he just downloaded a 45-page document. "Next week someone will be asking me about the specific document and I can say. 'Yes, I've seen it,' and that's how it benefits my work."

And just the month before, he called on a customer in California whom he had been e-mailing. "I felt like I'd been there before, I know these people and we're not strangers to each other. We exchange notes and pictures over the Internet, and you quickly find commonalities between you and your customers. Without our culture, that would not be possible. You would have to sit down for days to have the same relationship."[6]

Mark Koskiniemi, vice president for Human Relations at Buckman Labs, is thinking ahead about how to expand learning in the organization. "We can do it by hiring the latest and greatest graduates. But then what? That led us to distance learning and distributed learning that really have for the first time knocked down the socioeconomic barriers to education. We've leveled the playing field from Canada to Brazil to South Africa. The next step is for our associates to continue to grow and learn and educate themselves, then to refresh our education for ourselves and our children. You never know where the new knowledge is going to come from. The Bulab Learning Center has been created to fill the gap.

"There's a really important 'watch out for.' Don't expect the technology to do it all itself," Koskiniemi says. "It's culture, culture, culture. Top management has to support it; they lead by example. Bob is pushing the frontier with tools that we're providing. People who can use the tools get promoted. You don't need to bankrupt yourself on technology."

Customer Benefits

Although he is an engineer and a statistician (undergraduate degree from Purdue University in chemical engineering and an MBA from the University of Chicago), Buckman sounds at times like a communications theorist. For people to be effective, Buckman says, they need information that increases their "Span of Communication" and thus their "Span of Influence."[7] "Technology will allow you to change the 'Span of Communication' of an Associate, but it takes culture change to effect an individual's 'Span of Influence,' " he says.

"The speed at which you can communicate defines how quickly you can make money," Buckman says. "If I can respond to a customer in six hours anywhere in the world at any time, that's a competitive advantage. As the speed of communication increases, customer response time moves toward instantaneity [a Buckmanism]. That redefines competition. Any entrepreneur in the world will understand that."

Buckman says that to unleash the power of the individual, everyone has to "radically change their span of communication, and I mean radically. Anyone should be able to talk to anyone else inside and outside the organization. We want to close the gap with the customer. How do we increase our cash flow with the customer? By increasing our power on the front line. But that can only happen if the individual has good Spans of Communication and Influence."

Buckman's goal is to have 80 percent of the company "effectively engaged on the front line," that is, directly connected with customer needs. "If you're not doing something useful for a customer, why are you here?" He has only a few percentage points to go before having quintupled the number from 16 percent in 1979.

A company like Buckman is the latest in a long line of innovations centered on small groups working together. As a species, we've been working on this form of organization for a long time.

Team 101

Over thousands of years, human life has spawned myriad small groups. To see what is special about *teams* we need to understand what's common to all small groups. Then we can see what's particular to virtual teams.

Luckily, researchers show considerable agreement on how teams differ from *groups*—even if their precise definitions of them contrast.

Small Groups

Today, a very clear model of small-group characteristics stands with considerable consensus behind it.[8] Indeed, the general framework established in the mid-1980s has enjoyed a decade of testing and exploration.[9]

- Two or more individuals
- Interaction among group members
- Interdependence

This leads to a very short three-word definition of a small group:

Individuals interacting interdependently.

People become a group by virtue of doing things of mutual benefit together. A small group is *not* a random collection of people, like a crowd crossing a street or passengers on a plane. *Groups* of people have more; they have an interrelatedness and a common motivation that adds up to more than just a bunch of individuals.

A *collection of people becomes a group when the whole is more than the sum of the parts.*

It is very rare that a new small group arises out of nowhere. Usually, small groups arise from preexisting ones—the CFO network that grows out of a multinational finance organization, the pickup basketball team that follows the playground building project, the book club that grows out of the "art crit" group that grows out of the 50-something students at Massachusetts College of Art. Most small groups are part of networks and other larger organizations.

Individual *members* of the group define its boundaries. What allows people to say they are "in" the group while others are "out"? People who are on an e-mail distribution list establish themselves as members of that virtual group. If you are not on the list, you are not a member. Membership, as recognized by insiders and outsiders alike, gives a group its essential boundary.

The second element of small groups is *interaction*—people connecting with people. Communication, the means of connection that provides pathways for human relationships, is inherently a shared activity.

The third element is *interdependence,* which means what many people think of as "unifying purpose" or "shared goals." Interdependence—joint purpose and shared motivation—is essential to form individuals into something more, a group. The words *individuals interacting* are not sufficient to define a small group.

Synergy is the word Buckminster Fuller popularized to describe the "something more" characteristic. In virtual teams, ephemeral synergy arises from purpose pursued.

"We put the 'x' in dot-com" reads the in-joke marketing message among members of a product management group. Nonsense, anyone else would say. Not at all, replies the team. The "message" erupted in one of countless exchanges about how to position the product. The *x* itself then became a verb. For this team, "x-ing" something means applying the product's power to it.

Language, first invented in the earliest forager camps, continues to evolve all the time in groups today. Acronyms, stock phrases, and in-jokes are verbal indicators of group cohesion. Our company affectionately refers to our early product development stages as "hops." We collectively speak millions of dialects, whether in the small towns of Sicily or the web rooms of software development groups. They are our common tongues.

For millennia, small-group communications means that people talk to one another face-to-face, using the medium of sound waves traveling through air. We are genetically programmed to assume that most small-group communication is face-to-face. But reality is changing.

The move to virtual work is the most dramatic change in the nature of the small group since humans acquired the capacity to talk to one another.

Tasks Mean Teams

What are teams? The step from small groups to teams is short and simple. Both the scientific literature and the popular press express the distinction in the same clear way:

Teams exist for some task-oriented purpose.[10]

Orientation to task is what distinguishes teams from other types of small groups. While all small groups carry out tasks to some degree (as well as make decisions and support social interactions), task *is* the primary focus for teams. All other aspects are ancillary.

While purpose is fundamental to all groups, teams are specifically, deliberately, and invariably about results. Tasks are the work, the common process, that leads to results, the joint aspiration at the end. When they set goals, teams project their results and commit to the tasks required to carry them out.

Tasks also create team boundaries. Certain members with special skills must be part of the group for success. Different members shape and reshape the purpose and tasks of the group. Indeed, the goals and tasks often exist before the team identifies its members. The feedback loop between task definition and appropriate membership becomes a core defining process during a team's early development.

While task distinguishes teams from small groups, boundary-crossing differentiates traditional teams and virtual ones. It is the day-in-and-day-out reality of communicating, interacting, and building relationships across space, time, and organizations that makes teams virtual.

Four Ages of Small

We once had a cat named Small, named for E. F. Schumacher's famous dictum (and book), *Small Is Beautiful.*[11] When it comes to people organizing effectively, small is indeed beautiful—and very old.

Over the ages, we have become increasingly adept at being in small groups. When hierarchy came along, people did not stop meeting and performing in small numbers. When bureaucracy evolved, hierarchs did not throw down their scepters and call it a day. Industrial bureaucracies depend upon the small groups that populate their ranks and levels. While developing its own signature characteristics, each age also incorporates essential organizational features of the ones before it.

> Networks, the organizations of the Information Age, incorporate aspects of their predecessors: levels of hierarchies, specialties of bureaucracy, and clear membership of small groups.

Old forms do not, however, endure unchanged. With each new age, new versions of old forms supplement the organizational repertoire. In our most basic everyday life, we are shaped by human experience millions of years old. Awareness of our long history in small groups (Figure 3.1) offers a bountiful source of experience to call upon as we spread our virtual wings. It's in our social DNA.

Families and Camps

The mobile family, foraging to survive, is the basic social unit of the nomadic era. Relatively small, these families were partly self-sufficient and partly interdependent with other families. Together, they periodically set up camp in larger groups. Once in the camps, task groups naturally took shape. Hunters, gatherers, and traders joined forces according to circumstance and need.

Figure 3.1   Four Ages of Small Groups

	Nomadic	Agricultural	Industrial	Information
Families	Mobile family	Extended family	Nuclear family	Diverse family
Task Teams	Gatherers Hunters Traders	Farmers Herders Artisans	Position Specialty Professional	**Virtual Teams**
Social Groups	Health Leisure Friendship	Castes Classes Religious	Associations Special interest Clubs	Electronic groups Virtual communities
Decision Groups	House heads Camp councils	Rulers, elites Military units Owners	Legal Representative Committees	Direct participation Virtual government

The first teams were task-oriented groups in nomadic era camps.

Camps also stimulated relationships outside the family. These *nonkin affinity networks,* as the anthropologists call them, allowed people to have friends, share information, extend healing, encourage hobbies, enjoy leisure and recreation, and participate in adventures. Without cooperation across kin lines, humanity never would have gone beyond subsistence. These "virtual" kinships, what anthropologists call *fictive kinships,* were critical to human progress—and remain so.

The Agriculture of Groups

In the agricultural era, families grew larger and more extended. Farmers and herders, the new economic task units, crowded out hunters and gatherers. Skilled toolmakers evolved into artisans. With them came masters of the trade with their own small shops and apprentices. Society stratified into castes and classes. Religious groups proliferated as common spiritual lives integrated larger communities inhabiting bigger societies.

The great organizational structures of this time were ruling elites and military units. To protect land, agrarian settlements marshaled military hierarchies to coerce people.

But organized violence was not the only contribution of this age. The invention of hierarchy brought along a positive development: clear efficient authority structures with ranks and small group units combining into ever larger units. This innovation of multilevel social structure was a great leap forward in the human capacity to organize large numbers of people.

At the same time, the first cornerstone of capitalism was laid. Military and religious leaders became owners of land previously held by the groups who lived on it. In economic terms, ownership reverberates to our own day as the ultimate source of coercive authority—the right to hire, fire, and sell.

This timeless feature is the bedrock of hierarchical rights and responsibilities in companies. Executives confront an apparent dilemma when they try to team with one another because by their nature they are hierarchical decision makers. They actually have a dual nature—hierarchs who are guardians of supreme power and team members who are partners in power. Executive groups find it particularly difficult to be effective task teams.

Organization as Machine

In the Industrial Age, the typical family size shrank again, becoming more nuclear. While remaining key in society, the family abruptly ended its preeminence in the economic domain.

Instead, segmented, specialized work ruled. Task-oriented bureaucratic units became the basis for economic gain. Rules bound replicable operating units. The units in turn aggregated into larger mechanical processes that produced predictable results. Society viewed small groups of all sorts as interchangeable, replaceable parts of the machine organization.

The great social invention of bureaucracy is formal representation under law. Here, small groups stand for larger communities of people. New organizations defined by constitutions, laws, policies, and procedures created numerous bureaucratic small-group structures—from supreme courts to city councils.

The Information Era Small Group

At the dawn of the third millennium, increasingly diverse styles of families proliferate. The nature and role of the family are hot topics. Families are again a significant economic unit, not just as consumers but as joint ventures with two or more income streams.

At work, distributed, decentralized, flexible organizations are replacing colocated groups. The technological capacity to share information and the staggering increase in the ability to communicate provide fertile soil. *Virtual teams,* the new boundary-spanning, task-oriented working groups born of the Information Age, abound.

Crossing Boundaries

Buckman Labs is a sea of virtual teams that constantly form and dissolve. To solve a customer problem, a global virtual team comes together without anyone chartering it. The group includes anyone in the company who chooses to participate on a particular topic. When the discussion is over, the virtual team disbands.

Buckman's teams are quite different from traditional task groups comprising people from the same organization functioning in the same place at the same time—the conventional nine-to-five office and the assembly-line seven-to-three shift of industry.

We need some coordinates to explore the new type of team in this unfamiliar terrain (Figure 3.2). One dimension *is* familiar: distance over space and time. Another less obvious but extremely important perspective is that of organizational "distance."

Virtual teams come in different varieties, each with unique characteristics, that require nuances of behavior to be effective.

Figure 3.2   Varieties of Virtuality

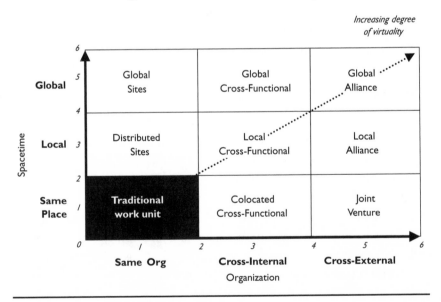

Distributed Teams

Distributed teams comprise people in the same organization who work in different places. They may operate interdependently, as is the case with Buckman Labs' research and development operation, distributed across all the company's sites. This contrasts with the branches of Fleet-Boston's First Community Bank, which operate relatively separately albeit under the same brand.

Teams with members in different places clearly have to solve the distance problem, and the further away, the bigger the distance problem. Perhaps just one person is situated remotely. Perhaps several are. Sometimes everyone is in a different place. It's all relative.

The ability to work at a distance reshapes the traditional headquarters-field relationship. Under the old model, site managers belonged to the same organization but rarely worked as a team. Indeed, branch offices, one familiar example of de facto distributed teams, often are encouraged to compete in a system that pits one against the other in the effort to maximize output and beat quotas.

When branches work together, however, they form virtual teams of people in the same organization situated in different places. The 47 branch managers of First Community Bank formed a team among themselves to address common service issues and to develop cross-branch priorities based on their own needs and shared learning. Branch teams face the same problems of crossing space and time as more organizationally diverse virtual teams. Local intergroup boundaries are sometimes more difficult to bridge than more distant affiliations because of competition over contiguous organizational borders.

Even if not distributed in space, virtual teams can be spread out in time. Teams of shifts and groups of managers and professionals-on-the-move share facilities—people in the same organization who use the same place at different times—but are not really colocated.

Cross-Organizational Teams

In traditional Industrial Age–type colocated teams, people worked side by side in the same space at the same time on interdependent tasks for the same organization. Several decades ago, even before the new communications technologies were widely available, one form of virtual team began to appear: the cross-functional team.

Today, cross-organizational teams are common. They comprise people from different organizations who work together in the same or different places. At Buckman Labs, an informal group of people—who number between 4 and 15 according to Buckman Lab's Alison Tucker— all work in Memphis, but for different Buckman organizations. Though their task is to brand the company's products, only some members of the team are from marketing.

In the classic cross-functional group, experts and stakeholders come together to solve problems or seize opportunities that require cooperation across organizational boundaries. Shell's Strategic Initiative Teams (see Chapter 2, "Networks"), which come together physically to develop a new organizational strategy for the 100-year-old company, include geophysicists, financiers, marketeers, production superintendents, executives, organization development consultants, and boilermakers. They continue their regular jobs while devoting the equivalent of another full-time job to the new Shell initiative.

As organizations span greater distances, the option to colocate people shrinks even as the ability to work at a distance grows. Relocation itself is increasingly difficult because of people's unwillingness to move and spiraling costs. Shortening project time frames underscore the lack of cost justification for moving people. Today's teams *must* form while remaining spread out.

Double Whammy

Of greatest challenge are those teams that are both distributed and cross-organizational, involving people from different organizations who work in different places.

Most work combines a pattern of individual and group tasks, time spent working alone and time spent working with others. For most virtual teams, *synchronous* interaction—shared time—is a scarce resource, whether face-to-face or at a distance. For best results, time together is planned, prepared for, and followed up on.

Time creates a complication that not even instantaneous communication can solve. As distance and time-zone crossing increases, the window of synchronicity in the workday compresses. New England is six hours behind Europe, and people in California leave work just as their counterparts start their next day in Japan. Even when real-time interaction is possible technically, it may not be practical.

Without face-to-face or other real-time interaction, this extreme but increasingly common form of virtual team tests the limits. How it deals with contentious issues virtually is as important as how greatly it shines in sharing information and solving technical problems.

How Virtual Are You?

Do you participate in or know about a virtual team? Where would this team or others fit on the two cross-boundary scales in Figure 3.2? Use the numbers along the side to mark judgments you make. Multiply the two scores to create a simple "virtuality index" for comparing different teams and networks.

Is there a starting point for boundary crossing? "Headquarters and field" typify the common pattern of distributed work. "Here" may be the organization and place where the leader sits, where the bulk of the team has workplaces, and/or where the sponsor or support system is located. Increasingly, however, no place is home (the zero point of each dimension), and everyone is relatively virtual. Then it is especially important to quickly open and populate an online place to contain the team's identity.

Consider all the members and stakeholders in your example group. Note where people are located to see the boundaries that the team crosses. Think about the impact of distance on a person-by-person basis to assess the likely frequency of face-to-face contact and the relative cost of the team getting together. The 50-foot rule (Chapter 1, "Why") suggests that people have to be very close together to gain the advantage of spontaneous interaction. Beyond that close range, cost and travel time increase with each greater distance. When people are face-to-face, take into account cultural differences in regard to personal-proximity "comfort zones."

The subscore on each dimension gives an indication of the general degree of difficulty the team will face in working virtually.

- A virtual team distributed in space and time, but from the same organization, is likely to find that communications and participation issues dominate its development. Consider how much time the team will spend together (synchronous) and how much asynchronous interaction it requires.
- A colocated, cross-organizational team is likely to experience difficulty establishing a common purpose and making decisions. Typically, you will need more time, more cycles, and more patience to deal with the details as you translate a broad, shared mission into goals and tasks.
- Virtual teams that are both distributed and cross-organizational will experience both stretched communications and stressful purpose setting. These are the teams most in need of new ways to work and technology-support infrastructures.

The People Boundary

By implication, traditional work means that people speak the same language and take their nonverbal cues from the same broader culture. Today, even when people are in the same location, the chances are high that they speak different languages.

Virtual teams break this traditional cultural boundary mold. When people occupy different places and come from different organizations, they can be certain that they will have to communicate across culture and custom with different languages. The language differences that virtual teams have to contend with are not all born of different country tongues. Two people from different professional upbringings can have almost as much problem communicating as two people who grow up speaking English and Japanese.

When teams go global, their language and culture issues clearly loom larger. However, all teams of the future will have to cope with the fact of increasing diversity in the workplace. Not only is the workforce becoming more diverse, but the task requirements of complex work demand that a more diverse group of people work together, whether in traditional settings or in virtual teams.

Sometimes colocated teams have even greater difficulty dealing with variations of language and culture than do virtual teams. Because they are less aware of their communication barriers, colocated teams do not necessarily create appropriate compensations. There is an analogy here to the relationship between distance and collaboration. Data show that people are somewhat less likely to communicate with a colleague upstairs in the same building than with one in another building.[12] When people know they are at a distance—culturally and linguistically as well as spatially— they are more conscious of the need to be explicit and intentional about communication.

More often than not, the first issue that arises for people working virtually is trust.

CHAPTER 4

TRUST

Virtual Relationships

"We're re-creating the complexity of the natural world in cyberspace and re-embracing deep, social archetypes," says David Sibbet, who describes his unique craft of graphic facilitation as "journalism put together with poster making."[1] Sibbett has pioneered the practice of facilitating groups with graphics. As meetings progress, graphics facilitators take multicolored notes on very big flipcharts, producing elaborate murals that simulate the group's "story in words and image, providing a way for groups to collectively uncover the patterns of shared meaning in their different perceptions." "Cyberspace will be equally complex. Already it is evolving beyond text and numbers to word, image, feeling, and social interaction. Do we navigate through our lives analytically? No, we rely on people we trust. We won't turn over millions of years of evolution just because we're using new tools."

Trust is the short word that underlies the years ahead. Online, we go through people we trust.

Benefits

People work together because they trust one another. They make deals, undertake projects, set goals, and lend one another resources. Teams with trust converge more easily, organize their work more quickly, and manage themselves better. Less trust makes it much more difficult to generate and sustain successful virtual teams.

Trust has always been important for groups. In the workaday world of the Industrial Age, it is more a nice-to-have quality than a need-to-have one. Times have changed.

Virtual teams are quicker, smarter, more flexible work groups in a sea of change. Highly adaptive organizations, these teams can cope with tumultuous complexity. For them, trust is a need-to-have quality.

Without daily face-to-face cues, trust is at once both harder to attain and easier to lose. Mistrust slips in between the slender lines of long-distance communication stripped of the nuances of in-person interaction. Business grinds to a halt when trust breaks down.

"Trust builds with the recognition of the contribution that everyone makes," says Pfizer's Hank McKinnell. "If you make a real contribution, people will trust you."

Trust is the elixir of group life, the belief or confidence in a person or organization's integrity, fairness, and reliability. This "matter of faith" comes from past experience, however brief or extensive. The importance of trust cuts across a team's life cycle:

- A new team requires trust to begin.
- It's the all-purpose grease for the ongoing hard work of the team.
- When it's done, a team leaves trust (or its lack) behind.

Successful virtual teams pay special attention to building trust at each stage of their development.

As trust accumulates—in teams, corporations, communities, and nations—it creates a new form of wealth. In the Network Age, *social capital* is as potent a source of value as land, resources, skills, and technology. To understand just how powerful an *economic* force social capital is, we travel back in time nearly a millennium.

Two Paths, Two Societies

Italy was in shambles as the curtain lifted on Europe's aptly named Dark Ages. Throughout the peninsula, imperial rule had crumbled. Banditry was rampant. Restoring social order was the government imperative of the time. With the dawning of the twelfth century, two radically different approaches emerged:

- Steep vertical hierarchies rose up in the south.
- Horizontal networks spread out in the north.

Hundreds of years later, these two paths reverberate still, not as faint echoes of the past but as powerful, pulsing shapers of the two disparate regions' cultures, institutions, and economies.

Beginning in the early 1100s, Italy's southern region fell under the organizing talents of Norman mercenaries. They superbly blended relatively enlightened feudal rule with Byzantine-style, complicated bureaucracy for the next few centuries. Then, following the deaths of a line of great kings, prosperity started to wane. The steep hierarchy passed to the landed autocrats.

This vertical, client-patron power structure remained intact for the next 800 years and is still spectacularly evident in the 1990s. The collapse of the central government to corruption, a mega-scandal known as "Kickback City" (in Italian, *Tangentopoli*), was nearly a millennium in the making. Meanwhile, Italy's central and northern towns became remarkable forerunners of twenty-first-century organizational design.

Inventing Credit

Not since the rise of Athens and the other early Greek city-states had the West witnessed such a brilliant light of self-governance as shined in Florence, Venice, Bologna, Genoa, Milan, and other cities and towns in the north of Italy. From the 1100s, decentralized centers of communal republicanism rose and prospered. At their core were voluntary mutual-aid associations of neighbors for protection from marauding violence and cooperation for economic prosperity.

> *"From the twelfth to the sixteenth century the feature*
> *that most distinguished Italian society from that in other*
> *regions in Europe was the extent to which men [sic]*
> *were able to take part in determining, largely by persua-*
> *sion, the laws and decisions governing their lives."*[2]

People formed myriad mutual-aid groups in many spheres, creating a "rich network of associational life"—in neighborhoods, among parish priests and religious societies, in political parties, and within "tower societies" that provided security. Key among them were craft and trade guilds, formed for social as well as economic purposes. A "vivid sense of equality" coursed through the affairs of these communities.

Most remarkable was the economic creativity unleashed by the growing civic communities. The northern Italian republics invented *credit*, adding this fundamental tool to the already known classic economic factors of markets, money, and law.

Before the innovation of credit, private capital could accumulate but could not travel further in the economy. Credit links savings and investment. It sets up an accumulating feedback loop whereby wealth can be used to create more wealth and economic growth. The prosperity of the communal north flourished through finance and commerce, which produced a different kind of affluence from that of the southern Sicilian Kingdom, which rooted wealth in the land.

What lay at the heart of the discovery of credit a thousand years ago? Nothing more complex than an essential human quality already old by then—*trust*. Credit (from the word meaning "to believe") is possible only when there is mutual trust. In the *Oxford English Dictionary*, the third definition of credit *is* trust. The more trust exists, the more efficient credit is. The cost of mistrust goes down. With widespread trust in northern Italy:

> *"(S)avings were activated for productive purposes to a*
> *degree inconceivable in previous centuries. . . . It was*
> *the widespread sense of honesty, strengthened by the*

> *sense of belonging to an integrated community, quite apart from definite legal obligations, which made possible the participation of all kinds of people with their savings in the productive process."*[3]

Northern Italy has maintained a rich, concentrated culture built on extensive intertwined horizontal relationships throughout the centuries, through plagues, foreign occupations, and periodic impositions of client-patron controls.

Emilia-Romagna: The Reprise

An unexpected visitor arrived at our office in West Newton, Massachusetts, in late fall 1991. He had a message that he said we could not ignore in the book we were then writing, *The TeamNet Factor*.[4] "You must tell the amazing story of what happens when many, many small businesses form networks," said Jean-Pierre Pellegrin, a French official at the Organization for Economic and Cooperation and Development in Paris. "Emilia-Romagna, then Denmark. Write about them." *Them* turned out to be a very big story indeed in north-central Italy.[5] The somewhat mysterious source of Emilia-Romagna's rags-to-riches story was the inspiration for the *flexible business network* movement around the world—where little companies become small giants by linking up.

After a century of centralized rule from Rome, Italy finally decided to decentralize its government in the 1970s. At the time that regional governments begin to form, Emilia-Romagna ranked eighteenth in income among Italy's 21 administrative regions.

Over the next decade, the economy exploded as hundreds of thousands of small businesses in Emilia-Romagna tied together into networks. It became the second wealthiest region in Italy, recording the greatest performance jump of any of the 80 European Community regions by the mid-1980s. Unemployment plunged from 20 percent to almost zero. By the late 1980s, there were 325,000 companies in this region of 4 million—an incredible ratio of one firm to 12 people, 90,000 of them in manufacturing.

Emilia-Romagna caught Denmark's attention. By the end of the 1980s, that country of 5 *million,* about the same size as the commonwealth of Massachusetts, intentionally launched a similar effort. Denmark's success proved that many of the Italian lessons are transferable. In these two countries, government stimulates thousands of networks, positively affecting the national bottom line.

Italy's experience in moving from centralized to decentralized governance mirrors that of many organizations. Its mandate comes long before its implementation. Italy's 1948 Constitution calls for the nation to decentralize and establish administrative regions. But it takes more than a generation for this to occur. Italy deliberately establishes an entirely new level of government in 1970. With the regions come new governments with fairly equivalent roles, rules, and budgets.

This rare event in a developed democracy offers a natural experiment: a set of governmental constants and a wealth of social, cultural, and economic variables encompassing the many extremes represented in Italy.

Harvard professor of government Robert Putnam and a network of colleagues seized the extraordinary opportunity to do very large scale social *science* in the field. Together they laid a baseline and tracked the ensuing institutional results. Putnam's book, *Making Democracy Work: Civic Traditions in Modern Italy,* summarizes their extensive findings and draws powerful implications for democracy and economic development in the Network Age.

They measured the performance of the new governments in three broad areas with 12 indicators:

- *Processes,* including cabinet stability, budget promptness, and statistical and information services
- *Lawmaking,* including reform legislation and legislative innovation

- *Implementation,* including day-care centers,[6] family clinics, industrial policy instruments, agricultural spending capacity, local health unit expenditures, housing and urban development, and bureaucratic responsiveness

Perception is at least as important as reality in politics. They tested these objective performance measures against citizen and community leaders' opinions gathered by surveys and polls and found them in close agreement.

Amazingly, Emilia-Romagna topped the authors' "good government" charts among all the regions.[7] Why?

The Hunt for Civic Community

While some regions thrived, others quagmired. These conclusions leapt out of the data—field observations, case studies, quantitative techniques, and statistical analysis—prompting the researchers to keep asking why. They liken their search for clues to a detective mystery.

The usual explanation, that good socioeconomics leads to good government, does not square with the data. Both the top performer and the bottom one started in 1970 with similar below-average social and economic indicators. Yet Emilia-Romagna in the north became the country's rising star, while Calabria in the toe of Italy turned in the most dismal performance. (See Figure 4.1.)

The answer, once they saw it, reverberated throughout the data:

- Indicators of good government correlate with . . .
- Places where people are joined in thick, overlapping networks, what the researchers termed "civic communities," that in turn map uncannily closely with the . . .
- Most horizontally organized types of governments of the medieval states as they existed in 1300.

Civic communities come about when people engage in horizontal relationships. They are "bound together by reciprocity and cooperation,"

Figure 4.1   Modern Outcomes of Ancient Social Capital

Institutional Performance in Italian Regions
1978–1985

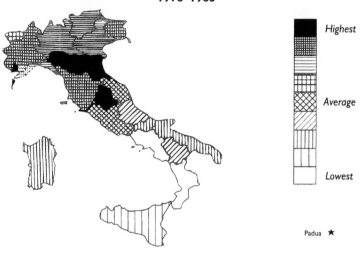

Highest

Average

Lowest

Padua ★

Republican and Autocratic Traditions
Italy c. 1300

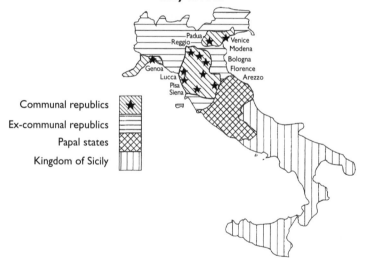

Communal republics

Ex-communal republics

Papal states

Kingdom of Sicily

Figure 4.1   (Continued)

Civic Community in Italian Regions

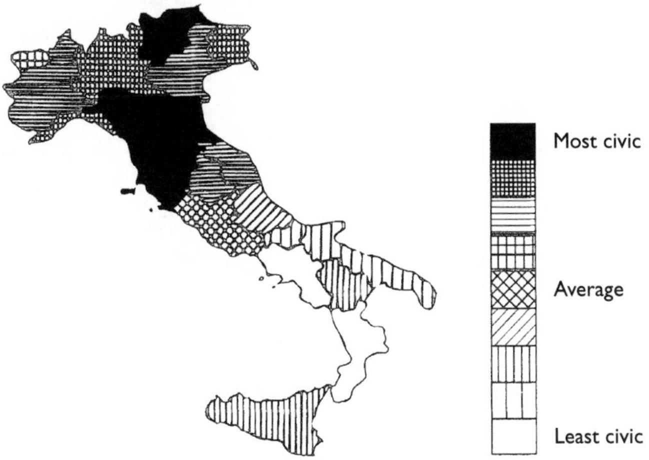

according to Putnam, rather than by vertical "authority and dependency."
Equality and trust, two basic human values, are at the core of civic culture. Civic societies are lush with social networks and associations of all
sorts, an observation Alexis de Tocqueville made regarding the about-to-
boom United States in his 1840 study, *Democracy in America.*

Many networks tightly braid people in Emilia-Romagna, which has
the top measures in both civic culture and institutional performance.
Putnam calls it "the site of an unusual concentration of overlapping networks of social solidarity, peopled by citizens with an unusually well
developed public spirit—a web of civic communities. Emilia-Romagna is
not populated by angels, but within its borders (and those of neighboring
regions in north-central Italy) collective action of all sorts, including government, is facilitated by norms and networks of civic engagement."

The results are simple and strong:

*Governments are better where measures of "civic-ness"
are higher.*

New Gold

In 1970, Bologna, once the intellectual capital of the medieval communal republics, became the new regional capital of Emilia-Romagna.

What fuels the unprecedented economic growth there and the creation of excellent government? What resources of capital enable such widespread creation of new wealth? Neither new land, natural resources, nor technology grace this ancient area. Not even human capital, meaning a highly educated and skilled populace, distinguish it.

What Emilia-Romagna did have in 1970 was an abundant stock of continuously renewing *social capital*.[8] Its spring of wealth has three tributaries:

- Trust
- Reciprocity
- Dense social networks

In the communal republics, extraordinary trust develops among myriad mutual-aid associations and allows the civic regions of Italy to invent credit. The lesson of the past millennium applies immediately to today's business networks.

> *"At the core of the mutual aid societies was practical reciprocity: I'll help you if you help me; let's face these problems together that none of us can face alone."*[9]

Today these seats of Western civilization again have shown how to spin old relationships into new gold.

Relationships among the players lodge social capital. Unlike financial and human capital, social capital cannot be the property of individuals or corporations. By its very nature, it is jointly owned.

People generate wealth in dense networks of horizontal relationships in two primary ways:

- By lowering transaction costs
- By increasing opportunities for cooperation

Transactions are at the heart of business. All transactions, commercial and otherwise, particularly across boundaries and over time, embody trust. Transactions have costs—heaviest when trust is low, lightest where trust is high.

Mistrust is expensive. Informal communication goes down and formality goes up: endless forms and legalisms, time and effort spent checking other people's work, drawn-out negotiations, political games and backstabbing, sticker shock at the cost of third-party enforcement, corruption, and crime. When trust diminishes, price goes up.

Left unrenewed and unused, social capital depletes, fragments, and disorganizes under the wear and tear of transaction costs. Mistrust makes networks hard to form and relationships difficult to maintain, further diminishing trust. Unchecked, this vicious cycle searches for a stable state. In a top-down culture held together by vertical controls, the norm to "never cooperate" stiffens in place.

But there is hope. Social capital also grows through *reciprocity* among people in *horizontal networks*. Reciprocity works when people

- Barter directly in the here and now.
- Bank benefits for the future, the barn-raising principle.

In barter, reciprocity is in equilibrium with an immediate and equivalent exchange, a trade of some kind. In barn raising, you do something today believing that it will come around to you in the future.

Future-oriented, barn-raising, cooperative behavior is the most productive type of reciprocity. It enables economic development.

Rotating credit associations, found in virtually all cultures around the world, show how trust creates new wealth. Revolving loan funds—from villages in Bangladesh where Grameen Bank funds new businesses to the Pine Ridge Reservation in South Dakota where small groups of microentrepreneurs pool resources—happen when everyone in a group contributes to a common pot. One member uses the collective pot, perhaps to increase his or her productivity (e.g., to buy seed or a plow). After experiencing the benefit, members, of course, continue to contribute. Why "of course"? Because in dense networks, where people know one another well; the cost of lost opportunities and the threat of ostracism are prohibitive.

Trust lowers the cost of cooperation, depositing money in the bank. Informal communication increases while formalities and paperwork recede. Negotiations are brief and conclusive. The need for "checkers" evaporates as people simply keep their word. No need to spend time supervising because everyone's involved in real work. With trust and relationships that are reciprocal, social capital accumulates. Without trust, it remains scattered and unformed. The more relationships you have, the greater the potential for crosshatches of trust.

Greed No More

"GREED, MISMANAGEMENT RAVAGE FISHERIES," reads the headline.[10] Near us, both the United States and Canada are invoking drastic measures to curtail the catch on the once-rich Georges Bank fishing grounds off the New England and Newfoundland coasts. Local economies are devastated. A precious resource is in dire danger globally.

Georges Bank is a real-world example of "the tragedy of the commons," whereby people ruin a place that they own in common by overuse. When everyone maximizes his or her own individual gain by exploiting a shared resource, they destroy a natural, common source of wealth. Add continuously improving technology, such as in ocean fishing, and the spiral to exhaustion accelerates.

The field of game theory has a name for this: "The dilemma of collective action" is one of several logical puzzles that speak ill of cooperation. According to the numbers, cooperation is either folly or, at best, rarely a rational choice. With such thinking, early game theorists make the science of economics more dismal than Malthus had ever imagined. In closed transactions where games are played in isolation only once, the winning strategy, they find, is for players to get as much for themselves as possible and never cooperate. Selfishness is logical and rational.

In isolated situations where there are no consequences in the future and relationships are top-down, people never cooperate, a predictable, suspicious, stable state. It's safer and more rational to always defect, to be mistrustful and exploitative.

However, when people play repeat games, the logic changes dramatically. People become more cooperative when their behavior in one transaction carries forward to subsequent ones. In "infinitely repeated games," cooperation suddenly becomes rational and practical according to later game theory studies.[11]

Game theory predicts, and Putnam's study demonstrates, that society holds together at two "quite different levels of efficiency and institutional performance." In one case, the informing principle is to "always defect." In the other, the motto is to "reciprocate help."

When the players connect in rich networks, "brave reciprocity" prevails. News about trustworthy and untrustworthy behavior spreads quickly and widely. Here the norm is different: "Cooperate with people who cooperate with you (or who cooperate with people like you), and don't be the first to defect.' "[12]

These self-reinforcing dynamics, reciprocity-trust and dependence-exploitation, reflect building-up and tearing-down forces. They are, respectively, *vicious* and *virtuous* loops, amplifying through positive feedback.

Trust, reciprocity, and networks all are mutually reinforcing, whether on the rise or on the wane.

Trust is at the personal core; reciprocity is at the interface; and networks tie it all together.

Networks facilitate communication and extend trust. When success spreads through a network, it stimulates more cooperation, providing models for others about what works. Innovation increases as the latest information and trends create a large-scale learning system in which many potential users share knowledge.

Innovation is stunning among Emilia-Romagna's hundreds of thousands of tiny, networked companies. As so many have observed about this region, it reflects a vital dynamic that simultaneously integrates vigorous competition and cooperation—"co-opetition"—among many independent players.

These lessons have a timeless quality. They apply both on grand scales and on intimate ones.

Capital Across the Ages

The twenty-first-century return to our millions-of-years-old roots carries a quiver of new collaborative tools of awesome power. Social capital is an old form of wealth, albeit a largely unacknowledged one. Suddenly, however, we have new ways to create and magnify it outside the confines of physical space-time limits. With the ability to reach across great distances without having to travel them physically, we are able to build communities of high trust that circle the globe.

Unlike human and physical capital, individuals cannot possess social capital. It lies in the web of relationships among us and mingles with other means of generating wealth.

Capital(s)

Capital, once simple, is itself complex in the new world:

- *Human capital* represents the value of the people part of the work equation, the skills and knowledge of individuals. The oldest form of capital, reaching back to the earliest societies, it is rooted in people's ability to survive in the world around them. As environmental challenges alter, so does the human capital required to survive and succeed. The hard work of applying human capital in the olden days has its corollary today in the round-the-clock efforts that typify crash projects on impossible deadlines.

- *Social capital,* an equally old resource, reflects the community skills that have coevolved with individual skills. People working together generate webs of social capital. Hunters and gatherers compensate for resource scarcity by pooling their communal smarts. Today, people can manufacture social capital abundantly everywhere all the time, no longer constrained by space or time.
- *Land capital* harks back to the economic basis of the agricultural era. With farming and herding, people use land in an entirely new way to provide a relatively predictable food supply. In domesticating aspects of nature, human beings take a dramatic leap in scale and civilization. What does it mean to own real estate in cyberspace?
- *Machine capital* is the great engine of economic growth in the Industrial Age. Technology rolls on with the laws of motion, remaking the world—everything from hand tools to locomotives. While people generate new fortunes with productive machinery, fields remain fertile. Land does not cease to have value as machines become dominant. Even at the beginning of the twenty-first century, people still perceive technology as the most potent force in economic growth. What is a machine when a chip smaller than a fingernail does the job of a whole factory?
- *Knowledge capital* resides in all the shared repositories of information and learning (most especially in the gray matter between people's ears). Cyberspace offers a vast new domain for this once limited source of wealth that is newly powerful and available in unprecedented ways. We've barely scratched the surface of what knowledge capital means.

The recognition of knowledge as a source of wealth and its intersection with other forms of capital is at the competitive cutting edge of the global marketplace.

Shared knowledge is the dominant productive source of twenty-first-century economics, with unanticipated consequences now unfolding at startling speed.

Virtual Capital

The debate about the value of capital is more intense than ever in the Internet world. Market capitalizations of Internet start-ups literally have redefined the meaning of value. Initial public offering–bound start-ups have none of the traditional indicators of investible companies— whether profits and customers or even products and revenues. *All* some of these companies have is their ideas and their relationships, which the market appears to value very highly. Indeed, "IPO" has become a verb.

Perhaps this makes sense after all. *All* forms of capital fuel today's networked organizations. Virtual teams possess human capital *in* their members and social capital *among* their members. They utilize physical capital that is *outside* people through their meeting facilities and communication infrastructures.

They also generate knowledge capital among people

- *Inside,* who have their own corporate memories and shared cognitive models.
- *Outside,* where information is shared in commonly accessible databases.
- *Between* one another, as they connect networks and pools of knowledge together while developing enduring relationships.

Regardless of their specific tasks, all virtual teams can increase their human, social, and knowledge capital. Human capital increases when more people work together in more places, meeting new challenges and acquiring new competencies. Social capital accumulates when virtual team members vastly expand the number and diversity of their relationships. Because of their physical separation, virtual teams have an obligation to make knowledge capital explicit and accessible.

Virtual teams stretch the bounds of human capability, offering value far beyond their immediate functions: They elongate the reach of social capital outside their immediate physical locales. Although many of their elements have ancient roots, today's virtual teams look out over vistas of virtual places never before seen by human eyes.

The new frontier is not far away; it is everywhere.

Creating Social Capital

All organizations, large and small, have some social capital that continuously grows and diminishes, a hidden source of wealth or a deficit that may presage a disastrous weakness.

> Social capital is "the structure of relations between and among actors,"[13] individual or organizational.

Can you recall a friendship or professional relationship that you established in one team or small group that later proved a valuable connection in another? Can you remember deciding to do business with a partner, vendor, or customer because of their preexisting reputation?

In starting our own company, NetAge, we pass the first test with a venture capital firm because of Leon Navickas, CEO of Centra[14] (which provides real-time online meeting services), a partner firm of ours that has funding from the venture capitalist. "You're prequalified because you're in the network," the funder says, referencing our relationship to Centra.

Imagine the potential in your organization for better, faster, smarter relationships based on a rich network of preestablished lines of trust. Each strong relationship has a multiplier effect built into it: The friends of friends of friends are potentially accessible through social networks of trust. The old adage, "It's not what you know but who you know," portrays the essence of social capital.

The negative side of social capital also pertains. "I don't have any hard data," another long-trusted partner tells us in reference to yet another firm that wants to do business with us. "But there's always something a little unclear about how they do business." We back off.

Do you recall cautioning others about people whom you came to distrust through work? Does a team experience leave a bad taste in your mouth that affects other situations or opportunities? Have you seen previously good relationships between people or companies strain or snap to the detriment of both? A bad experience also has a multiplier effect.

News of mistrust travels at the speed of speech, whether verbal or virtual, diminishing the capacity for collaboration within and between organizations.

It is better not to team at all than to team badly.

Social capital is a seminal idea growing at the intersection of economics and sociology since its 1988 introduction in a paper by University of Chicago sociologist James Coleman.[15] For the most part, the idea flies below the radar of public consciousness, but one mass-media peek came in an *ABC World News Tonight* segment.[16] It reported on where Harvard's Robert Putnam has gone with his work: the disturbing thesis that social capital is dangerously eroding in U.S. society as a whole. Putnam illustrates his point by many measures of declining participation in civic and social events. Among them is the telling observation that while more Americans are bowling than ever before, they are bowling alone rather than in once-popular bowling leagues.[17]

Virtual Trust

It is easier to form, launch, and sustain virtual teams in an environment rich in "the features of social organization . . . that facilitate coordination and cooperation for mutual benefit."

To work with people you rarely or never meet, you need some basis to believe in their expertise and trustworthiness. Clearly, a norm that supports dishonesty in some relationships rubs off on other relationships as the level of suspicion rises. The fragile sphere of virtual relationships requires a much higher level of trust than do conventional hierarchically controlled settings. Top-down control can mandate people to work together whether they want to or not. Virtual teams have only their shared trust in one another as their guarantee for the success of their joint work.

"The biggest thing that can undermine a virtual team is passive-aggressive behavior. You send me e-mail, I don't like it, I pretend I didn't get it, and you are damaged without recourse," says Keoki Andrus, a principal in The Launch Group[18] and a veteran of Microsoft and Novell, who calls this "virtual deception." People go to great lengths to fool the electronic gods, he says, reporting on one person who bragged about the tricks he used to make it appear that he had not received messages just so he could claim ignorant innocence. " 'I didn't get that' becomes the ultimate excuse," Andrus says. "There's no substitute for doing what you say you're going to do in building trust."

Michael Howland, president and CEO of Applied Knowledge Group,[19] believes "you can get signals from e-communication about how people are doing in the same way you can from physical body language."

He first tests the theory when he and his colleague, Andy Campbell, develop a prototype for a virtual field office for the CIA. The purpose is "to see if you could handle a major national security project virtually." They also use the project as a test bed to explore electronic body language. "We realized that you can see it. The same way we get voice tone changes in spoken language, you can see it in sentence structure. The speed of response or lack thereof is another indicator of where a person's coming from," Howland says.

When Buckman Labs grew into a global organization, questions of integrity immediately arose. Among the concerns that employees raised was whether to pay bribes in countries where this is customary. The issue prompts the development of a code of ethics that becomes central to the Buckman community. Among the 10 points in the code is this one: "That we must use the highest ethics to guide our business dealings to ensure that we are always proud to be a part of Buckman Laboratories."

Larger organizations that house good teams almost always express values in codes, philosophies, and principles. Invariably they include trust along with integrity, teamwork, and a commitment to the value of the individual. "The Eastman Way," a pillar of Eastman Chemical Company's corporate culture, declares, "Eastman people are the key to success. We must treat each other fairly and with respect, based on values and principles: honesty and integrity, fairness, trust, teamwork, diversity, employee well-being, citizenship, winning attitude."

The norm of reciprocity—you do something for me and I'll do something for you—recognizes that a favor received will somehow be repaid in the future. The oft-used phrase, "I owe you one," speaks precisely to the value of a reciprocal relationship. Business is awash in these sorts of "owe-sies."

Thick social networks are signs of healthy communities and businesses. The more involvement people have in community life, the stronger the economies of their regions. The same idea applies to business. The more activities that people engage in together, the greater their commitment to one another. Company picnics that include employees' families, online chat rooms where people can talk about their hobbies, and corporate support for community involvement all build social capital inside the company as well as outside.

Social capital both provides and comes out of good teaming.

Strategy

Although we stress the benefits of cooperation over competition, we realize that these two tendencies dance with each other. "Co-opetition" is the newly coined term for this uneasy dynamic of simultaneous cooperation and competition.[20]

The complements of competition and cooperation cannot be evenly matched. If they are, progress stagnates and change recedes. One tendency or the other must dominate to carry the process forward. In virtual teams, cooperation provides the greater driving force.

Cooperation is the survival strategy for virtual teams. When necessary, the smart cooperator is also an excellent competitor.

Cooperation sounds nice in theory, but should we heed the conventional wisdom that says "Nice guys finish last"? Apparently not. The mad partnering evidenced by Internet companies indicates that cooperation with competitors may be the only way to finish.

The tooth-and-claw competition of Darwin that many assume to be the natural condition of life is giving way. There is accumulating evidence that cooperation is evident at all levels of biology's kingdoms— from cells to big-brained mammals. It may be particularly evident in humanity's remarkable spurt of evolution over the past few million years. Cooperators seem to be the survivors. It's a strategy.

In the original logic of games, an aggressive competitor invariably wins over a willing cooperator because they played only single games, one at a time. However, if the game expands, with more rounds of play involving more people, then behavior has consequences. When the behavior in past games is known prior to future games, it carries a self-correcting social consequence. If you ruin another person and no one else hears about it, you can probably get away with it. Yet when your behavior becomes public, it suggests how you will play in the future. Others may not want to play with you.

The reasoning is common sense. If people know that I cooperate, they will want to associate with me. Together we can do more than we can separately. Cooperators win.

Perhaps the most famous event in game-theory history illustrates this view. In the 1950s, Robert Axelrod, a leading practitioner of games, staged a series of contests to find the best strategy for logically combining competition and cooperation. People proposed various strategies that were translated into lines of code. These in turn were put into the equivalent of an open cyberspace market so that games could undergo many repetitions. Anatol Rapoport, the mathematician and one of the original four founders of the Society for General Systems Research, submitted the winning strategy. It remains the undisputed champion.

With both a catchy name and the shortest code, Rapoport's "Tit-for-Tat" strategy is simple: Cooperate on your first move, then match the other player's response with the same strategy. You might call it "tough cooperation." In short:

Reach out, then respond in kind.

Open with friendship then respond to opportunities with cooperation and to challenges with competition. This strategy works even where there initially are only a few cooperators in a sea of competitors. Tit-for-tat cooperation slowly accrues benefits, whereas competitors can at best achieve a standstill as they beat up on each other.

The advantage of cooperation will only grow in the years ahead. At the same time, the payoffs from purely competitive strategies likely will diminish. In the age of information, the foundations that support competition are shifting dramatically from

- Material scarcity to information plenty.
- Limited information to information access.
- Anonymous players to trusted partners.

Scaling Up

The idea that relationships of trust and cooperation can have productive benefits has sparked a revolution in economic development. Social wealth, valuable in the business world, offers a powerful new development resource for people with limited human and physical capital.

From the United Nations Development Programme, which makes social capital one of its initiatives, to Silicon Valley, California, which has exploded economically through thick webs of relationships, social capital has been rapidly accumulating. Pioneers in business, government, education, religion, and nonprofit organizations have seen the potential of strategic cooperation and have benefited from it.

In her groundbreaking book, *Regional Advantage*,[21] AnnaLee Saxenian describes the culture of Silicon Valley as one that promotes collaboration across business and sectoral lines. She contrasts this "social capital building" environment with that of Boston's Route 128 region of the 1980s. There and then, leaving one company to go to a competitor was regarded as an act of heresy. From an economic standpoint, Saxenian observes that the recession of the late 1980s quickly reversed in Silicon Valley, whereas the Route 128 region still suffered well into the 1990s.[22]

Saxenian's analysis became the subject of conversation from coast to coast. While some in the Route 128 region were rankled (she reports having been *un*invited to give at least one talk), others were motivated. Numerous cross-industry collaborations erupted around Boston, hundreds if not thousands of new businesses started up, and it became just as difficult to hold onto an engineer in Boston as it did in Palo Alto. A strong economy now booms in both locations.

Such attempts to consciously build social capital are often the work of individual businesspeople like Harry Brown of EBC Industries. We've been following Brown's inspiring story of networking in the small-parts manufacturing industry for many years.[23] Entrepreneurs like Brown look beyond the traditional needs of their businesses—markets, employees, and funding—to the larger environment that makes it possible to maintain and capitalize on those resources. They recognize that unless highly trained people with the right skills are coming out of universities, the local labor pool will wither and the knowledge-based economy will idle. Issues like this concern civic entrepreneurs and their colleagues in regional economic development collaboratives.[24]

Great efforts begin with small ones. Small groups fundamentally comprise human societies at all scales in all sectors. Trust originates in small groups—families, friendships, and myriad formal and informal associations based on shared interests and common concerns.

To grow trust, small is beautiful.

We cannot avoid teaming. We can only team well or badly. Thus, we will accrue or deplete our corporate social capital with every small group in the organization, whether we consciously acknowledge the value of relationships or not.

Home is the ancient center of place-based trust networks. Home is now also another place altogether.

CHAPTER 5

PLACE

Home Is Where the Site Is

The last decades of the twentieth century see the "storming and norming" pains of the birth of the Network Age. Communism crumbles and market forces reign. A new economic world order prevails as nations scramble to stabilize their politics. Computers and networks fly past critical mass. Global electronic technology shifts into digital drive. Endlessly mutating bits erupt into the infinite cybercultures of the rising networked civilization.

Even before the Internet, Joshua Meyrowitz put words to what was to come in his 1985 book, *No Sense of Place*,[1] in which he says that electronic media are dissolving the historic connection between physical place and social space. In the "nowhere" of the Internet, time compresses and people behave differently. Where you are takes on new meaning—and offers new possibilities—when you can be anywhere.

Sun's Corporate DNA

Red-hot Sun Microsystems is the poster child for the Network Age. Started by a group of college buddies, Sun has been synonymous with networking ever since it shipped its first workstation, made in 1982, with a network connection based on a universal Internet protocol.

The company begins the twenty-first century with major claims to Internet indispensability: Sun computers run four-fifths of Internet backbone traffic and more than half of Internet service providers.[2] Triple-digit increases in Sun's stock price followed by multiple stock splits and skyrocketing revenues with good profit margins indicate how the financial markets view Sun. The company deserves its ownership of the trademark tag line that many others paraphrase:

"The Network is the Computer[TM]*."*

On the economic green of Silicon Valley that Sun calls home, there's always room for improvement.

Ten years after helping found Sun, Scott McNealy, the CEO, convenes a series of annual meetings for his senior staff. He invites speakers from the companies he most admires—Federal Express's Fred Smith in 1993, Motorola's then-CEO Gary Tooker in 1994, and Xerox's then-CEO Paul Allaire in 1995. Their talks target teamwork and customer satisfaction as major improvement areas for Sun.

Tooker's message particularly resonates with McNealy. Pointing to how teams profoundly improve quality at Motorola,[3] Tooker provides McNealy with the outlines of a model that Sun will follow. If Sun can apply its extraordinary technology strength to resolving its quality issues, Tooker suggests, it will have dramatic competitive advantage in the years ahead.

As a classic lean-and-mean company, Sun always has celebrated the independence and initiative of its individual engineers. Now, going it alone seems to have run its course. "The high-flying cowboy of Sun's culture doesn't work anymore," says John McEvoy, Western Area operations manager in Sun's Enterprise Services group. "We've grown too large. One person can't make it happen."

There always have been teams at Sun. It's natural for people to come together in teams to get their work done. What was about to happen at Sun, however, is new—the deliberate use of cross-boundary teams to tackle the company's most challenging issues. It would require ingenuity, delicacy, and a particular spin that can seduce Sun's freewheeling culture.

Sun's strength is technology innovation. Jim Lynch, the company's vice president of corporate quality, points to Java, Sun's paradigm-shattering innovation that spun the web into a sea of dancing icons. Java delivers tiny chunks of "nimble, interactive"[4] software across the Internet on an as-needed basis. Once released, Java became central to the company's offerings and the face of the Internet.[5]

"Java is not a technology idea that came about because we were improving processes," Lynch says. What became Java began in 1991 as a small off-site project whose purpose was to explore the next wave in computing. Propelled by a number of unexpected twists and turns over the next several years, the project eventually resulted in the release of Java source code on the Internet in 1995. If Sun is to deliberately create teams, it doesn't want to, cannot afford to, quell such creativity.

"It's extraordinarily complex when you're tampering constructively with a company's DNA," says Lynch, who takes on responsibility for SunTeams. "You have to be very careful."

Virtual SunTeams

Once McNealy and his staff decided to introduce teams, they moved quickly. In fall 1994, just a few months after Tooker's visit, McNealy and his staff met with leaders of Motorola's team effort. Motorola's widely admired model for teams proved particularly applicable to Sun, most especially because the two companies are in related industries. Five months later, Lynch got the go-ahead to launch SunTeams, which, since its 1995 start, has involved nearly a third of the company's workforce.

To kick things off, McNealy takes to the web waves on SWAN (Sun Wide Area Network). The company's vast computer network includes "WSUN Radio," not a traditional radio station, but rather an internal web site that transports all media—text, graphics, audio, and video. McNealy challenges people to enter a competition to solve the company's most vexing customer problems as fast as they can with small, cross-company "SunTeams." He proffers an appealing incentive: an all-expenses-paid weekend for members and significant others of the 16 finalist teams at a posh hotel in San Francisco. They'll compete for awards in the first annual "SunTeams Celebration."

McNealy succeeds in putting a Sun spin on teams—challenge, speed, and competition. Seventy-five teams sign up immediately.

To become a SunTeam, a group has to:

- Identify an important customer (whether external or internal) with a significant problem.
- Secure an executive sponsor.
- Agree to adhere to SunTeams' methodology.

By observing a common methodology, the teams work consistently, even though the content of their projects differs.

SunTeams' team architecture (its term), originally a blend of Motorola's and Xerox's team-building processes, continues to evolve, combining newer elements with even older ones. In 1999 McNealy decided to adapt Six Sigma, the breakthrough quality process made famous by its use at Motorola and GE, to Sun. Later that year, McNealy joined General Electric's board of directors coincident with that company's decision to bring e-commerce to all of its businesses. As a result, SunTeams is adapting GE's Six Sigma training approaches. In an interesting intertwining of corporate histories, GE obtained its original Six Sigma course—from Motorola, which initiated the process in 1987 and won the U.S. government's prestigious Malcolm Baldrige National Quality Award one year later.

With Six Sigma, statistically based methods are used to drive down defects in a process until the number reaches near perfection, or fewer than 3.4 imperfections per million cycles.

SunTeams is rising to the challenge. Since the late 1990s, SunTeams have solved more than a thousand significant customer-related issues, from availability (in other words, uptime) and eliminating what it calls customer "dissatisfiers" to redesigning internal processes and reporting systems. Calling SunTeams its "workhorse for addressing some of the company's key issues," the company credits the initiatives with saving millions of dollars per year.[6]

All of the teams—nearly a thousand since 1995—are virtual in some respect. Typically, team members are in different locations and time zones. In fact, they don't refer to their locations by their geographies; they call them *time zones* ("the AustralAsia time zone," for example). The teams, usually about 10 to 15 in size, comprise specialists in areas relevant to the problem being solved. They frequently include people from outside the company—suppliers and customers are members of numerous teams.

A typical SunTeam comes about when someone proposes an idea to a few others; together, they register to become an official SunTeam, gaining resources, support, and visibility. They work together intensively for six to nine months, sometimes a year, in the context of their day jobs. It's not rare for a particular SunTeam to spawn its own children. In the story we're about to tell, a successful effort to solve a quite substantial customer problem gave birth to another, and 60 percent of the original team moved to the new one.

The Glass House Gang

Sun needed to electrify its reflexes in responding to mission-critical customer problems, the result of what Lynch calls "time compaction." No one can afford to be down anymore. Uptime for Sun's customers is the difference between being *in* business and out of it completely.

We spoke to Lynch the day after the February 2000 hacker attack on a number of the Internet's most popular commercial sites. "Yahoo didn't have a business for six hours yesterday. When we sell a mission-critical system to Fidelity for its trading floor, for example, and it goes down, that's a major hit to Fidelity's business, causing a major reduction in its revenue, impeding them and their customers from doing business. When eBay or Yahoo's systems go down, they are 'out' of business."

So the Time-Based Notification team came together and set its purpose: to create a "reliable automated customer problem escalation process" for one of Sun's critical products. In 17 months' time, the SunTeam of 25 people significantly reduced the response time to report a mission-critical problem.[7]

Before the team's work, customer problems were escalated on a case-by-case basis. A "time-based notification system" would eliminate the vagaries of handling each problem idiosyncratically.

If a major customer like eBay or Amazon goes down, Sun now escalates the problem hourly. "No one has to watch the clock," says John McEvoy, the team's leader. "It's all automated. Customers like it. Each request starts an hourly paging process. Every 60 minutes we apply increasing levels of management and technical resources against the problem."

McEvoy says the automated process "gets them involved as a real team effort. It eliminates one or two people on site who say, 'Give me another 10 minutes and I'll have the problem solved' and then it's another 10 minutes."

This SunTeam brings together people from five major Sun organizations in nearly a dozen locations. They meet face-to-face three times during the year, once at the beginning to build trust and agreement on how they will work, then twice more at key review points. Subteams split off to tackle pieces of the problem.

They meet on the phone for at least an hour or two every other week. In between the conference calls, they use e-mail, one-on-one phone calls, and Show-Me, Sun's homegrown e-whiteboard program. All of their work is posted to their common web site that serves as home base for the team as it creates its web-based tool, WebEsc (as in web escalation).

Ed Hoff, leader for the team's follow-on effort, cites three reasons why the project works: the high trust level of team members; "significant confidence from senior management"; and the project being "driven at mid-management, which made it more grassroots."

The project proved so successful that the team sent 26 people to its successor, the Glass House Gang. (The Glass House is how computer people refer to the high-powered computing systems so delicate that they live behind glass walls.) Their task is to extend the escalation process to the rest of Sun's mission-critical products.

Even before the Glass House finishes its work, Sun is using virtual teams to monitor critical customer accounts.

"We design our products to be used under particular loads," Lynch explains, "and they're getting pinged[8] [computer talk for being contacted] millions of times a day. Failure, regardless of the source, is usually horribly complex. No one single person at Sun knows how to solve the problem when a major account goes down. This is the ground zero example. We have to put a team of people to work on the account, drawing on services and engineers all through a sequenced escalation process." Virtual teams lie at the heart of Sun's success.

The era is over when customers wait several days before a senior Sun person knows about their problems. Thrice weekly, the company's president and chief operating officer, Ed Zander, convenes a conference call with his staff. "Scott [McNealy] joins most of the time, and we go account by account for 20 to 30 minutes, looking at our most urgent and highest-priority customer issues," Lynch says describing how he begins his day. "We're solving problems faster and learning where we need to make process investments. Do we intend to do this forever? No, but we're doing this as an experiment to increase customer availability."

This, too, is a virtual team, with people calling in from wherever they are, Lynch says. "Ed can be in Barcelona, Scott's in New York, some are in California, and at 8 A.M. Pacific time, we all are on." And the solution depends on virtual teams. "We have to bring headquarters and the field together to get them [customers] backup."

Lynch picked up the idea from Cisco. Every night at 10 P.M. Pacific time except Saturday, Cisco's CEO John Chambers receives a report on a handful of the most important problem accounts. The two companies have strong ties; their products are complementary, providing the basic infrastructure for Unix-based networking, and Cisco's chief technology officer, Judith Estrin, sits on Sun's board.

"We've clearly established culturally that proactive effective teams are far better than individual heroics, and we have the infrastructure to go with it. The challenge is to expand the footprint of teams in the midst of the incredible transition going on," Lynch says.

Finance Net

Daniel Poon's cell phone rings at 5 A.M. in Hong Kong, waking him up. He's ready to talk about SunREVs, the team he leads. "The reason we were chosen to talk to you is that we're the most virtual SunTeam." His team has people in AustralAsia (one word at Sun), the United States, Hong Kong, Korea, Singapore, Taiwan, China, Australia, and Latin America. Therein lies the problem: Sun's salespeople, who are very virtual (they operate in many time zones), need accurate, timely financial information.

"They ring up finance and finance says, 'Give us a week or two weeks, we're doing a close,'" Poon reports. So his team sets out to solve this and other problems, including what he describes as the "Can you just plop this in?" problem. Many solutions get pushed down from corporate, but one size does not fit all.

So Poon and his colleagues grow the project from one that originally was managed locally in Australia, spreading it throughout Sun. The idea is to create the standard reporting system to support management throughout the company, right up and across to McNealy and his team. "That's pretty good," Poon says humbly.

A small group of about five do the conceptual design. When Sun-Teams anointed the local Sydney project, the team was 10 strong. Another ring of 20 became involved when management changed, followed by another 50 or so analysts, finance and sales executives, and vice presidents. In its first release the product has 300 users, a rather large virtual team of its own, along with its own user community. "I've been getting calls in the past two days about how it can be used in different contexts," Poon reports.

The project's beginning is classic Sun. It started out taking a third of Poon's time, then grew to three-quarters of his time while extending into other people's time. "It was very hard," he laments, "because it was grassroots and we didn't have the money to do it. We lived off an allowance from month to month and a programmer on a monthly basis." Then the idea of a web-enabled solution became very popular, helped by an e-mail from Scott McNealy himself. "He wrote to my boss and said, 'I don't want any more e-mail attachments. Give me a URL that I can access anytime, anywhere with reliability and accessibility. We're preaching this to our customers.'"

In short, SunREV dynamically reports the company's numbers on the web. It's the *place* where Sun's financial picture exists in the aggregate. The team worked for a year, never meeting face-to-face until six months into the project. Like other successful virtual teams, they communicate extensively via conference calls, e-mail, and shared web sites. Poon points out that his team doesn't have revenue management skills (the content of the project) but it does have information technology expertise. Trust is built on faith in one another's expertise and the benefit everyone involved can derive.

Of the 19 teams competing at the 1999 SunTeams celebration where SunREV appears, it alone receives the platinum award.

"We've Done Away with Paper"

Three aspects of Sun's virtual team program merit study by other companies because they are beacons of virtual team success: sponsorship, preparation, and infrastructure.

First, Sun insists that every team have an executive sponsor.

Sun did this one right from the start, encouraging employees to introduce the idea to the senior executives, who committed from the beginning and have stayed involved. McNealy's senior team members serve as the judges for the San Francisco finals each year, and they have adopted greater teamwork among themselves. To ensure ongoing involvement, each SunTeam has to recruit an executive sponsor whose role can be as simple as approving travel budgets, which can become an issue when people on the same team are working for different bosses.

Second, Sun prepares carefully for the SunTeam launch while leaving room for a great deal of flexibility and creativity.

Unfortunately, many companies decide to move to teams without a great deal of forethought. An edict comes down from on high to "form teams," with no supporting guidelines or resources. Alternatively, a company launches its team initiative with so much bureaucratic baggage that the effort is stillborn before it begins.

While Sun has put some basic processes in place, teams can be creative. This means that each team is free to develop its own agenda and schedule while also holding administrative overhead to a minimum. When teams experience unanticipated conflicts, they quickly resolve them themselves with guidance from the team sponsors.

Third, Sun has the collaborative technology infrastructure to support a large number of virtual teams.

Sun has been a boundary-crossing e-mail culture since it began in the early 1980s. An Internet original, Sun built a culture where people have long used e-mail the way other companies use the phone.

Possibly connecting the world's largest intranet in terms of numbers of web servers, SunWeb did not even exist in 1994. Virtually everything of value at Sun is on the web. At Sun, the web is the place.

Moving from Place to Place

"If you want to change an organization, the best lever is to change how it communicates," says W. R. "Bert" Sutherland, for many years director of SunLabs, the company's research and development group. "The big change of our time is what engineers call the 'time constant.' You can go around the globe in a matter of a few seconds in e-mail; the postal service takes days or weeks; in the windjammer days, it took months. A phone call is instantaneous if I can get through. E-mail is fast but not instantaneous and you don't need the recipient's attention. Different communication styles lead to different organizations."[9]

While organizations can increase their effectiveness enormously with the smart use of technology, heed what we have heard repeatedly from our on-the-ground virtual team experts: "It's 90 percent people and 10 percent technology." Social factors above all derail the development of many virtual teams. Understanding the new social geography of media, as Sun is doing, provides a powerful advantage in constructing productive virtual work places.

Increased access to information is a primary driver of change from hierarchy-bureaucracy to networks. Virtual teams depend upon the open exchange of information, both internally and externally. Still, there is a danger here.

Absolute openness will absolutely kill virtual teams.

As more information becomes more public, privacy becomes more precious. If all of its information and communications are public to everyone all the time, a virtual team will

- Have more difficulty creating its identity.
- Bypass critical needs for socialization.
- Remove essential supports for authority.

Issues of what is public, what is private, what is open, and what needs to be secure are central to virtual teams. In particular, these issues impact the design and development of cyberplaces, the true homes of fully realized virtual teams.

The Play Is the Thing

No Sense of Place,[10] Joshua Meyrowitz's breakthrough book, explores how electronic media displace our notions of what it means to be present, thus causing dislocations in our social behavior. The essential message of the book is that electronic media are dissolving the historic connection between physical place and social place.

Meyrowitz brings together the ideas of sociologist Erving Goffman, who conceptualized how social settings influence roles, with the mind-popping work of Marshall McLuhan, who describes media as extensions of the senses. Communications technology sets the stage for a whole new roster of roles as place expands into the ether.

Goffman says each role has two sides. Using the metaphor of a play, he describes the role as presenting its public face to the audience and its private face backstage, where the actors and director develop, rehearse, and discuss performances. Historically, belonging to a group means being able to go backstage. New people socialize into the group through their gradual introduction to the backstage. There they gain inside information. Promotion in a hierarchy means moving to ever more exclusive and private places.

Since time and place historically have been coincident, Goffman simply assumes the obvious, that groups communicate primarily face-to-face. Until now, the more subtle relationship between physical space and social effect has been obscured.

"It is not the physical setting itself that determines the nature of the interaction, but the patterns of information flow," Meyrowitz writes. If the social setting is an information system, then new media dramatically change the roles people play in how "groupness" is achieved. He places roles in three categories essential to virtual teams:

- Identity
- Socialization
- Rank

Identity

For the team to have its own unique sense of *identity,* its physical location matters less than its "shared but secret information." Members have access to this privileged information where and when the group gathers, providing them with a core sense of belonging. Such information separates members ("us") from others ("them") who do not have the same access. Backstage, the team discusses options, resolves conflicts, and makes decisions.

Suddenly, in the electronic era, people no longer must gather in physical places to "belong." Virtual teams tend to have very porous boundaries and may have little or no backstage. As private group places become public ones, group identity, an elusive quality hard enough to establish in the virtual world, blurs.

Socialization

New people become members of a group through "controlled access to group information," the formal and informal processes of *socialization.* Orientation and training are formal processes of socialization, while hints, tips, and suggestions convey crucial "how it's done" knowledge informally. People grow into groups over time. When access to a physical place governs availability of information, the whole group can watch as new members transition into full participants through their rites of passage.

Since it is physically impossible to be in two places at once in the face-to-face world, access to new places also used to mean that you had to leave old places behind. The electronic era suspends the Newtonian laws of motion. In cyberspace, people do not have to desert old places in order to access new ones. You can simultaneously be in numerous online places, joining new groups while weaning yourself from old ones.

You even can have parallel-process interactions: Attend your team's meetings by videoconference, push mute and take a phone call, check your e-mail, and talk to someone who walks into the room. Where, exactly, are you during the meeting—or are you dipping in and out of multiple meetings simultaneously? Far fetched? How often have you checked your e-mail while on a conference call?

Meta Greenberg, an organization development professional, reports on just how far people have taken the idea of multiple presence. "I have two clients at a telecommunications company who made a tape of 'ums and 'ahs,' rustling papers in the background. Then after a few hours on a long boring con call, they started the tape, left the room, and no one realized what happened. Boring meetings will not be cured just because they're not face-to-face. If anything, sabotage gets even more intriguing."[11]

As physical places give way to virtual ones, new members can instantly gain access to all of the group's information. Not surprisingly, traditional patterns of socialization are collapsing as transition stages become more difficult to discern.

Rank

According to tradition, *authority* depends heavily on access to exclusive places that house special knowledge. Elite clubs are obvious locales that demonstrate the power that comes with place. University libraries are another; if you belong to a particular academic club, you have access to its special knowledge that can literally make you an *authority* on a subject.

Indeed, the higher the group is in the hierarchy, the more these socially remote places convey a sense of "mystery and mystification."

Inaccessibility is a measure of status (or lack thereof). Members jealously guard backstage areas and carefully script performances.

Since the nomadic era, new media have increased the ability of leaders to segregate and isolate information systems. The consequence is that they extend their control. Here again, the electronic era is challenging these bastions of privilege. While it still may cost many thousands of dollars to join the country club, you need only pay your monthly Internet provider fee to enter into conversation with countless numbers of experts anywhere in the world.

Likewise, anyone with a connection to the net and a web browser now can visit thousands of university library home pages without ever registering for a single university course. Yet if that same person shows up at one of these libraries without an official identification card, access would likely be denied.

Another irony of the electronic era is that an anti-status symbol of the past is now an important tool to sustain authority in the future. Typing, once considered the province of the hired help, is a key skill in the electronic world. The effect of broader access to once-exclusive information has been felt nowhere more profoundly than in the upper ranks of hierarchy.

"Under Construction"

Privacy, an archaic feature of groups, remains essential for virtual teams.

> *Privacy complements openness as individuality complements group cooperation.*

In general, virtual teams face more hurdles in establishing their identities than do colocated ones. Shared, exclusive information is one way that a team develops a strong identity. For many groups, privacy is essential. Such is the case with Buckman Labs' (see Chapter 3, "Teams") online research and development discussion area, where patentable products are under development. Privacy is critical.

Corporate borders secure the absolute need for some information exclusivity in the competitive private enterprise system. Membership and privacy are invariably established at the enterprise level. There, an account on the corporate information system accompanies the badge with a picture for access to the physical facilities. At Buckman Laboratories, membership as an associate in practice means an account on the net and passwords to Buckman's online discussion areas. Some of the discussions are open to the entire company; others are restricted.

For decision-making and negotiating tasks, team privacy is essential. Openness to disagreements and an ability to tolerate yet manage conflict are at a premium in healthy boundary-crossing groups. Yet these qualities are even harder to foster in a fishbowl. The 10-minute video of SunTeams preparing their final presentations for the competition in San Francisco contains several amusing scenes poking fun at their need for privacy. Teams rehearse in private and present in public.

It is easy to design digital places that combine public and private areas, most simply through passwords and access lists. We have already noted that virtual team boundaries tend to be multilayered. Often they comprise a small core group, an extended team of less-directly involved members, and an even larger network of external partners and tangential people. Companies regularly configure multilevel virtual spaces, like eSun, from which all Sun information flows.

Internet sites allow public access to published information (press releases, annual reports, and the like). Internal intranet areas require authorization with access to plans and interim results. Completely private places are where teams discuss their most sensitive issues, such as new product development, budgets, and personnel.

By creating information places with graduated levels of access, virtual teams more easily and naturally stage the socialization of their members. At Buckman, for example, new associates begin by perusing the generally available information as a way to get to know the group's public persona. Soon they receive passwords that offer access to the regular inside information of the company's work. Later they are invited to join certain discussions with information that is proprietary to the group.

Executive Challenge

The social effect of increased access to information is most dramatic in the shrinkage of hierarchy. It's flattening, but it's not going away. For the most part, middle and supervisory management ranks are dwindling. Executive management is, if anything, becoming more exclusive and remote, a trend symbolized by the steep increase in CEO salaries. For all the personal aversion of many senior managers to computers (a dying generational artifact), the best and most powerful tools of digital technology have always been put at the service of executive information systems. This is not likely to change in virtual organizations.

Executives face the greatest challenge in virtual work. They above all must balance two apparently conflicting needs. On one hand, they must follow a general admonition to share information cooperatively and broadly throughout the organization. On the other hand, they have the strong requirement to protect the privacy of their own deliberations and below-the-waterline information (the disclosure of which might sink the corporate ship).

Paradoxically, at the same time hierarchical *boss-ship* is contracting, virtual teams and networks demand more *leader-ship*, not less. Many leadership roles are changing. Virtual team leaders often act more as coaches than as bosses. They are more likely to lead through influence than through coercion, and they are much more diverse in their sources of power. The behavior of protecting exclusive information from subordinates is sometimes too easily carried into executive team relationships. One unfortunate consequence of too much privacy is a corresponding diminution of cooperative pursuit of overall corporate goals by all the rest of the organization. Getting the right chemistry between public and private is hard.

Project teams are typically virtual, even if unrecognized as such. Usually they blend aspects of vertical leadership structures with horizontal patterns of expertise leadership. Teams need their own identity, socialization processes, and authority (decision-making) structures. Like vertical leaders, horizontally linked leaders of "communities of practice"[12] also need their private places. They, too, exchange peer-related information, debate standards, criticize rules, challenge orthodoxy, and otherwise prepare to meet their public leadership tasks. Membership in communities is usually by invitation only, based on expertise and/or roles.

*Communities of practice link people with common exper-
tise (such as technical specialties) or similar roles (such as
project managers) that address the need for horizontal
leadership across virtual teams.*

The Future of Place

"Can we sustain growth and performance as a purely virtual network?" This is the question that Paragon Biomedical, which runs clinical trials for major pharmaceutical companies, asks Gensler, the architecture, design, and consulting firm. Paragon's 150 people work mainly from home offices, "with state-of-the-art laptops, DSL lines at home (where available), and T1 lines into their offices," says Loree Goffigon, vice president and director, Gensler Consulting.

Gensler responds to Paragon's question and request for assistance with real estate designed to reinforce collaboration and connectivity. Their recommendations include building "corporate hearths" in each of Paragon's regions, ideal settings for face-to-face interactions. Now Paragon people can meet, train, and find workspace on demand in key locations, including Irvine, California, the company's original home.

"Philosophically, the creation of these places is about learning, access, and building community," says Goffigon. Her firm finds itself working with "a greater number of providers, including technology consultants, ad agencies, and graphic design firms. Our work is happening much more collaboratively and across a broader spectrum of organizational areas because the questions our clients are asking are more comprehensive and systemic."[13]

Metaphors from the physical world regularly tag the online one. People sitting at computers work on their own desktops while accessing group information on servers at sites. Desktops online may be a metaphor that in time will seem as quaint as horseless carriages. Regardless, some sense of place—like a site—will persist in the human online experience.

Site is a crossover term. It simultaneously stands for a building (or group of them), a computer or a cluster of machines, and an ephemeral collection of bits in cyberspace, as in a web site. Physical and online sites alike range in size from small to gigantic. At the small end of the scale are physical and online rooms. At the large end of the scale are sprawling corporate campuses like Microsoft's in Redmond, Washington, and vast cyberfacilities like America Online.

The United Nations Development Programme (UNDP) is perhaps the most electronically sophisticated group at the global organization. It uses electronic networking both to carry out its mission—to build more sustainable livelihoods for all—and to encourage more direct individual and community participation worldwide in the UN.

Shortly after the Internet began its phenomenal growth following the invention of the hyperlink and browser, the UN held the Fourth World Congress on Women in Beijing in 1995. John Lawrence (at that time the principal technical adviser at UNDP) and his colleagues "worked from behind the scenes," he says (echoing Goffman's language), to offer a global window into the event. Supported by the Education Development Center of Newton, Massachusetts,[14] the group "rented an electronic virtual room where anyone could come in to discuss issues that relate directly to agendas raised." During the summit itself, they scanned relevant documentation on to the Internet site as it became available. Annotated summaries of sessions were available during or just moments after events took place so that anyone anywhere in the world with Internet access could view and react to them.

As teams and organizations expand their presence online, they will continue to create online places that are analogous to the information resources available in physical places. Each organization that goes online invariably creates its own digital place, stocking it with information and products previously available only in physical places. Most often, this is simply a set of shared folders where documents are stored, usually organized by the content of the group's work. Group identity and process information are haphazardly organized and stored, if at all.

People create online places from the ground up. To do so, they use virtual analogs of desktops, rooms, offices, factories, malls, and communities. These and other familiar "place" metaphors serve as the building blocks for local cyberspace. We anticipate these metaphors will rapidly evolve from cartoonlike storefronts and graphical menus to increasingly sophisticated three-dimensional virtual realities that members will walk into and around. As the early computer-game-playing generations of kids grow up, they are incorporating the representational features of game technology into virtual team interfaces. Working in a virtual room is increasingly an *experience.*

Two Places

To operate effectively across boundaries, virtual teams become masters of media. They need to be media-savvy in two very important ways by creating

- *Product places* to prepare and deliver results, such as new products, decisions, reports, and plans.
- *Process places* to run their own organizations, because the actual time the team spends creating, specifying, designing, and managing itself is largely informational work.

Information Age technology products always have occupied a privileged position in the world of virtual work. They benefit from a basic axiom of going virtual.[15]

Digitize early and often. Start your results in digital form and keep them digital as long as possible.

The development of products in digital form offers one significant way that virtual teams can go beyond physical-place metaphors. This capability has been slowly developing for the past two decades.

Calypso

One early example of an astonishingly successful global virtual team is the Calypso Project that flourished in Digital Equipment Corporation's mid-1980s. It was in the company's heyday, when it had the world's largest internal network and was selling its popular MicroVAX computers as fast as it could produce them.[16] Through a then-unique process of virtual product development, this team created a revolutionary new minicomputer design. It was so robust that it served as the basis for a major product line, the VAX 6000 series. At the same time, the Calypso team built a production capacity that saw the first machines roll out simultaneously from three plants separated by an ocean. Everything was done in record time, and the project generated $2 billion in revenues the first year (1980 dollars!) and many billions more in the years following.

From the beginning, Calypso put its whole product design online. Thus it closed the loop on what had been a gradual transition through the 1970s in engineering and manufacturing design from analog to digital processes. The project's most intriguing technology innovation was its product database that contained everything from chip design to the metal "skins" of the machines. The product design itself was the team's "place."

Everyone on the team had access to the whole product database. At the same time, the communications system was designed to notify people only when changes were made in areas that they had previously specified as important to them. Thus, the product itself in its digital form became a highly specialized primary communications medium.

While a computer hardware design eventually must go from bits to atoms as a machine is made, software is a pure product of the digital age. Software is a truly ephemeral thing that naturally lives in virtual space. Software teams have always been at the leading edge of virtual work. Two key factors genetically code them for success. First, they have a commonly accessible online product focal point for their interdependent tasks. Second, they tend to have the necessary computer technology for communicating easily across boundaries. In our experience, the weakness of distributed software teams usually lies in their people and organizational issues, not in access to their common product or the availability of technology.

Some software efforts are not only broad in scope and complexity, but require agreements of a larger community to be useful. Such was the case with the late-1990s sudden appearance and stunningly rapid development of the open source Linux operating system. This was not the first time a community has created a product.

One early very successful Internet-based global software project was the distributed community that developed the Ada language. Military and other applications that require very fast real-time data processing for systems such as the Boeing 747 use Ada. Beginning in the mid-1970s, a core group of a half-dozen people engaged with a larger set of 100 key contributors in 20 countries. Together, they carried on a complex set of technical conversations over DARPANET, the military forerunner to the Internet. Over the multiyear course of the project's development, the conversation volume grew to 10,000 comments.[17]

Using your product as the lodestone for place does not have to be big and complicated. It can be as simple as a memo or report. At the University of Texas, Kathleen Knoll and Sirkka Jarvenppa conducted studies of virtual teams who had never met yet who were asked to produce common products. They analyzed data from 19 teams numbering from three to seven graduate students each at 13 different universities in nine countries who used only e-mail to communicate.[18] The best predictor of success for these extreme teams seemed to be a decision "during or soon after brainstorming, to work from a common document summarized from everyone's comments. This process seems to help the teams collaborate."

Teams that produced common documents early in the process generally communicated more frequently. They also had more consistent and even participation, showed less conflict, and evinced more satisfaction in the project. Finally, they demonstrated a "greater sense of team," meaning that they communicated "feelings, context, sensory information, roles, and identity."

Process Rooms

"War rooms" are one device that teams use to dive deep into a project and complete it.

Imagine instead "process rooms" on the web that bring people into virtual work. Here you can grow the intelligence of the team as people collaborate over time. Process rooms are where backstage interactions can occur and where you can share private information for the team. Though public web places have dominated early online development, we expect that private places on the web that persist over time will be the dominant experience of the future.

Process rooms are for both real-time team meetings and ongoing asynchronous storage, recall, and reuse of shared information. The room grows from an empty space at the start of a team's life to become progressively more organized and customized by the actions of the team itself as it molds the space to its particular needs. The team lives in the pulse of events that unfolds through its unique journey.

As a whole, a virtual team room provides an anchor point of reference for the workings of a coherent small group of people. It provides an inside and outside, an online social container with a boundary. While logins and passwords control the experience of access to secret information, they also provide an associated sense of security that the place is a safe space. Safe space is a very important design consideration and an underlying foundation for the establishment of trust virtually.

It is vital to create processes of orientation and training to induct people into the common place (group). Informal hints, tips, and suggestions can be found in an expanding set of online conversations. It is a major challenge for today's time-deprived fast-cycle teams to create appropriate rites of passage.

Physical places embody the traditional means for transmitting group culture. Teams have historically spent *time* in places structured by *length, width,* and *depth.* Virtual teams are spending *time* in cyberplaces structured by *people, purpose,* and *links*—the subjects of the next four chapters.

CHAPTER 6

TIME

The Virtual Pulse

People intuitively use the word *network* with a remarkable consistency that continues to surprise us. The idea evokes a clear, simple mental model, a structure of points or circles and connecting lines—nodes and links, vibrant with purposeful activity. Where people get fuzzy is in describing how a network or virtual team actually does anything coherent, how it moves in time.

Dimensions

As we see it, this is a problem of perception. To see something like a network or virtual team, you need to look at it from several points of view simultaneously. The people-purpose-links-time model provides four interrelated dimensions for seeing a group. With this model, you can hold something as distributed as a network and something as immediate as a virtual team—people linking with purpose over time. (See Figure 6.1.)

On the Wings of a Big Bid

April 24, 1991, was a big day at Digital Equipment Corporation, a peak day just before the long decline and eventual disappearance (into Compaq) of this groundbreaking company. McDonnell Douglas, now a part of

Figure 6.1   Four-Dimension Model

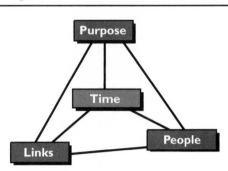

Boeing, chose Digital as one of two final bidders to become the computer systems integrator for its new commercial jumbo jet, the MD-12. To respond to this highly complex bid, Digital's core team of nine needed to expand to about 50 people—technical experts from across the company representing several dozen disciplines. To win, Digital had to rapidly create and make operational a team that would cross traditional boundaries.

A few days after Digital's selection as a finalist, the core team met to plan its next steps in Digital's Irvine, California, facility. Irvine is just a short ride south on Route 405 from Douglas Aircraft's Long Beach headquarters. The planning meeting was a raucous event, according to one participant. With phones ringing and people coming and going, the group still managed to churn out some of the essentials: a mission statement, a list of broad goals, a key-concepts graphic, and the invitation list for the second meeting a week later.

> *The group statement of purpose*—to win the MD-12 bid and prepare Digital to deliver on the contract—*expresses why the group wants to cooperate for mutual benefit.*

Two weeks later, the MD-12 Team numbered 30. It met in Irvine again to integrate new people, repeating the process the core group went through. The team reviewed the purpose, translated it into a clear set of goals, and began to assign tasks.

Ten days after that, a third planning meeting took place, this time in Massachusetts, near Digital's home base on the East Coast. Fifty people attended, representing engineering, manufacturing, and services. They reiterated all the aspects of the plan and subdivided into seven distinct Goal Teams. Each addressed a separate objective, each had its own leader, and each depended on people working together from different functions. Tasks were designed and assigned for each component part of the proposal to Douglas. Each Goal Team competed for management attention, organizational support, and allocation of overall resources, both within the team and with other parts of the corporation.

Down Select

As a close-to-the-customer salesman, Paul Beltis brought Digital the MD-12 project. As a longtime vendor to Douglas, Beltis invested in personal relationships and chance encounters at the customer site. Eventually, he detected the early signs of a new program that in time would need a systems integrator. *Systems integrators* tie together the disparate parts of an organization's computer installations. Since at that time, in the early 1990s, most companies bought their computer systems without much planning, it was a huge market.

Douglas did not list Digital as one of the original companies invited to bid on the program, which included IBM, Hewlett-Packard, Andersen Consulting, Computer Sciences Corporation, and Electronic Data Systems. Digital won its spot when a few of its people, including Ulf Fagerquist, a very senior and experienced executive, participated in Douglas's six-week MD-12 brainstorming session in summer 1990.

During that session, Digital positioned itself as understanding the *process* of product development. The building of the MD-12, with its complex partner/investor arrangement—each major supplier would invest its portion of the plane, including the engines, the wings, and the fuselage—was less an engineering and manufacturing issue than it was a process one. Digital's central message to Douglas was simple: "Integrate process and product," which Digital held to through the down-select process and its final bid.

Why did Digital make the final bid round, when it didn't even qualify for the first round? It sponsored a key customer event. In mid-March 1991, Digital facilitated and hosted a three-day meeting for the senior Douglas MD-12 executives in Digital's Irvine facilities. Under preparation for months, and delayed several times, the MD-12 general managers' meeting finally took place just as Douglas named a new MD-12 program manager. The meeting included his boss, the vice president charged with new product development. In this ideal, though intense, session, the importance of attention to process demonstrated its power in the team's development. Our role at this event and in the resulting MD-12 project was that of process consultants.

Three-Day Plane

The executive conference room was packed. There were 10 general managers from Douglas and six people from Digital, along with some laptops, an electronic whiteboard, a poster maker, and numerous dignitaries floating in and out.

With more than 200 years of plane-building experience in the room, the group devoted its first day to establishing purpose. They agreed on a mission statement, strategies, key concepts, and common assumptions. Here, preparation was critical. For several months prior, a Digital management consultant worked these elements in interviews with the Douglas managers and their staffs. The two weeks before the meeting were particularly intense, and the group experienced considerable success in this part of the process.

During the next day and a half, the group sketched out two plans, one for the following four months and the other for the subsequent five years. They defined phases, listed tasks, roughed out the logic, and estimated times, some in detail. The Digital team captured all this information in real time, both with traditional notes, flipcharts, and the electronic whiteboard, as well as directly into word processing on laptops and into other computer modeling tools. The software tools not only recorded the data, but processed it, too, generating several simultaneous views, including a schedule.

Because of the fast turnaround time, the group had its first view of the data within hours. It was able to revise its assumptions, enabling participants to see the effects of their changes. In 36 hours, they completed three iterations—run-throughs—of the short- and long-term MD-12 plans. By the end of the third day, the group began to make key decisions, as certain things become obvious even at the coarse level of detail.

This meeting reinforced Digital's message about the importance of process. While demonstrating its capabilities, it also obtained invaluable insight into the program. Significant personal relationships strengthened among people in the two companies, while Douglas benefited from a genuine service.

Six weeks later, Douglas selected Digital as one of two finalists. The other was EDS.

Three-Week Bid

Douglas formed technical evaluation teams to review the proposals. It assigned an official liaison person to the Digital team, whom Digital in turn invited to its team planning meetings. Douglas provided security badges and made offices available to all members of the Digital team; Digital then shifted its base of operations from Irvine to Long Beach. The aircraft company assured access to its people so that Digital could obtain the information it needed to propose solutions and make its bid. It sponsored tours of the MD-11 production facilities, its flagship plane. EDS enjoyed the same privileges.

At Digital, a handful of people suddenly found themselves riding atop a very big project, a systems integration bid two orders of magnitude larger than the average business in the area. When the game was over, it had become the "billion-dollar bid."

One day during the project, an MD-12 team member said, seemingly out of the blue, "158." His partner laughed. We were all standing in the Irvine hallway as a Digital employee from the United Kingdom walked by.

"158?" we asked.

They interrupted each other to explain that they'd been keeping track of the number of people involved, and the British fellow who just walked by was the 158th person to be associated with the MD-12 project.

In a few weeks, the Digital team grew from an ad hoc, mostly part-time group of fewer than 10 to a funded, functioning program of 50, with again that many active at any one time, drawing on and reporting to several hundred more.

To plan its work and get up to speed, Digital used the same process it employed with Douglas. The company held a series of three planning meetings over the next several weeks. In these meetings, the Digital team designed the organization that would guide it for the next four months until proposal delivery at the end of August. We called these meetings Work Process Design sessions.

The first iteration of the Digital team's own process was the raucous two-day event at the beginning of May. By the second session, the group had grown to 30 or so, people with much of the experience and life-cycle diversity (e.g., engineering, manufacturing, and product support) required to develop a comprehensive proposal. The packed conference room looked much like the MD-12 general managers' meeting held just across the hall eight weeks earlier.

Over the next two days, the group clarified its purpose, defined its goals, and formed Goal Teams. Materials developed in the first session seeded these tasks, which sped things up. With attention paid to leaving enough time for "bio breaks," meals, and schmoozing, each goal team brainstormed its lists of tasks, then reconvened with the other goal teams to knit together the overall logic. In the large group, people identified who would own each task, defined cross-functional relationships, and estimated how long each task would take.

With the same simple set of tools used in the March Douglas meeting, the team captured, displayed, revised, and redisplayed its planning data quickly enough to iterate it twice. People left with a 30-page handout of their joint work, including a directory of participants, a schedule, and a deployment chart of processes, milestones, and deliverables.

While the team accomplished a great deal in a short time, it was still in its very early shakeout period. Clearly, the group needed more time to complete sufficient planning, and, of course, politics and power problems erupted. Some gaps opened up, and the team realized it needed to involve other people. In the next few days, the team re-formed and headed east for one more two-day planning meeting the following week.

For the third meeting, each team member received a personalized MD-12 Program Handbook, containing basic information, key documents, the work process design, and results to date, with their names printed on the cover and the spine. Directories, task lists, models, schedules, and the like all had their places in the three-ring binder, which was designed to accommodate updates of more-current material.

With some new blood and a chance to absorb the experience of the previous week, the team ran through the process again. The goal teams, which now had formal status in the group, broke out tasks by specific deliverables, scheduled key meetings, and defined where they would have to make major decisions. They worked on the task logic, resolving vague and overcomplicated areas. People reviewed their commitments, including the cross-functional ones. They estimated resources and generated rough budgets. The meeting far exceeded most people's expectations, and Digital's MD-12 team was launched.

Three-Month Plane

During the third session, an ad hoc group formed—including people from several goal teams—to look at the whole life cycle of the MD-12 plane-building process. Digital had won bid status on its process promise. Now the task was to produce a plausible high-level process view of the plane as a whole. Digital would tie its technology solutions to the work described in that view.

A self-initiated team pulled together the available information and began the process of synthesizing an initial picture of the MD-12 life cycle. Three weeks later, Digital invited key Douglas general managers and their staffs to a presentation of its initial findings.

It was the ribbon cutting for Digital's "MD-12 Process Room"—the first of several process rooms at both Douglas and Digital. The odd-shaped room (a skewed trapezoid, widening from 12 to 15 feet along its 20-foot length) contained graphics of the vision, theory, and method of Digital's approach. Information covered the walls, gleaned from the March MD-12 executive meeting, from formal briefings, and from responses to recent information requests. The first draft of the MD-12 Work Process Framework occupied the "power spot" on the wall: It displayed the phases of the plane along one axis and the functions along the other.

The MD-12 Process Room opening was a success, the most important measure being Douglas's instant willingness to cooperate with Digital to flesh out the framework and to develop multiple process views.

Within hours, Digital hosted the first of 10 meetings over the next two months with various cross-functional mixtures of Douglas staff. New information replaced obsolete information, blanks got filled in, concepts jelled, and new graphics captured the shifts. All this information showed up on the walls of the Process Room.

Within a week, the MD-12 Process Room moved to a Douglas building at Long Beach. We took over a conference room in the program's executive suite with a window overlooking the runway where MD-11s are running their test flights. In this magical setting, we were able to bring the vision of the MD-12 alive and explode it onto the walls of the process room to keep the five-year 750,000-task program within the mental grasp of the teams of people that meet in the room.

This technologically enabled but physical process room sparked a vision of virtual team rooms online. Today, the technical capability to do this is virtually commonplace. It forms the emotional heart of the virtual room described in Chapter 11, "Navigate."

The End

As the picture of the MD-12 process stabilized, the Digital team tested its various solutions against the long-term view of the work required. In numerous technical meetings with Douglas organizations and experts, Digital's view gradually shifted from gathering requirements to demonstrating increasingly better solutions. By the time Digital submitted its proposal at the end of August, it tied all technology solutions to the required work according to the plane's life-cycle framework.

This story doesn't so much conclude as it does sputter out. Digital was the clear winner of the technical evaluation of the plan produced by the bid team, but the executives could not put together a winning business deal. EDS got the business, but the MD-12 was never built. EDS did, however, subsequently garner several billion dollars in long-term McDonnell Douglas contracts in the few years before Boeing consumed the whole company.

Digital, too, eventually sputtered out. Ken Olsen, who founded the company 35 years earlier, was gone within a year. Compaq eventually bought Digital, and the diaspora of its remarkable assemblage of talent accelerated.

Five Phases of Flight

Taking a trip is a journey, a story that can be told in five chapters.

The Flight

You are going to Washington, D.C., next week. You make reservations, set up meetings, and otherwise prepare in the midst of other activities.

A few hours before the flight, you begin a new phase of this journey. Between being home and being airborne lie a number of hurdles: packing; traffic to the airport; an unexpectedly full parking garage; the momentary panic when you think you've forgotten your tickets; lines at the reservations counter, lines at the security gate, and lines at the boarding gate, where you discover your flight is delayed. An hour later than you expected, you strap yourself in and the plane taxis out to the runway. In one breathtaking instant, the takeoff phase is over and you are in flight.

The flight itself is most of the journey. It's where you do the real work of getting from here to there. In-flight information comes from the crew in the cockpit, where they monitor sensors and adjust controls. The crew adapts to such variables as weather, traffic, and malfunctions by making changes during the flight, with the ultimate objective of a safe landing, ideally at the scheduled destination.

"In preparation for landing, please make sure your seat belts are securely fastened and your seat backs and tray tables are in their fully upright position." The flight attendant signals the start of the next phase:

landing. Landing and takeoff are the most stressful and dangerous events within the flight process. Hitting the ground almost always jars.

The arrival at the airport presents another set of obstacles—getting to a clear gate, opening the doors, deplaning, collecting your baggage if you checked it, and finding a car to take you to your end point.

With the flight complete, you arrive at your destination, a new status quo established. Thinking ahead (and remembering the morning's delay), you decide to confirm your flight home and inquire about times for that trip to the islands you have been thinking about. You are at the beginning of the next journey even as you arrive.

The Five Phases

The five phases of flight are metaphors for the five generic phases of any team's development, including a virtual one.

Beginning	Start-up	■ Preparation
	Launch	■ Takeoff
Middle	Perform	■ Flight
	Test	■ Landing
End	Deliver	■ Arrival

There are two periods of predictable turbulence: *takeoff,* the launch moment for teams, and *landing,* the test period for the team's work. Virtual teams also experience these predictable periods of turbulence in their development. Knowing about them in advance allows time for preparation so that they can be used to your advantage.

"It's just like skiing," Jeff, once a competitive downhill skier, analogizes. "If you check out the course ahead of time, you know where the bumps are, which means you can get momentum from them rather than being thrown off course by them. "Racers anticipate and pre-jump the bumps, gaining momentum from the bump's back side rather than being thrown for a loop by flying off the front."

Launch follows a sometimes lengthy start-up period. It also usually involves a relatively short but intense period of activities that produces a plan and defines leadership. Perform is when activity accelerates, where tasks are undertaken and results accumulate. But growth is always limited, and deadlines always loom. Work must be tested, brought in for a sometimes dangerous "landing," delivered to customers, and rolled out to users. A new status quo comes with the achievement of a goal that the next cycle of change will challenge.

Little journeys are contained within bigger journeys that are part of greater journeys, or vision quests. Start-up to delivery may happen over a matter of days, or the process may take years to unfold.

- *Start-up:* Long or short, in the initial period people assess and gather information. Exceptions accumulate as people speak out and ideas are tested.
- *Launch:* At some point, things jell—or they don't.
- *Perform:* If only we could live here permanently. People engage their energy and take huge strides in accomplishing real work as the overall effort achieves its objectives. There are problems and challenges, to be sure, but problem solving is the modus operandi.
- *Test:* Risks converge here. Success may blind us, and we may exceed the carrying capacity of our environment. The innovation undergoes strenuous testing before acceptance. Forces of resistance mount their final assault.
- *Deliver:* The process passes a final milestone. Here, the process may end, stabilize at a new status quo, or go into another cycle.

Life Cycle

A team is first and foremost a process: It has a beginning, a middle, and almost always an end. No team springs to life full-blown, and none lives forever. Words such as *conception, gestation, birth, childhood, adolescence, adulthood, midlife crisis,* and *old age* all apply to team life. Powerful results accrue when any team, virtual or not, consciously works its way through a life-cycle process.

Virtual teams are living systems, not machines. Everything about them is organic: They are made up of people with interdependent roles and a web of relationships aligned through shared purpose. As *living* systems, they are not biological organisms but rather social organisms, which have both a pulse and a life cycle.

A team's life cycle has its own rhythm, oscillating between coming together and going apart. This tempo obtains through the long-term patterns and peak moments of key gatherings, the overall life cycle, and the hour-by-hour churns of a team's daily life.

The proper metaphor—living system or machine—is critical to the understanding of virtual teams. It is hard enough to get face-to-face teams to "happen," to jell over time. It is doubly hard for virtual teams.

Teams grow. They take time to develop—and virtual teams tend to take even longer. Ironically, they don't really have the time.

Forming and Storming

Most organizational researchers and authors acknowledge and underscore this *growing* small-group truth: Team life is a process. Popular and academic studies alike agree on the general outlines of the basic team life cycle. Many people use Tuckman's 1960's model (or a variation) of the stages of small-group development.[1]

- Forming
- Storming
- Norming
- Performing
- Adjourning (usually omitted from the list)

This resilient model retains its freshness because it accords with experience. Countless teams use it as a guide.

Growth Curves

The Tuckman model agrees with a powerful general systems concept. It's a social application of a growth model that applies to everything from astronomy to biology to marketing. The S curve (known as the *logistic growth curve* in mathematics) is so common that Ludwig von Bertalanffy, the father of general systems theory, offers it as original proof that certain mathematical principles and patterns hold across diverse sciences.[2]

Consciously or unconsciously, virtually all successful teams follow this universal cycle of life.

When applied to a team, the S curve gives rise to some interesting ripples. Tuckman's model points to stress points, an important, overlooked feature of the life cycle, times of natural turbulence and potential conflict. By anticipating the likely stress points, a new, still-forming team gains a powerful advantage. Team members can use these natural points of commotion to give their process the energetic lift it needs—or they can be thrown off balance by conflicts that seem to come out of nowhere. While not all conflict is predictable, some of it is.

The Stressed S

The "Stressed S" is a generic process model (Figure 6.2) that we label in the flight metaphor: start-up, launch, perform, test, and deliver phases.[3] There are two major points in a team life cycle where stress is predictable—near the team's beginning and not long before its end.

In Chapter 10, "Launch," we show how to use this model and provide support tools.

Virtual teams must be especially conscious of their dynamics. Behavioral clues are spread out not only in space but also usually over longer time frames than they are with comparable colocated teams. It's easy enough to see when someone checks out of a face-to-face meeting, but how do you know if the person on your con call is checking e-mail (having used her mute button on her headset so that the tapping of her keys is not audible? This gets very personal for us).

Virtual teams need to design for this supercharged eventuality. Things go wrong all the time; projects are usually more difficult than you antic-

Figure 6.2 "Stressed S" Team Process

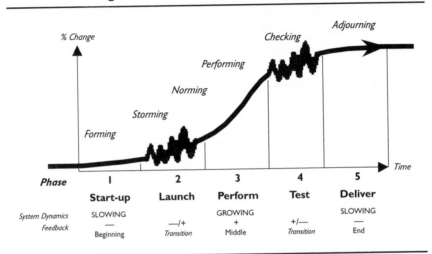

ipate. Completion is usually a beat-the-clock adventure. Smart virtual teams develop methods that anticipate the eccentricities of the life cycle and plan for stress.

Using the systems-thinking lens of feedback, it is apparent why these stress periods happen. Peter Senge, who brings systems dynamics and organizational learning to the center of contemporary management thinking,[4] describes two natural, complementary feedback mechanisms:

- *Slowing* is the dampening, stabilizing, conserving tendency that keeps change in check (negative feedback).
- *Growing* is the building-on-itself accumulating tendency that expands change (positive feedback).[5]

Slowing and growing mean going from one level of functioning to another. We must disrupt stability for change to occur. Then things can stabilize anew.

- *Phase 1: Start-up (slowing).* Feedback dampens and prevails. The idea for the team and its initial formation struggle against natural forces of resistance. The team's initiators generate interest, gather information, and explore ideas. It may take an excruciatingly long time for the fuzzy beginning to take off. No one may even clearly recall when it happens—or the collective "aha" may be breathtakingly brief. Either way, change of any kind struggles against the status quo.

- *Phase 2: Launch (transition).* As a critical mass of people with the same purpose comes together, the storm begins to howl. Before the team is really ready to perform, it must sharpen its vague purpose, establish leadership, make plans, find resources, obtain commitments, and acknowledge norms. This is the first transition. Poised between the slowing of phase 1 and the growing of phase 3, launch is the decisive phase. During this period, the team encodes its unique life-cycle code, punctuated with future moments of success and failure. Many virtual teams require a spark of creativity, a group "aha" that cements a core belief. This is where the group feels itself click and people begin to refer to themselves as "us." Some teams never get out of this phase. There are no guarantees here. It always takes painfully longer than anyone thinks that it will, and for virtual teams it often takes even longer still.

- *Phase 3: Perform (growing).* Most teams would much prefer to start right here. Growth is positive, accumulating, and exciting. Here the team does the bulk of its work. Results swiftly accrue and the team makes progress toward its goals, always satisfying. People meet and overcome obstacles. At its best, life is good and seemingly will go on forever. But growth cannot go on indefinitely without countervailing slowing actions that check and reshape it.

- *Phase 4: Test (transition).* Challenge time. Risks converge here. Success may blind us, and we may exceed the carrying capacity of our environment. The innovation undergoes strenuous testing before acceptance. Forces of resistance mount their final assault. The team must review results, finalize features, and limit resources. Meanwhile, time is running out and customers are waiting. All too often, this late-in-the-game second transition, from growing to slowing, is quite painful. Some teams end right here. Early participatory planning (e.g., customer involvement, regular reviews with stakeholders, and interim milestones) can turn this chapter into a triumph.

■ *Phase 5: Deliver (slowing):* Delivery is the endgame, when the team adjourns. The process passes a final milestone. Here the process may end, stabilize at a new status quo, or go into another cycle. The team delivers results, provides support, wraps up details, and in the best practices, ceremonializes its endings. Slowing is dominant here, dampening feedback as the team seeks to stabilize at a new level. It may be the end of one lifetime and the beginning of another, and its duration may be brief or long.

Together and Apart

Teams are dynamic. They manage tensions of stability and growth while moving forward. That same root dynamism lives in each of us, the conflicting pulls of being both "me" and "we." In team life, this plays out in significant ways, as patterns of coming together (aggregating into the "we") and going apart (dispersing to be "me").

We still can hear the echoes of the earliest groups in human history in organizations today. While archaeologists cannot excavate social organization in the same way that they can unearth shards of bone, they can infer a lot about it. By matching artifacts with direct observation of foraging societies that survive today, such as the !Kung of the Kalahari Desert in Botswana, we have a reasonable facsimile of the organizing process of early teams.

The same pulse that dominates team life today was there at the beginning. In the ancient life of nomads, groups of families came together and then dispersed on an annual cycle. Foragers followed the rhythm of the seasons dictated by their sources of food. Even today, !Kung households move to the same beat that literally "goes with the flow." Access to water moves the !Kung through seasonal cycles, causing groups of families to diverge and converge. The !Kung beat holds for the way most people work—they come together and then disperse. People work alone and then join up in a group. We do what we do best independently and then work with others to expand our capabilities. The basic social rhythm of human beings has not really changed in 2 million years.

The !Kung's major camp gatherings are like off-sites. These are special times and places for convening teams to literally "pull things together," to resolve conflicts, and to make decisions. They also are times of intense social interaction. Some managers regard the community-building aspects of such meetings as so important that they insist on them regardless of tight deadlines and budgets. As we inaugurate the age of virtual teams, such meetings become all the more important. Most people we talk to continue to stress the importance of face-to-face interaction to solidify virtual teams.

> *Face-to-face time is increasingly precious, a scarce resource in limited, costly supply.*

When the !Kung families come together, they suddenly find themselves living in a very different environment. Population greatly increases; numerous channels of interaction come into sight. Camps are alive with feasts and dancing, partying and ceremonies. Suddenly there are many hands to make light work. People hunt together and build common storage facilities, share resources and information, trade goods, and exchange tools. Perhaps most important, the camps are incubators for new families, where people make matches and find mates.

Camps of 25 and supercamps of 100 to 200 serve broad human needs for people to associate with one another. Multifamily camps arise from exchanges, interdependent relations, and repaid reciprocity. The same phenomenon occurs in business when multiple functions and teams come together. This provokes an ancient and natural tension between the family team and larger social organization. Even so, the cooperative act of sharing across organizational kin lines is critical. Without this necessary step, organizations cannot develop. They remain social isolates. As social psychology has found, isolates have poor health, are unhappy, and die sooner.[7]

Cooperate and Concentrate

The "together/apart" rhythm vibrates deep in all sorts of human groups. People congregate, then separate, not only over seasons but in the course of a day as well. Think about your day with some of your time spent alone and some time spent with others. Time-lapse videos in Steelcase-sponsored research show a remarkable pulse to team life.[8] Colocated teams of people come together for a time, then separate to do individual work—a together/apart fluctuation that replays many times over the course of the day.

Virtual teams have a harder time getting started and holding together than colocated teams. Thus, they need to be much more intentional about creating face-to-face meetings that nourish the natural rhythms of team life.

Activities that people undertake together and continue apart spark life. Establishing the life pulse is not hocus-pocus. It lives in how we choose to start things, whom we invite to participate, what agendas we create and plans we make, which tasks we implement, when we reach milestones, and how we bring closure.

"I believe that you clearly expedite [team processes] by spending more time on the front end and getting consensus," says former Eastman Chemical Company CEO Earnest Deavenport. "You shorten the implementation cycle as opposed to the opposite when differences and resistance come out in implementation."[9]

The moral for virtual teams who want to design their together/apart pulse is simple—and widely held by experienced team leaders and experts alike:

Invest in beginnings.

You will recoup time spent in the first two phases many times over in later phases. Mistakes, mistrust, unexpressed viewpoints, and unresolved conflicts all too easily introduce themselves and become part of operating norms. Lack of clarity around goals, tasks, and leadership hobbles the team in the performance phase. Failure to establish criteria and measures for results ensures a rocky ride during the inevitable testing phase regardless of whether the team is colocated or virtual.

Anticipation is the recommended prescription.

Real Time and Virtual Time

Coming together is a major challenge for virtual teams. For millions of years this has meant, of course, face-to-face. In the world of virtual work, togetherness means something broader—at-the-same-time (synchronous) events.

Most of the virtual teams that we've interviewed use telephone conference calls to provide some means of synchronous meeting, and many rely on videoconferences as well. Usually such same-time events include pods of people in different locales. A regular weekly meeting of one Ernst & Young International CIO team is a videoconference, tying together four people in New York and another five in London.

The people at Buckman Labs have found, as have many other companies, that a very active online conversation can be fast-paced enough to seem almost real time. Buckman's early chat facilities allowed people who had never met (and might never meet) to have on-screen conversations where they talked about their families and hobbies. The major advantage of these sessions was that they quickly built a modicum of trust and usually caused affection to develop among the participants as they glimpsed one another's private lives.

We recently sat in (virtually, via conference call from Massachusetts) on a Pfizer team meeting with people on videoconference in Groton, Connecticut, Sandwich, England, and New York City, with everyone clicking along through their virtual team room on the web. Such meetings are taking place around the world, in different combinations, stretching everyone's ability to comprehend the technology and the experience.

While the range of synchronous options is growing rapidly, as is the bandwidth required to carry rich real-time interactions, a new channel has been added to the human repertoire: non-real-time, or persisting *asynchronous*, communications. Threaded discussions, online conversations that resemble verbal exchanges, are the most common example. Portals, intranets, and extranets localize all the communication media into continuous digital campgrounds. These "virtual water coolers"[10]—reminiscent of the !Kung gathering around Kalahari water holes—offer entirely new options for shaping meaningful aggregation in virtual teams while supporting their dispersion.

Stretching Time

Time is an essential dimension of human organizations, whether virtual teams, enterprises, or nations—and it poses a dilemma. With the blurring of the line between home and work, complaints prevail about lack of time. To see how immersed we are in time as groups, we need to expand our limited view of time as a ticking clock.

Calendar Time

Clock time is, of course, important. This is the physical level of time, the precise slicing of which is emblematic of the Industrial Age, with its foundations in Newtonian mechanics. Calendar time, the daily schedules of minutes and hours that repeat in patterns of weeks, months, and years, tends to dominate our lives.

"There's never enough time" is directed at the limited hours in the day to do everything we need or want to do. For people working together, dates mark meetings, task deadlines, team milestones, holidays, personal commitments, and the needs of family life.

Agendas and schedules are tools for creating and anticipating our futures. Learning how to create agendas for virtual team events is a vital skill for twenty-first-century leaders. While the agenda maps the minutes and hours of time spent together, the overall schedule ties together days and weeks. Schedules may just include same-time events, or they may expand to all activities, including different-time ones. Which brings us to looking at time as process.

Process Time

The together/apart pulse reflects biological characteristics of time, organic rhythms of human processes that syncopate life. This is time in "chunks" of duration. In working life, these show up as events and tasks, process components.

This is not time marching on. Rather it represents the results of human choice and design—why, when, and how we'll meet; why, when, and how we'll divide and do the work. In practical terms, this is "project time," and its signature display is the *Gantt chart*, typically a bar chart of tasks showing start and finish dates along an axis of calendar time.

For all but the simplest teams, project management is a critical and often overlooked ingredient for successful distributed work. Colocated teams can quickly share ideas, correct misunderstandings, and work through problems. Virtual teams need to be more explicit in their planning and their plans. Clarifying goals, tracking tasks, and accounting for results all are part of elaborating process time in a manner visible to all members of the team. The team embeds this detail in a larger context.

Phase Time

Processes have beginnings, middles, and ends, repeating cycles of change. For human groups, change and growth are stories in larger stories. All groups within groups within groups are on journeys within journeys within journeys. In the big picture, this is evolutionary time.

Cycles are made up of phases and represent time on a larger scale, the really big chunks of lived time. We have phases of our lives, from childhood to wisdom. Our organizations go through phases of development and change as well, so team dramas are often within the context of larger organizational dramas. And we are all immersed in the really large-scale drama of change in our global civilization, each grand age another phase of human existence at the leading tip of the planet's evolution.

It is notoriously difficult to see the phases we're living through in the moment, particularly since we are prone to see work move along faster than it actually does. Hindsight is the wonderful educator on the impact of phases. Recognizing phases and changes between them is often a key contribution of an outside observer (facilitator, consultant).

The tool to use to manage cycles is high-level life-cycle planning. Put your virtual team or network into a development context. Beginning with the end in mind, as Stephen Covey suggests, imagine the *feeling* of a successful process as it moves along through its early struggles, jelling turbulence, and daily progress to final test and delivery by a product development team. Design to the phases with as much anticipation as you can muster; then ride the inevitable waves of change as you live them.

And what is it that pulls/pushes groups of people through time? It is *shared purpose.*

CHAPTER 7

PURPOSE

Why We Work

The time by car between any two of Tennessee's big cities—Memphis to Nashville, Nashville to Knoxville, Knoxville to Chattanooga—is under five hours. In our search for great virtual teams, we make the drive east from Nashville in the center of the state on I-40 on an early summer's night. The sun setting behind us colors the sky ahead, painting the peaks that become the Appalachians the shades of their names. Here, where Tennessee, Virginia, and North Carolina converge, the Blue Ridge meets the Smoky Mountains.

Smoky blue turns to black by the time we top the last hills to our destination. Suddenly a surrealistic "whiteprint" of light flashes below us, shimmering strands of luminescence that sparkle for acres, pipes pushing up to 90-degree turns and then angling down into elaborate twists of conduits. A spaceport? A city of the future? Tucked away in the small town of Kingsport is one of the world's largest chemical manufacturers—and an acknowledged world-class management system.

Turning Hierarchy on Its Side

It was in this valley conveniently situated on both a navigable river and railroad that, at the urging of a local entrepreneur, George Eastman decided to invest in a defunct chemical plant in 1920. He needed a reliable chemical supplier for his developing photography business some 700 miles to the north: Eastman Kodak Company in Rochester, New York.

Three quarters of a century later, Eastman Chemical Company, which spun off from Eastman Kodak in 1994, is a $4.5 billion global operation with 15,000 employees manufacturing 400 products. Although you cannot go into the corner store and buy anything with the Eastman label, you would have a hard time not buying something with an Eastman product in it. Need a toothbrush? An Eastman chemical is an ingredient in the plastic handle. Soft drink and liquor bottles, painkillers, peanut butter, tires, carpet, mascara, stonewashed jeans, brake fluid, garden hoses, thermos bottles, latex paint, tennis balls, and, of course, Kodak film all contain Eastman chemicals.

Today Eastman Kodak is still Eastman Chemical Company's largest customer, but it is only one of 7,000 who buy its products around the world. Nestled in the northeast corner of Tennessee, Kingsport is the chemical company's world headquarters. Manufacturing operations stretch across six American states, Canada, Mexico, The Netherlands, Malaysia, Argentina, Wales, Hong Kong, and Spain.

Teams Every Which Way

In 1993, Eastman became the first chemical company to receive the U.S. government's highest kudo for quality, the Malcolm Baldrige National Quality Award. We first reported on Eastman in *The Age of the Network*.[1] There we told the story of a traditional firm that reinvented itself as a networked organization while still retaining important elements of hierarchy and bureaucracy.

It took a quality crisis of business-threatening proportions—and nearly two decades of work—to move the company to the network structure it now has. The company began its renaissance in the late 1970s when it lost market share of a major product due to poor quality. With a focus on traditional quality approaches and a lot of common sense and creativity, Eastman went about redesigning how it does its work, from the shop floor to the very top of the company. Today, *everyone* works in teams—and usually in multiple teams.

Ask people at Eastman why they win the Baldrige Award and they will point to their quality philosophy that rests on team alignment. "It's a consensus style of management," says Earnest Deavenport, who became Eastman's CEO in 1989, "that is much more based on team than individual decisions. There is more empowerment of teams than you find in a conventional organization. Many fewer decisions get bumped up to me to make individually."

Eastman is a complex mix of permanent, temporary, face-to-face, ad hoc, geographically distributed, culturally diverse, vertical, and horizontal teams. Some have traditional team leaders. Some rotate leadership. Some are quite formally chartered. Others less so. There are multiple executive teams and hundreds of shop-floor teams.

Almost all Eastman teams cut across space, time, and/or organization boundaries.

Eastman has all types of virtual teams. It has shift teams that are responsible for keeping operations going around the clock. Short-term project teams are invariably cross-functional. While sometimes co-located, more often these teams follow the typical pattern of coming together and then going apart. They meet as necessary to plan and align their work, then carry it out individually or in smaller groups.

Longer-lasting process teams are distributed and cross-organizational—for example, customer and supplier teams. Although most virtual teams need some face-to-face time together to function effectively, especially at the beginning, they can become more virtual over time. Eastman has a supplier team, for example, that had many face-to-face encounters when it began, but increasingly fewer as time passed. Once the group established trust and set up its processes of interaction, it continued to make quality improvements without meeting. The virtual team functioned asynchronously in different places and organizations.

Quality

Because Eastman is a manufacturing operation, good teamwork on the shop floor is synonymous with good quality in its products. One of its earliest "improvements" came as a simple recognition in the late 1970s: The four shifts per day are simply one ongoing team spread out over 24 hours.

"At that time, we had a 'tag and you're it' shift change mentality, four different people around the clock running four different shift teams," says Will Hutsell, Eastman's senior associate in Corporate Quality. Very little information passed between shifts. When one shift left, the next would come in and readjust all the control room dials, as though the people before them had no idea what they were doing. Operators had to ask permission to make any changes, and, of course, they punched time clocks.

During the initial implementation of continuous improvement efforts, Eastman took groups of the shift foremen off the job for quality management training. Instead of working their normal shifts, they came together as a group for training and planning improvement projects. These foremen (who are now called *team managers*) then went back to their work areas and held team meetings with their operators to develop plans for implementing the projects.

Change came quickly. The operators had the skills and information they needed to do their work without asking anyone's permission. In time, they stopped punching time clocks. Operations improved enormously and control rooms were clean. Eastman was on its way to a Baldrige.

Today, Eastman's training process is a sophisticated operation that reaches across the company. For example, to be trained as coaches, people leave their jobs for 12 weeks of intensive education in modern management thinking, skill building, and practice. Initially, the company set up training programs and had people attend individually, but found that approach not to be very effective. So groups of managers started attending together, creating sufficient critical mass of shared experience in the organization to sustain the learning when people returned to their jobs.

At the same time that Eastman reinvented work on the shop floor, it also made many other significant changes that raised the trust level in the company:

- It equalized benefits across the organization. Everyone has the same vacations for years served and everyone has access to the same healthcare plan.
- It eliminated the traditional performance appraisal system that distributed people's performance across a bell curve, replacing it with an employee development system.
- After experimenting with team rewards, it stopped them because it proved impossible to draw indisputable lines around "the team." Individual teams depend on the overall interteam environment; they cannot succeed without it. Eastman now has a company-wide bonus program tied to the company's performance.

Begin with Purpose

All Eastman teams have a vision and a mission, and most have charters and sponsors. In many cases, teams accept a written charter with a signing ceremony that commissions the teams.

"Because there are many teams at Eastman, it is essential that we always define the purpose of each team," Hutsell says. Without clear purpose and an established process for defining it, confusion, not quality, would rule at Eastman.

"Typically a broad charter is put in place and the team is empowered to see if it makes sense," he says. "The team can modify its own makeup." Using Eastman's Quality Management Process, teams pay attention to such questions as: Do we have the right purpose? And do we have the right membership? This helps keep teams on track.

"You must look at the purpose," Hutsell cautions. "Only when you have that right can you get from here to there." Eastman's early attempt to use one of the most fundamental quality tools, *statistical process control* (a quantitative method for improving quality), failed when the company tried to implement it without fully making clear its connection to purpose.

From Intent to Results

> *The best predictors of virtual team success are the clarity of its purpose and the group's participation in achieving it.*

Eastman teams thrive in a culture infused with purpose. Purpose starts at, but is not dictated by, the top. The senior management team is the keeper of the Strategic Intent, the document that contains the company's vision ("To be the world's preferred chemical company") and its mission ("To create superior value for customers, employees, investors, suppliers, and publics"). The senior management team is also custodian of the document known as *The Eastman Way*, which sets out its values and principles. The document makes explicit the culture required to support teams working across organizational boundaries. It also serves as the touchstone for innumerable changes that make a difference in the day-to-day working life of Eastman employee-owners.

While written down and published, the Strategic Intent is also a dynamic document. It serves as the framework for overall long-term company strategy and shorter-term initiatives known as *Major Improvement Opportunities* (MIOs). Everyone in the company is involved in the planning process. Organizations bring the knowledge of their part of the business—specifically including customer needs, competitive comparisons, company and supplier capabilities, and risk assessments—together with the Strategic Intent to develop Strategic Alternatives. These are then formally submitted to the Eastman executive team that forms the overall strategy and makes selections among alternatives.

With the strategies set, the organizations develop goals, their own MIOs, and their criteria for success, known as the *key results* areas. With concrete measures in hand, the virtual teams develop plans using Eastman's Quality Management Process, in which everyone in the company is trained. Eastman's version of the familiar plan-do-check-act continuous improvement cycle adds a step at the beginning. Before "plan," there is an "assess organization" step where the team focuses on clarifying its purpose in interaction with customers and in alignment with the company's strategy.

Early in its team journey, Eastman made a mistake that many companies do: They convened teams and focused on the mechanics of the meetings, such as following agendas and drafting plans, without giving the teams a clear purpose. That turned around when the teams took on specific projects with clearly defined expectations. Eastman values time spent gathering information, developing and choosing among alternatives, creating implementation plans, monitoring and documenting progress, celebrating results, and even formally disbanding. The process itself generates continuously increasing value.

The Eastman "Pizza" Organization

For people interested in organizations, Eastman is famous for a unique depiction of its organization chart, its "pizza with pepperoni." Hierarchy, bureaucracy, networks, and teams all have their place in this organization-in-the-round (Figure 7.1). The company expects people to communicate horizontally, not vertically. There is no going up a chain of command, across to another function, and then coming back down another chain of command to get something done.

Deavenport created the now-famous circular chart in 1991, he says, because he wanted "to signal the organization that this was a different structure, a networked structure, a team effort, not business as usual. We're all in this together." While the chart preserves the logic of hierarchical levels, "the artist in you has to come out to see the pizza chart as different from a hierarchical one," Deavenport commented.

Eastman used a truly cross-sectional approach in showing how its hierarchy, bureaucracy, and network fit together in a twenty-first-century organization. The central and foreground position of the then-chairman and CEO, Earnie Deavenport, symbolizes hierarchy. Structurally, his position anchors the hub-and-spoke locations of the six major corporate components. Bureaucracy is well represented both in the general use of specialization and purpose (every subgroup has a unique name and mission) and in specific components devoted to maintaining traditional bureaucratic functions.

Figure 7.1   Eastman Pizza Chart

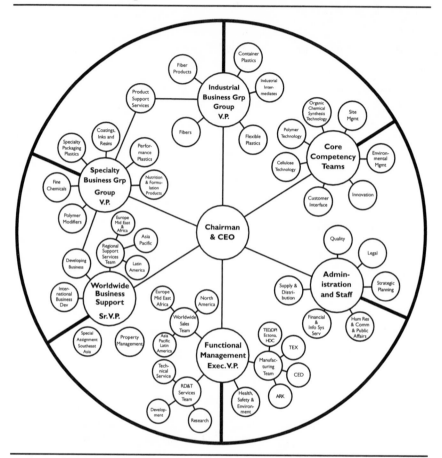

What made the Eastman chart uniquely indicative of an Information Age networked organization is its periphery. This heavy outer circle attaches directly to all the major components and represents the direct connections among the divisions. Deavenport talked about the "white space," where collaboration takes place and work gets done. In the circle, he repeated, "no one is on top."

"Work gets done across and within and between functions. Major processes in the organization have to go horizontal. A lot of important work doesn't get done in the vertical sense," explained Robert Joines, a former manufacturing vice president.

Still, there's a place for hierarchy, he said. "Sometimes Earnie [Deavenport] had to make decisions no one else can. You can't stamp out hierarchy and run an organization. You have to have vertical alignment. To be successful, you have to learn to do both of these together. Our interlocking teams are a hierarchy in a sense, and then we *turn hierarchy on its side.*"

Authority

Nothing is more important to the virtual team than its clear purpose. Discovering it is the team's first priority. Once found, purpose locks into place the source of virtual legitimacy and power.

Hierarchical groups can fall back on force as their source of authority. Bureaucracy can turn to rules and regulations. Virtual teams and networks require something more to mold and hold them. When new organizations emerge, so do new premises of authority and power. To see how authority works in the Network Age, we need to start at the beginning.

Four Ages of Power

Charisma and tradition rule nomadic cultures.

Nomadic authorities had the ability to influence others, but not to force them to do anything. Leaders, including those surviving today, claim authority by demonstrating competency, inspiring passion, and recalling the voices of the ancestors.

Eventually nomads rooted permanently, tending farms and building cities. Hierarchy arose.

Hierarchies use force to defend resources, maintain social stability, and control technology.

In business, the people who sit at the top of the hierarchy—the owners—have the power to hire and fire, to give out rewards, and to inflict punishment. They may promote and demote employees, grant and refuse raises, acknowledge people or place them on probation. The extraordinary power of owners is nowhere more evident than in their exclusive right to start, buy, sell or merge a business as a whole or in parts. When Shell Oil Company partnered with Texaco to create three new companies to handle their downstream retail business, 7,000 Shell employees and a comparable number from Texaco changed companies. Today Shell, tomorrow Equilon, and there you are having to bond with a new culture with your arch competitor that never existed before.

When agriculture gave way to industry, brute force yielded to the rule of law.

Bureaucracies use rules, regulations, policies, and procedures to gain authority. In this rule by law, bureaucrats get their power from their place in the administrative structure. Traditionally, each rank has its own legal perks.

Purpose is central to all small groups and teams. It takes on a new aura in virtual teams. Because traditional authority is minimized, they need some other guiding force.

Virtual teams develop an inner authority based on everyone's commitment to shared purpose.

Strategic alliance teams comprise people from different companies. They lack common reporting structures or policies because people in them come from different hierarchies. In cross-functional teams (the best-known virtual team), no common authority figure may tie everyone together until they reach the CEO level.

Knowledge

In the beginning, someone has an idea. It spills out in a meeting or on a phone call and maybe gets firmed up on an e-mail. Conversations begin, others are inspired and recruited, and presto: A virtual team has the essential glue. Inside or outside formal channels, within a company or between firms, ad hoc teams self-legitimatize through common purpose.

A new species of authority often appears long before it becomes dominant. Law emerged thousands of years ago in the hands of Hammurabi and Solon, much earlier than the rise of constitutional governments like the United States that subordinated military force to democratic rule. From laws, rules, and regulations, industrial bureaucracies constructed new dominant modes of authority.

Just as each age strengthens a previously limited source of authority, so does it bring a new basis for power, the other half of the governance equation.

> *In virtual teams, power comes from information, expertise, and knowledge, the new reservoir of wealth.*

Peter Drucker regards knowledge as so critical now that he uses the plural—as in "we need multiple *knowledges* to survive."[2] His advice: "One cannot manage change. One can only be ahead of it." Knowledge workers are capital assets, not costs, he says.[3] How did people become so valuable? Today's tasks require brain, not brawn. Specific expertise is in great demand. Experts have always had power, but not the kind they have today.

People come together with hope that by combining efforts they can achieve something great. To get to their desired results, they divide up the work. Most tasks require people with specific skills, capabilities, and experiences. Such folks have power to the degree that their participation is critical (Figure 7.2).

Virtual teams have an especially tough job. They need to cope with all the traditional power people *and* they must harness the information and knowledge-power people.

Figure 7.2   Sources of Authority and Power

	Source of Authority	Source of Power
Individual	Charisma	Personal
Small Group	Tradition	Affiliation
Hierarchy	Ownership	Reward/punish
Bureaucracy	Law	Position
Network	Purpose	Knowledge
	↓	↓
	Goal-Based Authority	*Task-Based Power*

- Though the jury is still out on how companies will reward and punish virtual teams, hierarchy clearly has far less influence in the new world.
- The importance of position varies enormously in virtual teams. Some individuals come to the virtual team as anointed leaders. In others, everyone temporarily (and sometimes uneasily) sheds his or her rank and takes on a new identity. Formal positions still exist, but they do not necessarily determine who takes precedence in virtual teams.
- Because of their ability to reach anywhere for members, virtual teams can easily include people with a wide diversity of knowledge and skills. By deliberately seeking difference, the team reaps the creative benefits of a broader range of viewpoints and expertise. Diversity becomes the differentiator.

Everyone on a virtual team needs to be expert in something the group requires. The more important the work, the more highly valued the required skills. Like architects, consultants (relatively pure instances of people with expertise power) build teams to work on a specific project, then build another team to satisfy the needs of the next project. Each team's members differ depending on its requirements.

Why Cooperate?

Purpose sustains and initiates process. It is the source of life for all teams, the inner fire that gives them their vitality. Virtual teams face two particular challenges that differ from those of colocated teams.

First, it costs more to mature purpose in virtual teams, both in terms of the length of time it takes to mature and in the literal expense of bringing together distantly situated people. On the other hand, a well-set purpose can be a source of economic benefit: Coordination costs fall when committed people align around the same goals.

Second, purpose is more important when people are all spread out than it is when a boss is watching over everyone's shoulders.

For resource-lean and information-rich virtual teams, good organization design that mirrors the work makes for better results. As the team carries out its original intent, the organization re-forms to address new goals and the next pieces of the work. People reconfigure continuously. Today, it's Don, Kate, and Keith working on Pfizer. Tomorrow it's Kate, Jeff, Jen, and Carrie working on the offering. The day after that it's Annie, Jeff II, and Jessica working on recruitment. Our organization, like most others, constantly re-forms, organically adapting to the dynamic unfolding of the work.

Compatibility Rules

Virtual team success or failure begins with the relationships among people and goals. Nearly a half century of empirical research demonstrates the power of cooperation in teams.

Social psychologist Morton Deutsch was the first to use goal interdependency to predict how well people work together. He asked whether people see their goals as cooperative, independent, or competitive relative to one another. The more interdependent the goals, the more successful the team.

- *Cooperation* occurs when people have compatible goals. When you succeed, I succeed. Confidence and trust are expected behaviors. Cooperation generates positive feelings of family and community as people share and integrate information.

- *Independence* results when goals are not related. Your success or failure has no bearing on mine. I do not expect any support or hindrance from you. Aspirations are personal and relationships between us are less personal. We all do our own thing and have no need to share.

- *Competition* follows from incompatible goals and the belief that if you win, I lose. Your success diminishes mine. I not only expect no help but I anticipate hostility and prepare accordingly. To prevail in competition, rather than integrating in cooperation, people hoard information and use it as power.

Dean Tjosvold, Professor of Business Administration at Simon Fraser University in Canada, is at the forefront of team researchers who are bringing a wealth of learning from hundreds of studies into real-world practice.[4] He reports that myriad studies document this simple fact:

Cooperative goals motivate team members.

When goals are compatible, people strive to succeed and work becomes meaningful. Cooperation brings added benefits of helping others, feeling good, and storing goodwill for the future. It spurs information sharing and greatly expands insights available for planning, problem solving, and execution. Confident of success, people believe that others want them to do well. They have more fun, which translates into more positive feelings about work. Most important to problem solving and related tasks, a wide range of studies confirm that cooperation results in higher productivity than competitive or independent work.

Researchers' conclusions about competition within teams aren't surprising. Competition does not motivate people to share information, plan together, or find the best path for producing results. Competitors do not expect others to help or encourage them. What competition can do is to galvanize the team as a whole against another team. It motivates people who believe they have superior ability and are likely to win, but it demoralizes people who have (or believe they have) lesser abilities and experiences. Competition also can motivate when tasks are simple and information needs are low, providing that most of the people believe they have a chance of winning. However, since sharing information is the lifeblood of a virtual team, competition within hinders or scuttles success.

Motivation

Whether intentional or not, tasks and rewards always generate cooperation, independence, or competition.

- Joint rewards for group tasks promote *cooperation.* When cooperating, people assume that everything is fair and expect corresponding rewards. They pool their talents, offering and using individual skills and competencies as needed by the tasks. People appreciate creative conflict as a tool for finding the best answer.
- Unrelated tasks, separately rewarded, encourage *independence.* Quotas or sales targets measure individual success, separate explicit external criteria. People use their abilities to further their own goals. They avoid conflict, regarding it as a distraction from separate pursuits.
- Codependent tasks—separate pieces of work that *require* a winner and a loser—create the environment for *competition.* Such systems need rules to regulate the games. People use their abilities against one another. They avoid conflict entirely or deliberately escalate it to gain personal advantage.

Most work situations are complex and involve a mixture of motives. Tasks that are set up interdependently require cooperation. At the same time, people compete for attention, praise, promotions, and raises while taking pride in their individual accomplishments.

Typically, people encourage cooperation within a team to better compete with outside groups. One familiar archetype of this behavior is a great sports team—for example, the 1970s Boston Celtics basketball team's legendary internal teamwork propelled them to one championship after another. Such us-against-them behavior is considerably more tricky in work organizations. Many a successful team that bonds into a tight family also excludes and competes with outsiders. Unfortunately, outsiders to the team may still be insiders in the organization. A company with many teams ultimately wants all of them to cooperate for the good of the enterprise.

However cooperation fares inside the corporation, can we still safely assume that competition takes over at the enterprise boundary? For hundreds of years, the simple rule has been to cooperate internally and compete externally. This maxim is under fire. Countless alliances explode across corporate boundaries. The Internet ties companies closer to vendors and customers. Competitors and noncompetitors cooperate all the time, wedding partners as unlikely as the Muppets and Ford Motor Company.

Discovering Purpose

Purpose sparks life in virtual teams. This discovery brings people together, builds trust, and gets things going. To survive, teams must turn their purpose into action, using it to design their work and organization. Some teams receive a fully formed charter; others go off with a vague sense of desired direction. Some team members think that setting purpose is important; others do not. Most team experience lies between these extremes, as people struggle to understand and express their purpose.

Purpose is the campfire around which virtual team members gather.

We use the word *purpose* to stand for a broad range of terms—from abstract *vision* to increasingly concrete *mission, goals, tasks,* and *results.* Although teams may vary from organization to organization, how they relate to one another is important. Purpose is a little system of ideas; it expresses itself differently across the organization while synthesizing common harmonies.

Vision before Mission

Vision is the inspiration for purpose-driven organizations, the source that generates the flow of work. When articulated best, vision includes a compelling picture of the achievable, highly desirable future. Vision is also the realm of values and philosophy, the intangible but crucial culture of ethics, norms, and the intrinsic value of people that bring life to virtual teams. It does not have to be long.

Eastman's vision is short and simple: "To be the world's preferred chemical company." The word *preferred* carries both the customer focus and the implied strategy of superior quality. Other organizations create lengthy vision statements. The Massachusetts Teachers Association, with 75,000 members—one of the largest unions in the Commonwealth—has a vision statement that covers a page. Regardless of length, it's the painting of the future.

Mission is the simple statement of what the group does, the strategy that expresses its identity. Though usually more specific than the vision, it remains abstract. A flower importer answered marketing expert Ted Levitt's famous recurring question, "What business are you in?" with one word: *love* (not transportation or agriculture). In a world of fast-changing markets, this question usually goes to the heart of organizational transformation and the teams it spawns.

Goals state what we're going to *do*, translating intangible lofty visions into palpable, practical results. They reformulate the mission—the singular overall goal—into a few manageable sub-missions. Goals provide motivation, the starting point for work process, the original formula for dividing work into its components. Goals allow you to see desired outcomes in the future. Embedded in goals is the strategy for turning vision and mission into positive results. The smarter the goals, the better the strategy. Discovering this virtually takes time.

Tasks are "the doing," how the work gets accomplished, the actions that arise as goals go into motion. Invariably expressed in action verbs (e.g., *develop, design, identify, create*), tasks specify the actions that members take. Tasks are the team's signature, its mark on its world. Purpose becomes quite practical when people do their tasks. But because they are in constant motion, tasks can be somewhat slippery to the materialist grasp.

Results thud into place as the concrete outcomes of purpose, the "done." Reports, presentations, events, products, decisions—outcomes that everyone understands—clearly express purpose. The team creates *something* through its work. For a task action to be complete, there is always a result (however grand or poor) within a given period of time. It is in the nature of the task-oriented team to produce and judge itself by its end products.

Since we are genetically programmed to see results as "things," it is often hard for virtual teams to make their results concrete and tangible to people. Making results explicit is one of the primary benefits of creating online places to do collaborative work.

The Path

To put purpose into motion, plan.

The better the planning, the more effective the process. Better processes mean less time, less cost, and more customer satisfaction. Many groan at the thought of planning, harking back to numerous memories of shelved plans, quixotic decisions by higher authorities, or perhaps detail to a level of mind-numbing minutiae. As bad as planning can be, there is simply no other way. The virtual teams must build purpose refinement into its work process. This means planning.

We all know how to plan—in a general sort of way. We do it all the time by following a basic pattern that we use repeatedly every day: the path. Each time we envision a result that we act upon we conjure up a little bit of planning, whether it's going to the kitchen to get a cup of coffee, to the store to get a magazine, or to the web site to get some information. We have an image of what we want in our minds (a goal) and we rehearse the steps (plan the tasks) that will take us to where we want to go (the result). Then we set off.

Goal → Tasks → Results

These interrelated terms reflect the universal pattern of work: a motivating source, a target at the end, and steps that connect the source and the target over time.

Short paths or long journeys, the logic is the same. Most of the journey lies in the middle, between goals and results, in the province of tasks, the doing. While tasks are points along the path, the pieces of work that fit together over time, process is the sequence of actions. Each task is itself a little bundle of activity. Results do not just appear by magic at the end; they grow over time in the course of doing work and performing tasks.

Results

There is a natural flow to purpose. Like mountain streams seeking springs, purpose runs from the heights of abstract vision to concrete valleys of results. Putting purpose into action over time produces a dynamic picture of work (Figure 7.3).

Vision flows into mission, which becomes the highest-level goal. To accomplish the overall purpose, segment mission into subgoals, the first steps toward the division of labor. Tasks are the specific steps taken to achieve results. Some steps are serial, each dependent on the one before. Other tasks are independent and parallel, coming together at the end or interdependently across tracks of parallel activity. Most of the work of virtual teams is a mix of these modes.

Corporate Breakdown

Virtual teams truly are microcosms of the organizations that spawn them. This becomes increasingly evident the higher the group is in the organization. At the top, the senior team most literally and directly expresses that truth. There, all the work components come together and the organizations of all the major players cross boundaries.

Figure 7.3   Flow of Purpose

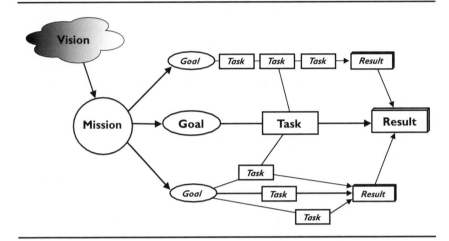

Put into the language of purpose, the organization's structure provides a way to break down its work. Look to the interplay between goals
and tasks to see this little-recognized but profound fact of business life:
Goals at one level generate tasks at the next level, where the assignment
is in turn taken on as a goal. Cross-hatching work across levels is a familiar, natural, and practical way to organize teamwork. Although not a conventional framework, the goal-driven view of work offers teams a
perspective on how their work interrelates (Figure 7.4), essential for
extensive enterprise-wide virtual teamwork.

Pfizer Pharmaceuticals Group cascades its goals, says Joe Bonito, who
heads the company's organizational effectiveness and consulting efforts.
President Hank McKinnell's goals "go down to line executives, who
translate them to marketing and research. It's an excellent system."

Where does the vision come from? The board of directors, representing the owners (i.e., shareholders), sits at the top of the organization together with the highest ranks of senior management. In most
business organizations, senior management generates the vision and
provides direction, whether bold or timid, vivid or obscure, conscious
or unconscious. They establish a hierarchy of goals based on what the

Figure 7.4   Corporate Purpose Breakdown

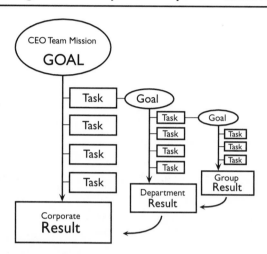

owners want: profit, growth, social objectives, and other returns of import to them.

To reach these positive corporate results, the company creates value through its work. Most permanent organizations segment the work literally, setting up divisions and departments (both derive from the same root word meaning *divide*). Each has its own mission—for example, marketing, research and development, engineering, production, sales, and distribution departments (functions) or divisions based on factors such as products, geographies, or industries. To make its contribution to the joint work effort, a large organizational component like marketing may further subdivide its piece. Internally, it creates its own departments and groups, each of which has separate charters (written or just understood) based on the work assigned from above. This sequence replicates down and throughout the organization, with each group doing its own work and defining expected outcomes.

So it goes down the line, with a person from this level serving on an implied cross-functional team while also serving as head of the team at the next level down.

Detailing

While the importance of discovering purpose does not by itself distinguish virtual teams from traditional ones, the depth and clarity of its expression does. The purpose problem is twofold for virtual teams:

- Crossing boundaries of space, time, and organization only further complicates already complex communication. An inherently messy process of creating a coherent, productive, and lasting purpose in the early stages of a team's life is even less tidy for a virtual team. It needs dense and frequent communication.
- Once developed, the team must make the purpose and plan explicit in symbols, words, diagrams, tools, handbooks, and persisting virtual places. The plan must stay updated, flexible, and adaptable in order to serve as a coordination hub for distributed work.

The problem with a complex purpose lies in people's need to grasp it simply. Establishing purpose requires first a conceptual solution, then a display solution, and finally a navigation solution.

"Periodically, we go back to our original purpose, our shared mental model. Building such a model has been extremely helpful in communicating across geographies and cultures. Some teams produce explicit pictures of what their mental models have become in terms of numbers and graphics. It gives us a vision of where we are headed that allows us to plan for what we need in terms of specifics such as logistics, sales, and technical service," Eastman's Hutsell says.

Interactive digital media offer a wealth of untapped potential for virtual teams to expand their communication capacity. At the same time, the expression and direct use of the power of purpose really comes into its own with the web and intranets.

Mental models, whether expressed as outlines, lists, diagrams, or art, are easily displayed on the web. These models then become portals—quite literally as clickable links and maps—to layers of more detail about goals, tasks, results, people, resources, organization, and every other kind of information that may be important to a team's work.

Mental models—ranging from broad perspectives on the market, estimates of risk, and organizational strategies to budgets, product designs, work processes, and agendas—have been the province of hierarchy. Typically, they are locked in the boss's head or file drawer, developed through experience, and communicated to others as needed. This works in a slow-paced world of simple purpose where people are not expected to think for themselves. But fast-paced virtual teams facing complex problems need to share a conceptual framework for their work. And that, in essence, is a people problem.

CHAPTER 8

PEOPLE

On the Ice Together

NCAA Division 1 men's college ice hockey teams are small—around 20 players in total. The typical number of skaters on the ice at any one moment is 12, six on each side. Each player has a position, a role, but when they go into action, skating as fast as they can with their eyes on the puck, one another, and the goal all at once, it's hard to tell who's doing what. Team movement mesmerizes: The puck flies; a stick catches it and splits in two; its owner whirls backward; players streak across the ice and crash into one another; the fans scream, "Skate! Shoot!" We are glad none is our child.

It's such an exhausting sport that every 60 seconds or so, all the skaters head for their respective benches to rest as fresh replacements climb over the boards and onto the ice. The speed of the whole operation is dizzying, with teams and subteams forming and re-forming, depending on the task at hand. Coaches keep the process moving: They call players, suggest plays, and draw configurations on pieces of paper that players crowd around to see.

At crunch time, they abandon typical rules. The number of people on the ice becomes unbalanced from one side to the other. In their first face-off of the twenty-first century, Yale is down 1 on Harvard's ice (home teams usually have an advantage). Coach Tim Taylor pulls his goalie in the last two minutes (the deadline), replacing him with an additional forward. That gives Yale six offensive players against Harvard's five. It is an all-out drive to reach the goal(ie), and the team needs all available hands.

Such is life in virtual teams. Small numbers, constantly shifting. Some people go all out while others rest, then just as quickly they switch positions. Operating with commonly agreed protocols, virtual teams invent new ones in the crunch. All available hands means everyone is "on the ice," a requirement for keeping up in Internet time. Everyone focuses on the same goal, each has a role, and when the team is in high action, leadership moves from person to person. You're at the center now, then on the side while someone else leads. The team leader or coach (or maybe both) keeps an eye on the whole, making sure everyone is playing, participating. Every move is a play; learning to play is the key.

"All of Us Smarter than Any of Us"

For Hank McKinnell, Pfizer's president and chief operating officer, "Virtual teams are a big part of the way we do business. We don't have all the good ideas in the world and we're in different places." Searle (its comarketing partner for the drug, Celebrex®) is in Chicago; Eisai Company Ltd. (its comarketing partner for the Alzheimer's drug Aricept®) is in Japan. "You either learn how to do virtual teams or you travel."[1]

With its acquisition of Warner-Lambert, Pfizer is the world's second largest pharmaceutical company. Today McKinnell is talking about bandwidth. He is excited about the company's videoconferencing system, which links the 5,000-person sales force at real-time speed.

The future is a monumental challenge for companies like Pfizer. Each day of its final drug development process costs $1 million in direct expenses. Use multiples to calculate the lost market opportunity for each of those days. At the same time, the company is expanding the number of compounds it develops simultaneously, while integrating one of its competitors. The company's people epitomize specialized knowledge workers. They practice science and produce ideas in a rigorous sequence that involves industry, government, and consumers. Anything, everything that speeds up processes while maintaining quality is to Pfizer's advantage.

"We have cross-functional, collaborative virtual teams at every level," says Joe Bonito, Pfizer's senior director for Worldwide Organizational Effectiveness. "They are the way we develop our products, and our competitive advantage lies in our ability to work with our 'co-promote' partners."

Pfizer brings its global product development teams together to launch them, then sends them off to carry out their plans virtually. "We have a large catalytic event that gets people face-to-face for a period of time to build trust and personal connection. We develop shared aspirations, clarity of purpose, goals, and an action plan," Bonito says. Then the teams return to their home locations to carry out the plan.

Pfizer's Central Research organization is experimenting with a combination of face-to-face meetings and up-to-the-minute virtual team rooms. "Teams are just such complex things, and virtual, cross-functional teams are several orders more complex," says Jim McCarthy, senior adviser in its Team Effectiveness group, which supports the company's research and development teams. He cautions: "You really do need to do your homework if you're going to bring your teams online. Your job is to diffuse complexity. It's a very different process, and part of the battle is having people understand that there is value in doing work differently. People tend to see things online and believe that they have to interact with everything. You just need to think of web-based team processes as sets of just-in-time tools; use only what you need when you need it."

Hank McKinnell, a laptop-carrying executive, is a good role model for the company. He's a Ph.D. who in his college days programmed an IBM 1401 in machine language. "I moved the wires around in the back of the machine," he remembers. Pfizer was the first pharmaceutical company to put its annual report on the Internet in 1994.[2] The experiences that have helped McKinnell most in his career? Joining Pfizer, spending half his work life outside the United States, and learning to type in high school.

"I started 28 years ago at Pfizer in Japan, so a very early part of my experience was learning consensus. I've been in the minority several times in my career, and that made a real impression on me," McKinnell says. "The demographics of the workforce are driving us. We can't count on nine-to-five, five days a week, largely male and white employees. It's just not like that anymore. We have to draw the best and brightest from all segments. Diversity benefits us when there are more people around the table holding different views."

"It's a challenge when we have to team up with people who are different," says Bonito, who sees "a shift from resistance as the senior executives have said teamwork is the way we want to manage our business. Even if we underestimated how hard it would be to work with Searle or its parent, Monsanto, we've gotten smarter. We're becoming more transparent about how decisions get made and how long they take. In our organization, it's pretty clear to us who can make what decisions. But when you work with partners, you don't know who makes what decisions at what levels."

"It took 150 years to build this company," McKinnell says, referring to Pfizer's beginnings in Brooklyn, New York, in 1849, the year of the California gold rush. We have a very successful organization; it's not broken, but we want to fix it *before* it gets broken. We've recognized the benefits of cross-functional teamwork. The silos are disappearing."

Reinventing Government

The National Museum of American History in Washington, D.C., houses an exhibit heralding the start of the information revolution. A female mannequin stands in a nineteenth-century office, while a male wax figure in a Victorian business suit watches her. She literally is *cutting the red tape* that binds brown accordion folders stuffed with papers. On this day, the organization of information makes its next big move—into the newly invented wooden filing cabinet.

Bureaucracy, a word first used by Thomas Carlyle in 1848 (he called it the "continental nuisance"), institutionalizes the storage of information, embodied in the written word. In fact, the now extinct root word *burel* means a writing desk. This treatment of written material where ideas are physically encased, typically with only private access, is quite different from its treatment in networks. "Information wants to be free," Stewart Brand has been saying since PCs were invented.[3]

On a steamy end-of-August dog day in 1993, most people in the capital had left for vacation. Yet across the street from the museum, the vestibule of the Mellon Auditorium, with its three-story-tall marble columns and oak floors so old that they could no longer be sanded, was crowded and noisy with 200 people.

They were registering for a conference. Its purpose? To launch a network of federal employees who participated in the first stage of "reinventing government." We were there as designers and facilitators of the three-day getting-started process.

Reinvent the U.S. government? Isn't this the proverbial oxymoron? Even if you could, skeptics say, would you want to?

In 1993, the United States was not the only country looking at reinvention: Australia, Canada, Denmark, Great Britain, France, Sweden, and New Zealand, as well as a few less likely candidates (Italy, Mexico, India, Chile, Palestine, South Africa, and Germany), were but some of the countries that were reinventing. Virtually every state in the Union has had some type of reinvention effort under way, as have hundreds of cities and towns, including such differing places as New York City, Youngstown, Ohio, and even tiny Sanford, Maine, where then–police chief, Gordon Paul, became an expert in quality and networking.[4]

All this governmental introspection is easy to understand. Like most other centuries'-old organizations, the U.S. government no longer can cope with its problems in the same way it has in the past.

The twenty-first century is about speed and information, knowledge and competence, complexity and wisdom. The nineteenth century was about slow, steady progress, factories and railroads, clockworks and mechanisms. Industrial Age organizations ill serve the turmoil of the Network Age.

Launching NetResults

Marion Metcalf was one of the original 200 "crusading federal bureaucrats" who staffed the government's 1993 National Performance Review. A graduate of Brown University with a master's in city and regional planning from Harvard, she joined from the Justice Department where she'd worked for a number of years. NPR had an exceptionally cross-boundary design for a government initiative. The "volunteers" from 22 major agencies went to NPR for five months, forming 33 cross-functional teams, including 11 "systems" teams that looked at department-spanning issues like finance and organizational design. Their mandate was to come up with a plan for reinvention.

The rule for the agency teams was that people could not "reinvent" their own departments. Metcalf, for example, whose day job was in the Enforcement Office at the Immigration and Naturalization Service, served on the Department of Labor team. For the systems teams, "NPR recruited recognized reformers (by networking to find out who they were!)," Metcalf explained,[5] mentioning Vincette Goerl, then a financial manager at the General Services Administration (now chief financial officer at the U.S. Forest Service), who worked on the Financial Management Team.

The beauty of this design was that it depended on the real experts—the people who, on a daily basis, ground out the federal government. No one knew better than they the pain of securing 23 signatures for a simple travel voucher or the labor-intensive paper-pushing process that could make buying a PC a three-year ordeal. Many generations of PCs develop, grow, and die in that time.

NPR invited numerous management consultants to address the staff at brown-bag lunches and keynotes. Tom Peters kicked off the Labor Department's reinvention effort with a packed house of 1,500 at the Mellon Auditorium. Joseph Juran, Peter Senge, Daryl Connor, and Shoshanna Zuboff, to name just a few, along with executives from many companies coping with complex change, got their 15 minutes, many in front of Vice President Al Gore, who sponsored the reinvention campaign.

We became involved because Metcalf had a sore throat. Our third book on the development of networked organizations, *The TeamNet Factor,* was still in galleys when Seattle-based Robert Gilman, publisher of *In Context,*[6] read it on a flight to Washington. When he landed, he called Al Gilman (his brother and Marion's husband), who was at choral practice,[7] which Marion had skipped due to her sore throat. Marion and Robert started talking, and she explained her new assignment working for the vice president. The toughest problem, she said, was getting agencies and internal departments to work together across boundaries. Robert told her about our book, and soon we, too, were volunteering at NPR in summer 1993.

By early August, Carolyn Lukensmeyer, NPR's deputy director at the time, who was working with Andy Campbell (then an organization development director at the CIA), Metcalf, Goerl and a handful of others, asked for our help. "I'm a believer in networking," says Bob Stone, who at that time was director of NPR. "Carolyn said that there are these people with ideas about networks and we ought to be working on it. In recent years, my leadership style has tended to let people follow their hearts if they thought there was something really worthwhile."[8]

People were wondering what would happen when they returned to their home agencies. Their experience had turned them into evangelists. How could they go back to, in many cases, their dreary, paper-pushing, meeting-infested, low-results jobs? Couldn't they stay connected in some way, continuing to exchange ideas while actively working to implement the recommendations? Stone's nod of the head gave the go-ahead to launch a *people network* that would link the returning army of reinventing-government believers.

Six hundred people were invited, and a third showed up in that last week of August. They stayed together over two days, with dozens coming and going, simultaneous break-out and plenary sessions, late-night huddles, boxed lunches, and palettes of flipcharts. In the same auditorium where the president presents the annual Malcolm Baldrige National Quality Awards, NetResults[9] named itself, crafted a set of goals, expressed its preferences for how to communicate, developed a plan, and agreed upon a mission statement:

"To serve as a communication vehicle and catalyst to facilitate broad participation, stimulate leadership, and support the goals, strategies, activities, and achievements of continuous government improvement."

Operating only informally, NetResults soon linked thousands of people in different agencies through face-to-face meetings, informal exchange of memos, and via the Internet,[10] where fly scads of conversations, e-mails, opinions, articles, drop-in chats, and online computer conferences.[11]

The NPR web site carries the history and accomplishments of the overall effort: size of government reduced by 350,000; elimination of nearly three-quarters of a million pages of internal rules; and savings of about $137 billion, to name a few. The top goal for Year 2001? "Achieve outcomes no agency can achieve alone."

"There's no way to tell how much good you're doing in such an effort," says Bob Stone, who retired as "energizer in chief" of NPR in 1999. The net result is most evident, he believes, in the networks and networking spawned by the people who participate: Financial and procurement executives from across government remain tightly linked[12]; information reaches places the same day that formerly took months to arrive; and people like Metcalf receive awards for encouraging greater cooperation.

"This isn't a technology thing," Stone says. "This is a communication thing."

The Net Results

Marion Metcalf received a standing ovation from a packed Riverside Baptist Church in Washington, D.C., on December 17, 1999. It was her memorial service; Metcalf had died suddenly the previous Saturday at the age of 44. Her family, friends, and colleagues were celebrating Metcalf's life, including an award just the month before from the U.S. Immigration and Naturalization Service Commissioner and the Government Technology Leadership Award. She was the team leader for INS's Green Card team that overhauled how the agency's lead product would be produced.

When Metcalf took over the project, "INS had only one facility producing the [green] cards, and it just couldn't keep up with demand. To make matters worse, INS had created more types of cards over the years. This meant different systems producing the different cards. But INS has put those days behind it,"[13] wrote Joshua Dean in Gov.Exec.com, which also gave Metcalf's team an award.

Such was her challenge when she arrived. New technology choices caused a stalemate, while the old system was so antiquated that no one wanted to use it any longer. Typical government silos prevented people with good solutions and new approaches from being able to implement them.

"She understood that her job was to be a manager, not a single-handed problem solver. She understood that what she was managing was a crosscutting team, not a standing-line organization," says Al Gilman, who himself coleads a worldwide working group for the World Wide Web Consortium.[14]

What Are We Going to Do with(out) Marion?[15]

There were few dry eyes at Marion Metcalf's memorial service as her brother Larry repeated this phrase. Friends and family came from across the country, including people who knew her best online.

Metcalf's NPR experience turned her into a prodigious online networker. Although severe congenital scoliosis prevented her from straightening her limbs (thus the refrain, "What are we going to do with Marion?"), she angled toward the keyboard and typed as fast as anyone you've ever seen. She helped launch NetResults, posting hundreds of messages, set up web sites for government, nonprofits, and friends, kept in touch with a family listserv, and became a guiding voice in SPIRIT, the women's conference housed on Caucus's[16] online network.

Her death was shattering to this small electronic community. "How, I wonder, can it be that someone can become such a big part of my life when I only met her three or four times?" wrote Jennifer Sutton, a University of Oregon graduate student who traveled across the country to read poems at Metcalf's memorial. "I sent her lots of things I read. And so often she would respond with such probing questions, intelligent insights."[17]

Sutton is blind. Such is the power of networking in the Network Age.

Stress

While it's not easy to be a member or leader of a team, it's even more difficult in a virtual team deep in the flux of change. All the self-doubting questions that any team member asks ("What am I doing here? Do they need me? Am I included? Who's the leader? How aggressive do I need to be? Will I measure up?") are even more exaggerated when the group lacks daily face-to-face contact.

Doubts, concerns, perceived problems, and boredom mingle with excitement, opportunities, caring, satisfaction, and even exhilaration. To be part of a team is to continuously work a dynamic tension deep in the heart of being human.

I must simultaneously be "me," an independent individual, and "we," an interdependent person in a group.

Each of us grapples with this tension between the need to *separate* or *differentiate,* to enhance our *individuality,* and the need to *integrate*— to bond in groups.

Complements, Not Opposites

Cooperation requires independence. This apparent contradiction is the challenge of working well with other people.

Too often, the individual and the group post to opposite sides of the wall, each vying to prevail in a win-lose contest. We characterize entire cultures as individualistic (United States) or group-oriented (Japan).

In reality, *me* and *we* are complements, not opposites. This is the key to resolving the paradox.

Virtual teams arc high-connectivity organizations.

To a significant degree, virtual teams self-manage. For them to succeed, people must be independent and capable of making quick yet thoughtful decisions. Virtual people need to know more, decide more, do more. Clear agreements on purpose coupled with personal commitment comprise one part of the equation; open, accessible, comprehensive information and communication environments are the other. These make possible the ongoing conversation that is the team's process.

Sture Karlsson, managing director of an internal service company that is part of TetraPak, the Swedish packaging company, puts it this way,

"People must know more about the vision and purpose when they cannot lean on the side of the organizational box they belong to."

It gets more complicated if you are simultaneously a leader of teams of people who work for you *and* a member of teams of peers and bosses. "Me" is me personally, but also me representing "my team." "We" is the family feeling of "me and the people who report to me," *and* it is also the language of "me and my peers" with the person we work for. How can people be both "me" and "we?"

The CEO View

To see *me* and *we* across the boundaries of a virtual team, adopt the "CEO view," a fundamental personal and virtual skill.

Tom Botts, Natural Gas Director for Shell U.K, is trying to build a cohesive group from three distinct organizational cultures and multiple ethnic ones. "The key is not just getting people to know one another but knitting them together. They need a compelling story that everyone can hold. How and why does this thing fit together?" he asks.

"They need to not just affiliate with their units but with this long value chain of gas products and services. We've had some success in getting people to grasp the bigger picture." Botts has put together the Gas Leadership Network of the top 40 people in the Gas Directorate. "The first time we got together it was very stilted, and everyone was very cautious," he remembers. "We did an exercise on stereotypes and the same stereotypes emerged group by group. We tacked them up on the wall and they all were identical. You could feel tension go out of room. Now, a year into it, the Gas Leadership Network is really demonstrating its leadership capacity and making a real difference in the business."

Metaphorically, leaders are like Janus, the Roman god of beginnings and endings, who guards doorways. The god of portals has two faces, one that looks in and the other that looks out.

The Janus leader views life from the boundary—looking inward to the group itself and outward to the environment.

The CEO's view is a natural Janus view. The top-level leader sits on the organization's boundary, balancing internal needs and capabilities with external assessments and strategies. Internally, the organization is a web of relationships, while externally a web of relationships enmeshes the organization itself. Not only at-the-top leaders, but leaders at every level sit on boundaries. Simultaneously they peer up and down and in and out.

From Janus's view, people are *holons.* People are both wholes and parts. Holon means *whole* ("hol-") and *part* ("-on"). As individuals, people are parts of groups; as leaders they stand for the whole.

Arthur Koestler originally coined the word *holon.*[18] It concisely expresses the idea that everything (atoms, cells, solar systems, cars, people) is simultaneously a *whole* in and of itself and a *part* within something larger.

Usually called *hierarchy* by scientists, the holon is a central principle of general systems theory. It is the idea that everything—life and the universe and everything in between—structures itself in levels, "subsystems comprising systems within suprasystems." Mathematicians talk about "sets of sets." Nobel Laureate Herbert Simon called hierarchy the "architecture of complexity."[19] (See Chapter 11, "Theory.")

Simple word, complex idea. We use the holon (hierarchy) idea every time we use money, outline a report, store a file, find a reference, or check an organization chart. When we go up a level to a higher authority, broader scope, or more abstract view, we use the holon idea literally. We also use it when we go down a level to more detail, narrower scope, and more-concrete views.

Strange a word as it is for most people (though The Police used it in an early-1980s song), holon can stand for organizations, small groups, and individuals. Stripped to its mathematical essence and used in the context of technology, a holon is a *node.* People and virtual teams are nodes in networks. A node may be simple—one person—or it may unfold into a whole universe. America Online is only one node on the Internet, but millions of people are attached to it. A team is a node in a larger organization, and it comprises member nodes linked into a network.

Members, leaders, and levels resolve the me/we paradox. They turn flesh-and-blood huggable people into intangible hard-to-grasp virtual teams.

Members

The experience of finding oneself on too many teams is not unusual. Most people are members of multiple groups. We all take part in a constantly changing personal pageant of many small groups simultaneously—family, community, friendship, and affinity groups as well as task-oriented work teams. In each group and team, we play different roles. People are not parts of groups in the same way that hearts are parts of bodies. Only in the extreme (slavery, for instance) does a group own people body and soul.

Like people, roles are integral to groups. People animate roles that belong to the group.

Roles

The role mediates between an independent individual and his or her expected behavior in the group. What sociologist Erving Goffman calls the basic "unit of socialization," roles naturally arise informally in small groups and are more felt than visible. In larger organizations, roles tend to take on more trappings through titles, written job descriptions, and personal contracts.

Although you cannot see them, you experience the importance of roles by talking about your part in a group: "What is my role?" or "That role's already filled" or "I can fill that role" or even, as you are leaving, "There's no role for me."

Roles translate between me and we, between the bottomless complexity of individual people and the comparative simplicity of playing a part in a group.

Roles are easier to see in their more formal presentation as *positions*. People usually diagram positions in relationship to other positions; organization charts show which person reports to whom. Positions clearly belong to the organization that sets them up and can just as easily take them away.

An open position—a formal role—stands by itself as a sometimes-gaping hole in an organization, an empty place in the structure. When a person steps into a position, a classic dynamic arises between the characteristics of the particular person and the legacy of expectations that the role conveys. Once populated anew, the role both shapes and is shaped by the person who occupies it (Figure 8.1). This becomes even more complex when the team is virtual.

People also carry their formal positions into the many teams they join. Sometimes this is appropriate; sometimes it is not. In virtual teams with limited face-to-face interaction, roles rise in importance. Consider that in virtual teams

- People typically play multiple roles, often many more than in conventional teams.
- Roles require greater clarification. Expectations need to be made more explicit than in colocated teams.
- At the same time, role flexibility is essential because the process is dynamic and roles change constantly.

Me

Respect for the individual is a core value of all the great team companies. The trick is to develop greater cross-boundary capabilities without diminishing—better yet, while enhancing—the independence of individuals and teams.

Enhance independence as you strengthen interdependence.

Figure 8.1 Roles Integrate "Me" and "We"

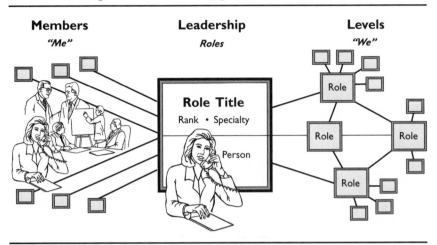

Independence permeates every level of organization—from people as members of teams to teams as parts of larger organizations to the independence required of companies in alliances. All groups need a minimal level of independence and decision making in relationship to the larger system. Virtual teams need even more.

Independence can never be complete or absolute; not for people, teams, companies, or nations. Independence is always a matter of degree along a range from "too little" to "sufficient" to "optimal" and, finally, "too much."

Because virtual teams need higher levels of *interdependence* in roles, they require correspondingly higher levels of relative *independence* and voluntary behavior in the individual members.

Leaders

One leader makes for a good sound bite, but it takes more than one to lead a successful virtual team.

Insofar as the sudden proliferation of virtual teams is in some ways a harking back to a simpler way of organizing, it is instructive to look at how the most original teams handled leadership. In forager societies, there are many informal leaders. Among the !Kung tribe in the Kalahari Desert in Botswana, a foraging society that has survived thousands of years in spite of tremendous threat, leaders influence but they do not force.

Traditional anthropology interpreted such systems as being without a leader (*acephalous*, meaning "no head"). Then in the late 1960s, University of Minnesota anthropologists Virginia Hine and Luther Gerlach confirmed that this is actually a form of many-headed (*polycephalous*)[20] distributed leadership. Herbalists, hunters, midwives, warriors, and other particularly skilled or knowledgeable people take the lead as circumstances require. To one frustrated researcher trying to identify a single local leader, a !Kung elder said,

> *"Of course we have headmen! In fact, we are all headmen. . . . Each one of us is headman over himself!"*[21]

Virtual teams take a page from the !Kung book. As organizations that require much more leadership than conventional colocated teams, they nevertheless have much lower overall coordination cost. This only works if everyone understands and assumes part of the expanded virtual leadership burden.

Grasping a Group

Decades of research on small groups and teams have turned up this major insight: The only universal role observed in groups is leadership.

> *Virtual teams are leader-full not leader-less.*

Leadership is pervasive in virtual teams. The leadership structure as a whole is an inclusive set of related roles of leaders and followers. Reuben Harris, chair of the Department of Systems Management at the Naval

Postgraduate School, has identified six basic leadership roles that virtual teams require:

- Coordinator
- Designer
- Disseminator
- Tech-net manager
- Socio-net manager
- Executive champion

The transformation of a person into representing a group by way of leadership is a miracle of social construction. Leaders are convenient handles to help members and outside observers alike grasp groups.

When confronted with complex ideas, people have a habit of using one part of the idea to represent the whole.[22] "Wall Street" stands for the complexity of U.S. financial markets; the "Oval Office" stands for the presidency and Executive Branch of government.

The phrase, "I belong to Gail's group," shows one person representing a whole group, nowhere more obvious than in the role of the CEO. Here, a person stands for a corporate entity that may include thousands of people, "speaking for" the organization externally and "speaking to" the group internally.

The habit of simplifying complexity by grasping a prominent part can translate into single-pointed leadership. Cultures even build in this view. Such is the case at one major company that requires every project to have a single "designated responsible individual."

Although virtual teams may have single leaders, multiple leaders are the norm rather than the exception.[23] Virtual teams that deal with complex issues and problems invariably have shared leadership, regardless of the titles they use for convenience.

Many authors of books on teams simply assume without discussion that a team needs a single leader. A few distinguish, as we do, between formal leadership (governance), which may be singular, and the broader multiple leadership that always arises in a successful, healthy team. "In successful teams, leadership is shared," states Glenn Parker unequivocally.[24]

In the earliest teams, the camp teams, leadership was informal and distributed, based on influence rather than authority. We are in many ways returning to the organic structures of that era, albeit with a fantastic new capability to create nonterritorial spaces and share information.

Social and Task Leaders

Virtual teams typically have at least two kinds of leaders—social leaders and task leaders, a distinction first made in the 1950s:

- Task leaders are oriented to expertise, activities, and decisions required to accomplish results. Productivity measures task success. This is of central importance to virtual teams, since here "task rules."
- Social leaders arise from interactions that generate feelings of group identity, status, attractiveness, and personal satisfaction. Group cohesion measures social leadership success and is equally critical to virtual teams sustaining themselves.

In a traditional hierarchy-bureaucracy, social leadership simplifies and formalizes as a place in the authority structure. Task leadership boils down to one core expertise. A typical role title reveals both the social and task aspects. Consider the vice president for manufacturing:

- The vice president is a designation of social rank, a level in an authority structure—the *hierarchy* part of the title.
- Manufacturing is a label of task specialization, pointing to an area of expertise—the *bureaucracy* part of the title.

How do you convey rank online? New interactive media such as e-mail pose unforeseen problems to the existing authority structure. In work areas, for example, space displays importance (a closed office versus a cubicle), signs offer titles, and choice of attire differentiates employees from executives.

> *Rank—having it and using it—is a major challenge for virtual groups.*

A new team often defines its expertise roles before it locates the members who populate them. This is in itself a step toward virtuality. Imagine a team that does not yet exist. It is most often the search for the right people, those with needed expertise and experience, that leads to different locations and organizations—and the consequent formation of a virtual team.

> *While rank is confusing, specialization is booming in virtual teams. Your area of expertise most often defines your role in task-oriented virtual teams.*

"I can't think of any project that we do on our own. There is just too much to know and there are too many specialties in the built environment," says Gary Wheeler, leader of the Chicago office of Perkins & Will, the architectural, engineering, and interior design firm and past president of the American Society of Interior Design. Wheeler's office is just completing a project for ADC, the Minneapolis-based broadband company. "We did all the program interviews over their intranet site, allowing up to 5,000 people the opportunity to give input. We got 30 to 40 percent response where normally we get 10 to 20 percent. We're involving people from HR, IT, facilities, and management on the core team. We validated our findings with them, then shared them with leadership. A great deal was done via the net." This is a completely new way to work for a company as grounded in place as an architecture and design firm.

Managing the challenges of virtual team life also brings the opportunity to involve the best minds and most experienced people, wherever in the world they may be. In time, great teams will become the norm as we climb the learning curve of distributed work.

Levels

Big organizations are made up of smaller organizations that are made up of even smaller groups. Small groups tie together organizations from the front line to the executive suite to the boardroom.

As the basic unit of organization, how big is a small group? How big is a group of small groups? Does being virtual make a difference in size?

At the Virtual Table[25]

The number of people on a team is one of those things that appears so obvious that it is easy to miss its significance. All teams, after all, have a size that refers to the number of members. Size also accounts for the internal communications burden and the number and variety of interactions and relationships that the team requires.

The size of a colocated team is rather immediately apparent, and membership is usually clear. In virtual teams, size often becomes fuzzy, swelling and contracting as individuals come and go. Virtual membership boundaries often have degrees of "centralness" or "bands of involvement"—a core group, an extended team, and an external network of partners (Figure 8.2).

> *Millions of years of experience indicate there are two natural breakpoints in the size of small groups: 5 and 25.*

Experienced team leaders, researchers, and popular writers alike agree that the ideal core team ranges in size from four to seven members. This is, not so coincidentally perhaps, the same size as a typical Stone Age family and not very different in size from many families today.

Is there a lower limit to team size? One debate among researchers is whether two people, technically known as a *dyad,* are enough to constitute a group. Three people, so some thinking goes, bring enough diversity to qualify: Three nodes offer multiple communication pathways and the possibility of subgroups and cliques.

Figure 8.2   Rings of Involvement

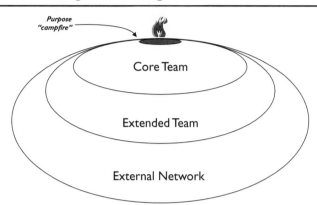

Purpose "campfire"

Core Team

Extended Team

External Network

For us personally, this is not a question: Two *can* team. As friends, lovers, spouses, parents, business partners, and even coauthors (this is our sixth book), we surely are a very small but very complex group. Even two people can play many roles with one another, with a great diversity of communication (and potential for misunderstanding) between them.

Is there an upper limit on how big a team or small group can be? People suggest differing numbers here, but generally 15 to 25 people is the upper limit. When you get to 25, however, small subgroups typically form. Some writers offer different rules for measuring the size of small groups, such as "the number that allows everyone to know everyone else" or "whatever size can form a functional unity."

Teamnets

Teams do not exist in isolation. For millions of years, teaming occurred in camps and groups of camps (Figure 8.3). This remains true today, even if "the camp" often goes unrecognized.

The nomadic family yoked together between four and seven people as its basic socioeconomic unit, the same size as today's typical team. From time immemorial, these small units naturally congregated into larger associations. Camps involving clusters of four to six families appear to be as universal as the family itself. The Olduvai Gorge in Tanzania, for example, reveals that base camps of 25 to 30 people existed as early as 1.7 million years ago, at the very beginning of the Stone Age in the Lower Paleolithic era.

Researchers call this "the magic number 25,"[26] five camps of five families averaging five members each. Twenty-five is also the number of people in most everyone's "persisting lifelong network." These are the folks who are closest to you throughout your life, staying with you despite job changes, divorces, births, deaths, and moves from one locale to another.

With more than 25 or 30 people, a comfortable meeting becomes difficult and starts to turn into a conference, and people cease to be entirely familiar with one another. All of this becomes more murky, however, when people are online. How many people can maintain a reasonable conversation online? We suspect that, for now, the same number applies to virtual teams. More than 25 people on a core distributed team leads to loss of intimacy required to sustain meaningful communication.

At the next level, nomadic era camps invariably joined up in a supercamp, a local network of four to ten camps or so who together identified the foraging territory of a "local group."

Figure 8.3   Early Evolution of Team Levels

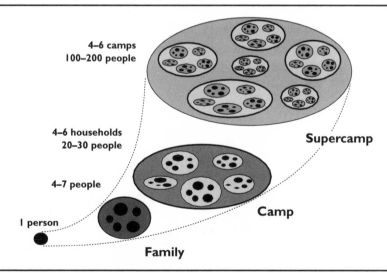

These supercamps are comparable to a large group of 100 to 200 people, another natural cleavage point in modern organizations. W. L. Gore & Associates, the folks who brought Gore-Tex to the world, keep their plant size to a maximum of 150 to 200, which founder Wilbert ("Bill") Gore believed was the number at which human achievement peaks. Larger than that, he said, and people start to get in one another's way.

When people call a group that is bigger than a handful or two of people a "team," they usually are referring to a "team of teams." This is a group that has a common set of cross-team goals and interdependent tasks—what we call a *teamnet*, a network of teams.[27] Understanding the appropriate internal team structure is an often overlooked design issue. People sometimes make these often contentious subgroup definition decisions too early, too make-it-or-break-it-confrontationally, or too unconsciously and off-handedly.

> *There is no one "right" size for virtual teams. Size depends first on the task at hand and second on the unique constraints and opportunities of the situation.*

Generally, the more complex and diverse the task, the larger and more diverse the team needs to be—more expertise, more people. Although more people bring more talent, they also bring along the need for more coordination, and that generates its own problems. Adding people helps performance up to a point. Then the law of diminishing returns sets in. Before long, more people degrade performance.[28] After a limit, which seems to vary by task, more people may actually do less. Sound familiar?

Big, big, qualifier: Since these rules regarding size come from millions of years of experience with colocation, it is only a starting point for estimating the appropriate sizing and clustering for virtual teams.

Virtual teams can be successful only if people cooperatively manage and coordinate membership and leadership. With the skills and infrastructures in place to multiply and share leadership, we are seeing some teams explode the apparent limits on productive size. Virtual teams tend to have relatively smaller active core groups and larger overall memberships.

No Team Is an Island

For fast, flexible, productive, virtual teams, the work shapes the organizational structure. Indeed, it is in their internal work design that the intelligence of the group manifests. The process, categories of work, and relationships shape the interactions and ongoing conversation that is the team "thinking out loud."

With each new level of organization, new team roles and responsibilities emerge. A group with an identity itself becomes an "individual." The team acts and is perceived as a unit at the next level of organization. Teams that are really humming often become very inwardly focused, sometimes creating bonds that rival family ones in strength.

Warning: Virtual team success can breed insularity.

Management movements like quality and reengineering created a new myth: *the team as hero.*[29] While this recognizes the renewed importance of small groups, it also can invest the team with rampant, competitive, isolationism. Independent teams without interteam interdependence can fragment corporate structure.

We are in danger of moving from isolated bureaucrats sitting in specialized boxes to isolated teams of disconnected specialists.

The *team-alone* syndrome dominates many businesses and other organizations. Individual teams spring up as challenges arise that the existing hierarchy-bureaucracy cannot manage. Generally unconnected to one another, these teams are rarely part of a conscious strategy to grow the organization to meet the challenges of accelerating change.

Some companies are already working in twenty-first-century, virtual team style. For Pfizer, Buckman Labs, and Sun Microsystems, virtual teams are, over time, a key business strategy. They offer competitive advantage for meeting challenges of speed, cost-effectiveness, and quality in a global, customer-focused, rapidly changing economy.

How is this possible? Because the human ability to connect has increased exponentially.

CHAPTER 9

LINKS

Being in Touch

> *Only connect! That was the whole of her sermon. Only connect the prose and the passion, and both will be exalted, and human love will be seen at its height. Live in fragments no longer.*
>
> —*Howards End* by E. M. Forster[1]

Connecting across Centuries

August 19 is the national day of mourning in Nepal. Two young boys walk down Pulchowk Road (which links Kathmandu to Patan), steering a cow dressed like a clown. They're headed for Patan Durbar Square with Walkman stereos strapped to their heads. There the prime minister will tell jokes, front-page news in *The Kathmandu Post*. Mourning lasts for a year in Nepal, and then it's time to give it up. Laughter is the national cure.

Just around the corner and housed in a little clump of small buildings is the International Centre for Integrated Mountain Development.[2] ICIMOD has been around for a while, protecting the resource-rich, 2,100-mile-long Hindu Kush–Himalaya mountain range, home to more than 140 million people in Afghanistan, Bangladesh, Bhutan, China, India, Myanmar, Nepal, and Pakistan.[3]

Many of ICIMOD's constituents live in remote villages where, as in much of the world, there are no phones, satellites, or any other distance-spanning technologies save the foot. It can take a month for an ICIMOD letter to reach northwestern Nepal and at least another for the reply to return.

Back in ICIMOD's charmingly modest headquarters, messages and information zip around the world, thanks to a very fast communication line[4] that links it directly to Singapore. The organization, itself a collaboration of eight regional, four Scandinavian, and two European countries, has been online since April 1, 1996, when it declared "full-scale connectivity for electronic mail as well as its own Homepage on the World Wide Web."[5] Clearly, Nepal, like much of the world, bridges the ages. In terms of access to technology, we are both in one another's backyards *and* we are universes apart.

Wrapped around our planet is the *connect*, the way to communicate at very low cost regardless of where we are in time or space. Spontaneously and with little planning, perpetual global conversations have erupted in a finger snap, making next-door neighbors of people in Yellow Springs, Ohio; Bangalore, India; and Banjul, The Gambia. No single organization owns the Internet, the earth's interconnected computer network of networks. No authoritative hierarchy governs it. And it has grown faster and in more directions than ever predicted. It's affecting the world in ways we never imagined.

Some people, like writer and electronic community pioneer Howard Rheingold, saw what was coming. In 1984, he wrote, "Before today's first-graders graduate from high school, hundreds of millions of people around the world will join together to create new kinds of human communities, making use of a tool that a small number of thinkers and tinkerers dreamed into being over the past century. . . . The computer of the twenty-first century will be everywhere."[6]

Rheingold went online for the first time in 1985 and, like a few tens of thousands of other people, got hooked.

"No one really predicted that this little subculture of the 1980s would become the web of the '90s and would change everything," Rheingold says today.[7] "We didn't see all of the e-commerce and portals and a jillion web pages, not developing as quickly as it has. It was just a little subculture for 20 years that began . . . with 1,000 people. The growth curve has been extraordinarily rapid recently, but existed for a long time. It's the 'network effect' that Kevin Kelly[8] wrote about. Emergent properties from networks of people of certain sizes."

The Internet is an electronic technology that makes it possible for people to "only connect." The Network Age is all about the ability to develop relationships that endure across space and time. Geography is no longer a barrier to people's capacity to work together (co-labor, hence the word *collaborate*) and braid communities.

Telecommunications and the global economy have arrived for millions of people, bringing with them new partners in daily work. Colleagues can sleep to opposing clocks and still belong to the same team. This is true, but it is not easy. The explosion of links across every conceivable boundary is staggering in its complexity, as languages, cultures, governments, distance, and the mysterious nuances of human behavior all play their parts.

The technology network *supports* the people network. Those who regard the technology alone as the network miss the point. Networking means people connecting with people, which happens whether they're sitting around a conference table, checking messages, pressing phones to their ears, staring at computers, standing by fax machines, or opening the increasingly rare specimen of handwritten mail.

But the technology *is* amazing, and truly different.

Circa 2086

Motorola's product road map goes out to the year 2086. According to the plan, that's about the time, give or take a few years, you'll "be able to translate yourself from place to place *Star Trek*–style at the speed of light," says the company's chief technology officer Dennis Roberson. Johns Hopkins has already taken the first step toward the transporter, he reports. "They've translated a molecule. They've figured out what's there at one end and re-created it at the other."

Won't those who are reading (or writing) these words need replacement parts in order to be around to witness, or better still, experience, this? "We're working on those too," Roberson replies.

"Because We're Motorola"

The company that got its start with five employees and the assets of a bankrupt business of battery eliminators (which allowed battery-operated home radios to operate on ordinary household current) was the first winner of the prized U.S. Malcolm Baldrige National Quality Award in 1988.

Motorola's past, present, and future lie in distributed communications. The company makes the devices (pagers, phones) themselves, the chips that power them, and the systems that carry their signals, what Roberson describes as "a very large universe." The company is responsible for so many distributed communication innovations that it has its own impressive museum at corporate headquarters in Schaumburg, Illinois. There you find a time line of push-button car radios, walkie-talkies, color TVs, pagers, cell phone systems, and global satellite grids that reach individuals. Fuel cells that are an order of magnitude higher performance than anything existing today, life science chips, and bioinformatics inventions (where biology and computers converge) also emanate from Motorola Labs.

Arriving in 1998 at Motorola from NCR, where he pioneered perpetual videoconferencing among continent-spanning engineering sites, Roberson found a 155,000-person organization operating in 116 countries and engineering efforts in 55 countries. It was a giant holding company with many autonomous businesses: police and fire safety communications; the service trades; cell phones; communication infrastructures; satellite systems; semiconductors; and, what Roberson calls "everything else, including world leadership in" automotive electronics, telecommunications electronics, digital ballasts for fluorescent lamps, and energy systems, including batteries and rechargers. The "Internet had also begun to dawn on Motorola," so fledgling efforts were under way in that area as well.

So many disparate businesses operating independently spawned considerable inefficiencies, particularly in regard to communication, and the task of pulling all of Motorola's communications components together fell to the communications business veteran, Merle Gilmore.

It was a monumental task that began by colocating a small cross-organizational team. They "established an outpost in the Motorola Museum," Roberson reports. There, their tight skunkworks of people from around the world met around the clock "with person on top of person, pulled together in open cubes, not even separated by office walls." Their purpose was to make sense of all of Motorola's many disparate communication businesses.

They used the usual small-group tools to communicate: e-mail, phone, fax, face-to-face meetings, and videoconferencing. The official launch of the Communications Enterprise, the new organization that resulted from the group's work less than six months later, took place on a large scale when "75,000 people were brought together for a meeting that was telecast all over the world to Motorola locations with moderators standing in each of them."

In reality, they were not all present because, as Roberson puts it, "Some thousands preferred to sleep at 2 A.M. For them, videos were sent out, which then moved into a regimen of quarterly updates that have migrated to webcasts. Now people attend major announcements at their desktops at their convenience. I'm downloading the video while I'm talking to you."

Motorola makes heavy use of its own devices, in particular, its two-way pager/communicator technology, which "because we're Motorola, is standard gear for most senior professionals in the company."

The two-way pager communicator, PageWriter 2000, "offers you the opportunity to multitask and be working in semi-dead time," Roberson explains. "You can talk while attending a meeting or even while presenting to a group." Our call arrived when he was in a meeting. "Are you ready for phone interview?" his page from executive assistant Diane Lesner read. Yes, he replied in two keystrokes. On a busy day, he estimates that many senior people in Motorola send and receive 50 or more pages. "You're trying to make decisions very quickly and this means you can be running transactions constantly. We all sit in too many long meetings that include vast voids of mind-numbing information."

Roberson is a high-energy person. The first time we saw him in person he ran from the back of a large ballroom, hopped up on the stage, and opened with an animated cartoon of himself flying around the world, projected from a PC that he operated himself.[9]

The Worm Hole

At the time, Roberson was CTO at NCR, where he accomplished something that technology executives rarely do: His megaproject, involving more than 1,000 people in 17 locations, met the market four months ahead of schedule. The computer his team developed was a behemoth than can be meaningfully described only by the weight of the disks it uses: Its 11-terabyte (a million megabytes) version weighs 20 tons. Such "terabrutes" manage massive amounts of data for banks, large retailers, telecommunications companies, and the like.

"We used various communications mechanisms to keep this very, very far flung team together," Roberson said at the time, including "videoconferencing taken to its logical next step—a continuously open line so that you could have a meeting anytime you wanted to."

The team affectionately nicknamed it "the Worm Hole." Think of it, he said, as "a portal of instant transport from one place in the universe to another." The reference comes from the opening credits sequence of *Star Trek* TV show *Deep Space Nine*, which suggests just such an intergalactic phenomenon.

The Worm Hole links three NCR engineering sites (Naperville, Illinois, Columbia, South Carolina, and San Diego, California) with a high-speed, full-bandwidth, always-on audio/video/data link.[10] By the time we "met" Roberson, there was a fourth link, at the company's headquarters in Dayton, Ohio.

We were escorted to an ordinary-looking conference room. Inside were three 32-inch TV screens along with a control pad to operate their cameras. Each screen served a different purpose: One was an electronic overhead projector casting foils onto a screen. Another was a standard PC monitor for real-time information sharing. The third was for people to see one another—and there was Dennis Roberson himself in South Carolina. He stood up and extended his hand electronically. It was a perfectly clear line, with no delays or weird movements.

Because of the top-quality connection, there was no strobe light effect or the sometimes not-so-humorous delays that people associate with what Roberson dubs "traditional" videoconferencing. "It was the only room of its type that I'd experienced where you really could forget that you were not in the same place," he explains. The teams added some nice touches. "The grain of the wood on the table was the same in both Columbia and San Diego." By angling the cameras properly—there were two or three in each location—the desk in one Worm Hole blended right into the desk on the monitor at the other. "It was just a bright engineer who thought of that level of detail," he pointed out. "That sort of thing really helped create the feeling of 'being there.' "

With their three-hour time difference, the group in the east often was eating lunch while the one in the west was not (or vice versa). "Someone was always saying, 'Can I pass you a sandwich?' People thought they should because they felt like they were in the same room."

The Worm Hole was important for organized meetings; the system could accommodate up to three sites simultaneously, with as many people in each location as could comfortably fit into the 18- by 24-foot conference rooms. "The next step was when the doors were left open, and people did in fact 'meet in the hall.' Someone yelled out through the tube and you would have meetings that took place on the fly."

How far away were the engineers from the Worm Hole? Roberson stood up, and we manipulated the camera to follow him as he walked to the door. "Oh, they're all within about 50 feet," he remarked with a sweep of his arm.

Cellular Implants

A half decade later, Roberson observes the downside of that story: In the Worm Hole, you have to be there. "If you put Worm Holes everywhere on earth, you still don't create an environment that people want to work in on an everyday basis. When people here in the U.S. are working, people in Asia are sleeping. How do you keep connected on a continuing basis when you're working with teams that span the whole globe?

"We're moving to web-enabled devices that detect where human intervention is required, sending pages or short messages to individuals who send actions back to the machines, telling them what to do next, in the process expanding from people-to-people (or P2P) communications to people-to-machines (or P2T(hing)) communications, and for completeness, yes, thing-to-thing (T2T) communication is also on its way. Given the global nature of the Internet, the next logical step is that you can be connected anywhere in the world. Via GSM[11] [the global standard for mobile communication] you can be almost anywhere literally today and still be connected. You're even freed from your laptop with handheld or even wearable mobile devices connected through the Internet.

"You can be involved in design on a continuing basis with people working with you around the world. You're always connected and that's a downside—you can never get away from work. The upside is that if you have critical projects and you have other responsibilities, you can continue to contribute, from virtually anywhere. You can be on the beach in the summer and find a few quiet moments to keep your project moving in very efficient ways, or during intermission in a school program, or even while waiting in line for a new driver's license or for a doctor's appointment. Traditional downtime is now translated into available uptime.

"Face-to-face is sometimes mandatory. But these days the vast majority of my one-on-one communication is time-disconnected, and that is different from the Worm Hole. I do more transactions with e-mail and two-way pages than I do over the phone or in person. 'In person' for me now means giving presentations or being presented." For Roberson to meet one-on-one with his boss, Motorola president Bob Growney, more than once or twice a month is very rare.

"That's not to say that we don't communicate all the time. It's crucial to maintain ongoing regular communication in the midst of very busy schedules: two-way pages, e-mails, quick grabs in hall, sometimes even in front of audiences, but our traditional 'one-on-one-time-with-the-boss' is minimal."

Communication can be global as well. Roberson was in China doing his e-mail when "in came a flurry of e-mails from Chris Galvin, Motorola's chairman and CEO [and grandson of its founder]. Six to be exact. He had just landed in the Middle East, where he downloaded his e-mails. One was hot and of considerable interest to me. Chris had copied Bob Growney, who'd just gotten into his office in Schaumberg at 7 A.M. So Chris was online in the Middle East, I was in China, and Bob was in Schaumberg. We sent back and forth a dozen e-mails and moved to a relatively decisive point around the technology issues that Chris had raised. We were very, very far away physically but nonetheless very close timewise even though we were using not-quite-state-of-the-art e-mail."

The company provides security for such conversations through local dial-in numbers in most major cities around the planet, which "is what you want when the CEO, COO, and CTO are having a conversation."

"The trick is communication," Roberson says. "How do you keep in touch, have the right kind of contact, in the right ways? There you need an array of tools that work very effectively, many of them very traditional, but a few approaching state of the art. We now need to be able to pass around 10-, even 50-megabyte files that high-bandwidth connections have enabled.

"One of our costs now in more remote areas is stringing very high performance cable. We have a network that we've built around the world. The base pipes are necessary and critical, but alone they are not sufficient. You need the software that runs on top of it to enable the communication. We now have a consistent e-mail system in place worldwide, which didn't exist a few years ago, and we've connected everyone up to our internal secure Internet. We have a very large web presence, as many high-tech companies do, so that everyone has access to the same information at the same time. It gives the global context, and everyone is connected globally."

Motorola, through its research arm, Motorola Labs, is also pushing communication to its logical boundaries in the nearer term: telepathy and telekinesis. "I'm not talking about the science-fiction version. The fact is that as you give people ever greater communication capabilities and research continues on how the brain works, we will be able to compose messages in the brain and transmit them through electronics to other people and things," says Roberson. He points to the prospect of microprocessors-based "systems on a chip" in light switches, door handles, household appliances, and even shirts that communicate. "You perform telekinesis [moving objects at a distance] by communicating with Internet-protocol-addressable chips that are thither and yon," he explains.

"So that's good for the base level. Now you need to overlay a whole set of processes for how people will use these tools. You need to know what to expect when you have 2,000 people around the globe in nearly 20 different sites, as we do in the Global Software organization. Common processes are the key to this highly distributed organization. Well-chosen, properly defined, and continuously updated processes are indeed at the heart of effective communications across Motorola and indeed all major corporations.

"When you're into grand challenges—changing the world, making a visionary statement of the future, this is better done face-to-face. At

Motorola, we have the opportunity to literally change the world. If people think that's too lofty a goal, I revert back to PowerPoint slides and show how the walkie-talkie revolutionized military activities, and the cell phone is continuing to change the world."

Four Ages of Media

Marshall McLuhan woke people up to the weighty impact of media on human experience with his 1964 book *Understanding Media.*[12] His memorable phrase, "the medium is the message," summarizes his insights.

Imagine being asked to do something. Your interpretation of the request depends on whether the requester is your boss, subordinate, partner, or competitor. It also matters whether you receive the message in a face-to-face exchange, a handwritten note, e-mail, or a printed memo sent to everyone.

Many communications theorists separate the content of a message from its context. They point to the *metamessage*—the relationships, status, and interpretive cues that ride along with the literal symbols themselves. Scientist-philosopher Gregory Bateson calls these bells and whistles the "command" part of the message.

McLuhan goes a step further. He says that the transmission medium itself powerfully influences the total communications experience. That is, there is (1) the message, (2) the affect (influence) it carries, and (3) the medium by which it travels—a meta-metamessage so to speak.

> *The most basic message any medium sends is whether it expects, allows, or makes possible a response. Virtual teams need to maximize their use of media that enable interaction.*

History of Communication

A signature style of communication typifies each era of human civilization, just as a signature organization does. In fact, different media usually are key features in differentiating the big break points in history.

- Speech shaped the nomadic era and the formation of storytelling small groups and camps.
- Writing emerged in the agricultural era and made large-scale hierarchies possible.
- Printing spread specialized knowledge in the bureaucratic Industrial Age.
- In the Network Age, electronic media are shrinking the planet to the "global village," McLuhan's famous phrase.

Each era—small group, hierarchy, bureaucracy, and network—brings its own capabilities that accumulate over time. Instead of new forms of organization wiping out the old, they incorporate them. Thus, today's network benefits from and includes the positive aspects of its organizational predecessors: the specialized functions of bureaucracies, the levels of hierarchies, and the coherence of small groups.

As the new impacts the old, it brings modern variations to recurring themes. The virtual team is a new form of small group made possible and necessary by new forms of communication. While we now have geographically distributed small groups, we still retain access to the variations spawned in each previous era. Command-and-control hierarchical teams, such as military units, and rule-based bureaucratic groups, such as executive committees, are still with us.

Successive waves of change may have reduced the globe's nomads to vanishingly small numbers. Yet the echo of communications in that age still reverberates distinctly in all human life in the twenty-first century.

Time has not diminished the importance of oral communication.

Writing, the second great leap in communication, makes speech enduring and transportable. Words, when written down, persist and can move independent of the writer. Printing in turn incorporates writing, making it available to larger numbers of people. New electronic media incorporate all previous ones. The inventions of the new include the innovations of the old.

Each type of media has features that influence effectiveness, cost, and accessibility. In particular:

One-way media broadcast actions.
Two-way media enable interactions.

This fundamental distinction—whether a medium is one-way or two-way—shapes virtual team communication. Virtual teams must produce products and interact across distances fractured by delays in time. One-way media are great for delivering products (and orders), but they do not enable the interaction (and goodwill) required for people to work in virtual teams. Imagine Motorola's distributed software organization of 5,000 people, which literally operates around the clock with work handed off from one of its eight centers to another, trying to operate with one-way media only. Impossible.[13]

Technology has moved the human world of small groups from the assumed state of colocation in place and time to the option of working together at a distance. This change has been thousands of years in the making. For virtual teams, the conditions for communicating across space and time boundaries are intimately involved with the nature of their technology and how interactive it is.

Virtual teams are beneficiaries of this long evolution of communications technology. Media, once developed, do not go away.

We do not generally lose older forms of communication as we acquire newer ones.

We organize the varieties of ways that people and organizations use to send and receive information in the Communications Media Palette (Figure 9.1) by the four ages.

Each great era of communication carries a common set of advantages and constraints summarized along these dimensions:

Figure 9.1   Communications Media Palette

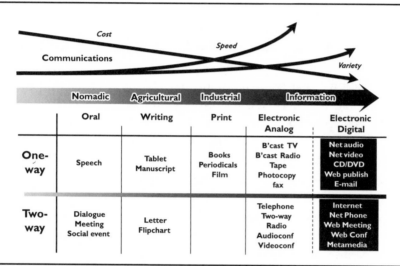

	Oral	Writing	Print	Electronic Analog	Electronic Digital
One-way	Speech	Tablet Manuscript	Books Periodicals Film	B'cast TV B'cast Radio Tape Photocopy fax	Net audio Net video CD/DVD Web publish E-mail
Two-way	Dialogue Meeting Social event	Letter Flipchart		Telephone Two-way Radio Audioconf Videoconf	Internet Net Phone Web Meeting Web Conf Metamedia

- *Interaction.* How far apart people are physically and how many people any medium can reach influence interaction, the back and forth (or lack of it) of communication.
- *Speed.* The pace of message production, the speed of its transmission, and the rate of its reception govern the swiftness of communication.
- *Memory.* The ability to hold and use a message depends upon its storage, its ease of recall, its difficulty in modification, and its reprocessing capability.

Speech

To speak to someone else without the aid of technology, both sender and receiver need to be in the same place (colocated) at the same time (synchronous). Consequently, a speaker can reach only as many people as the voice will carry to.

The physics of sound carries voice through the air. The receiver's capacity to hear and comprehend speech rule reception. Given the requirement of shared space and time, speaking offers a medium with no appreciable delay between sender and receiver.

People retain what they hear only in the private places of their individual memories, not in the communication medium that links them. Unlike e-mail, for example, that records itself, speech evaporates. Reconstructing a remembered conversation has caused more than one argument. People interpret conversations privately, separate from the medium itself. In short, real-time oral communication has little inherent storage, recall, modification, or reprocessing features. Continuity persists through an oral tradition passed from memory to memory.

Speech encompasses all the possibilities: one-to-few-to-many channels that are both one- and two-way. Speeches, workshops, seminars, and briefings are predominately one-way, sender-based; conversations, meetings, and social events are all two-way and interactive.

Talking to one another is the work of small groups. The foundation is same-time and face-to-face. Rooted in our cultural genes, the oral communication made possible by the telephone is the heart of same-time connection that is free of place.

Written Media

Very roughly speaking, written languages, both alphabetic and ideographic, coevolved with the agricultural economy and the rise of hierarchy. Egyptian hieroglyphics and calendars, for example, developed 5,000 years ago, setting the stage for the Early Dynasty period and the rise of the first great cities. Writing offered options to message senders—from inscriptions on stone that have lasted for ages, to painstakingly penned and copied manuscripts, to the remarkably flexible medium of paper documents.

Writing represented a profound break with the limitations of the spoken word. Senders and receivers were no longer required to be in the same place at the same time; they could be in different places (distributed) at different times (asynchronous). The number of people reached by writing, while in principle virtually unlimited, was in fact quite small. The costs of production and transportation, together with the literacy required for individual use, capped the number of possible writers and readers.

Slower and more cumbersome than speaking, written interaction occurs when people exchange letters and notes. Delivery depends on the transport technology, which in the agricultural era included domesticated animals, wheeled vehicles, and boats, as well as fleet-footedness.

An individual's capacity to read governs the speed of reception. This adds up to a general delay between sender and receiver, dependent mainly on the distance between them.

The advent of writing freed communication from the constraints of space and time because of its most important quality in memory terms: the ability to be stored. Suddenly, human beings had a way to capture communications and make messages explicit, public, and permanent. While writing on paper is a great way to store ideas, its ability to help people recall or modify communications is limited. Witness how much time you spend riffling through files and piles looking for a particular piece of paper.

Words on paper are the ancestors of today's asynchronous media. Both signify a *conceptual leap*—from ephemeral thought to expressing it in concrete, transportable symbols. Using language and the alphabet to convey meaning remains central even as asynchronous communication possibilities erupt.

Print

Historians cite the invention of the printing press and the production of the Gutenberg Bible in 1456 as key early developments of the Industrial Era. Printing is primarily a one-way medium, whereby single senders can reach great audiences of receivers through proclamations, books, and other printed materials. Newspapers, magazines, and newsletters are print media where a few senders (publishers, writers, and advertisers) reach large audiences of generally passive readers. Monographs or limited run publications offer some small-scale options, but until the advent of computer-based desktop publishing, the cost of production had been so relatively high that printed media have had limited value for interactive communication.

Like writing by hand, printing breaks the bonds of space and time. Unlike writing, print reproduction is comparatively easy; the time and cost differences between a print run of 1,000 and 10,000 are marginal. Very large numbers of people are reachable through print.

Print production, however, is much more complicated and slower than writing. It involves not only the time required for writing, but also the time of transferring writing to the print mechanism and the time of printing the product itself. Speed of delivery is again dependent on the transport technology, which greatly increased in the industrial machine era. Speed of reception, however, remains constrained by the speed of reading. These factors create what is usually a substantial delay between sending and receiving, rendering print almost useless for sustained interaction.

Like writing, printing provides storage integral to the medium. Its recall, however, is still limited to remembering the location of the information and then physically combing through material to find it. Modification is, if anything, more difficult in printing than in writing.

Atoms and Bits

It's been a century since relativity and quantum mechanics liquefied the Newtonian absolutes. Most of us point to the mid-twentieth century as the visible beginning of the transition from industrial to postindustrial eras. In the new millennium, technology, culture, economics, and organizations all are in the process of completing a fundamental transformation.

Half a century deep into the Information Age, we can recognize its major stages. In 1964, McLuhan described the media of our time as "electric," remarkable by the almost instantaneous nature of communications based on principles of electromagnetism. Writing in 1995, Nicholas Negroponte, director of MIT's Media Lab, drew a fundamental distinction between *Being Digital*[14] and *being analog.* From Negroponte's point of view, analog TV shares more with books than it does with computer-based digital media.

In the analog world, *atoms* deliver information. We move molecules in the air, ship paper around, or modulate the structure of electromagnetic waves. In the digital world, *bits* deliver information. Bits are pure information, representations of on-off switches. They deconstruct the analog world into ephemeral strings of binary relationships and reconstruct them wherever. An analog book deteriorates over time, but a digital book is potentially timeless. An analog book occupies physical space, whereas a digital one occupies none the eye can see.

This very big difference between atoms and bits profoundly influences virtual teams. Accordingly, we separate the atom era from the bit era.

Atoms

Broadcast TV and radio, videotapes, audiocassettes, and the like are all one-way analog electronic media. They allow senders to reach groups of receivers at virtually any scale—from local to global. The boys with the cow and their Walkman stereos in Nepal are analog.

The telephone has been the most important addition to the human repertoire of one-to-one communication since the evolution of speech. It has made a new species of interactivity possible. Telephone conference calls and voice mail are group-oriented analog media. The same is true for traditional videoconferencing and its offspring, desktop video-conferencing. Analog electronic reproduction extends to print through media such as fax.

People often remark on the distributed nature of electronic media. However, this non-place-dependent feature does not distinguish them from earlier nonoral forms. Senders and receivers of writing and print can be just as far apart as the people who communicate via electronic media can.

In terms of time, however, there is an enormous difference. Electronic media completely fracture the constraints of time, offering real-time and non-real-time connections, or even both together, such as recording a broadcast for replay. These media extend to virtually unlimited scales, reaching billions of people at the same time (during the Olympics, for example).

Electronic communication effectively travels at the speed of light, a distribution speed that has no parallel in nonelectronic media. For introduction and reception, however, analog speed slams into real-time barriers. An hour's worth of information broadcast or viewed on a tape still takes an hour to meaningfully view (fast-forward aside). How quickly people can speak and listen limits the speed of the telephone connection. This is the real-time restraint of the analog world.

In memory terms, atoms offer little in the way of fundamentally new capabilities. Like writing and printing, electronic media can store communications, but provide limited support for recall and modification without additional digital capability.

While these media seemed to extend communications to vast global reach, over time it is the interactive qualities of these media that will be the really big story. Electronic real-time media offer opportunities for interaction that is essential to virtual life.

Bits

ENIAC, the first electronic computer, was unofficially turned on at the end of World War II. In early 1945, ENIAC help to compute some last-minute calculations for the first atomic bomb. The birth of the digital era is linked with the nuclear explosions in August of that year, which sundered human time into an irrevocable "before" and "after."

Despite their dramatic entrance, computers stayed in the background for the next quarter-century, generally supporting the centralized, routine bureaucratic needs of the Industrial Age. They fueled the rise of IBM to the pinnacle of global companies. Computers subsequently shrank from mainframes to minis, led by then-new companies like the late Digital Equipment Corporation.[15]

When the computer-on-a-chip escaped from the labs in the mid-1970s, the digital revolution began to flower and directly touch everyday working life. It gave rise to the now-ubiquitous personal computer (PC) and companies like Apple ("computers for the rest of us") and the striking "WinTel," which combined Microsoft's operating system with Intel's chips to monopolize the world's computing resources in the 1990s.

Somewhat simultaneous with the rise of the PC has been the development of computer networks, initially created to spread out use of the incredibly expensive mainframes through time sharing. These trends converged in the 1980s, heralded by the Macintosh, a PC with built-in networking. The network is now the central computing paradigm, linking computers of every size and capacity, from massively parallel super-computers to mainframes, minis, workstations, desktop PCs, portables, palmtops, and chips embedded in all manner of appliances. More than one company has used the slogan that Sun Microsystems made famous: "The network is the computer."

The total computing capacity available to society consists of both the individual devices and the network connections among them, what some call "the matrix."[16] This combination has given rise to "computer-mediated communications," in the parlance of early researchers in the field of *digital media*.

Like their analog counterparts, electronic digital media offer an array of one-way options, some (such as digital TV) still relatively new at the start of the millennium. Internet audio and video provide both one-way and two-way capabilities, although bandwidth limits are slowing their growth. The transmission of graphics, audio, and video requires bandwidth that is vastly greater than that needed for transmitting simple (ASCII) text such as e-mail that is almost instantly replicable and can reach millions or a few.

The new media also offer something else: *interactivity*.

Bits really shine in interactivity, exploding the limits to human organization and allowing a vast expansion in virtual group capability and variety.

The options of one person communicating with another, of a few communicating with a few, or of many communicating with many others flow almost seamlessly from one digital variety to the next. E-mail ranks with the telephone and face-to-face dialogue as a powerful and pervasive personal medium. Digital technology also allows the point-to-point exchange of files (including digitized print documents) and replicates the telephone system through Internet telephony. Small groups have a growing list of digital media available that allow a few people to communicate with a few others—from same-time online chat and electronic meetings to time-disconnected computer conferencing and topical discussions.

Digital media and especially the ubiquitous Internet represent historically unparalleled expansions of interactive capability. Just what is different?

The Digital Difference

As with every media since writing, digital media support communications across space. Like analog electronic media, digital communication may be real-time or time-disconnected; it's effectively unlimited in terms of the numbers of people it can reach.

All computer-based media take full advantage of the speed of light. This is especially true at the nanoscale of the chips themselves, imperceptible to our natural senses. Production and reception speeds are not limited to real time. They may vary enormously according to the type of data being prepared and communicated. A database almost instantly produces information at processor speeds, whereas you type an e-mail note in real time.

The big difference, what makes it so effective for interaction, lies in its vastly increased memory capabilities (see highlights, Figure 9.2). This pertains not simply in storage, which all post-oral media share, but also in memory's other aspects. Recall is integral to digital media. One can peruse vast quantities of information in moments, or even seconds— needles picked instantly out of the proverbial haystacks of data. Modification is unlimited; it is easier (and incomparably faster) to turn bits on and off than it is to retype a page. Take a stroll down memory lane to compare the act of editing a document on a computer with retyping pages on a typewriter. (Typewriter? What's that?)

Figure 9.2   Media Similarities and Differences

		Oral	Written	Printed	Analog Electronic	Digital Electronic
Interaction	Space	Colocated	Distributed	Distributed	Distributed	Distributed
	Time	Synchronous	Async	Async	Sync/Async	Sync/Async
	Size	Small	Small	Mass	Unlimited	Unlimited
Speed	Produce	Speaking	Writing	Write+Print	Real-time	**Variable**
	Deliver	Sound	Transport	Transport	Electronic	Electronic
	Receive	Hearing	Reading	Reading	Real-time	**Variable**
	Delay	None	Some	Lots	None	None
Memory	Store	None	Integral	Integral	Integral	Integral
	Recall	None	Limited	Limited	Limited	**Integral**
	Modify	None	Limited	Limited	Limited	**Unlimited**
	Reprocess	Separate	Separate	Separate	Separate	**Integral**

Reprocessing is unique to digital media.

No medium other than the computer-based one can reprocess its own stored information. Computers can compress, split apart, and recombine information in infinite varieties. The medium itself makes possible computer-enhanced images, data compression, packet switching, language translation, content filtering, and morphing, to name just a few of its capabilities.

It is not just what you can do with the bits that is so exciting, but what you can do with the content itself. Of special interest are the digital connections that can link concepts, data, pictures, diagrams, and all manner of media. We have barely scratched the surface of the cognitive capabilities that digital media offer to virtual teams and the organizational networks they undergird.

The underlined hyper*link* is a brilliant bit of conceptual invention that represents only a wisp of code, yet its use can construct a practically infinite set of interconnections. Each connection on the web is embedded in a potentially meaningful context. It exactly captures those aspects of technology, interaction, and meaning that we seek to convey by using the word *links,* which stands for the multilayered concept of communications.

Digital also connects people interacting in old formats in entirely new ways. Online conversations, meetings, and conferences—real-time and time-disconnected—provide a new array of interactive media. They open abundant possibilities for communication among many senders and receivers—from groups of a few to vast numbers of participants.

The digital medium is the ultimately flexible one. It can take on the shape and contour of any of the others, from a highly centralized mass medium to a completely decentralized interactive one. Most remarkably, it can be all forms at once, available to match the right medium to the right need. For a virtual team that is working anywhere at any time, digital technology dramatically expands its communication bandwidth—professionally, organizationally, educationally, psychologically, personally, intellectually, emotionally, and socially.

Communicating

While communication has been critical to group life since the beginning of human time, today connective technologies are exploding exponentially. They enable small task-oriented groups to perform in extraordinary new ways.

Communication has quite a diverse set of dictionary definitions in current usage. Key elements of the future are wrapped up in multiple meanings of the word *communication* that pull in different directions. The word works, however, because there is an essential interdependency among all the different meanings.

A simple example distinguishes the different but interdependent elements of communications. Physical phone connections are passive *media*. Jessica calls Jeff and the phone company records *interaction,* a measurable stream of communication at a particular time from this node to that. What is not recorded is the tangle of *relationships,* the interests and passions of the moment, the trust that threads the notes carried along the wire.

Links, the wonderful, vital term riding the global web wave and sweeping through the Information Age, is a short word for communication. At one end are concrete physical media like wires and telephones and even conversational airspace; at the other end are the elusive, mysterious relationships among people.

While "purpose" (see Chapter 6) flows from abstract vision to concrete results, communication links flow in the opposite direction. They move from the potential of actual tangible connections to the obscurities of human bonds. Between physical connections and human relationships lie interactions, the moment-by-moment, blow-by-blow stuff of daily social life (Figure 9.3).

Figure 9.3   Communication Links

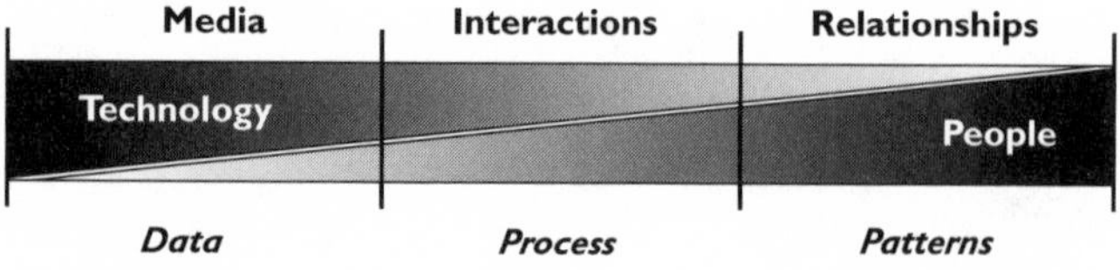

> *Links are physical media that enable interactions that spawn and maintain relationships.*

Many Media

Physical media provide the communication channels, the means of interaction. Channels exist quite separately from people or what they want to communicate. As technologies, they are passive and offer only the potential for communication, not the act itself. They are necessary, but not sufficient.

Choose the medium appropriate to the need:

- Face-to-face helps build trust.
- Real-time media keep people in sync.
- Asynchronous media create the ability to link over time, the persisting online meeting place.

As for human groups with rhythms and pulses (see Chapter 5, "Time"), we need to connect both in real time and over time. While face-to-face interaction is synchronous, it stands apart from all other modes of communication in the genetic depth of its rootedness in the group psyche.

Talking Across Boundaries

Interactions are all about process. To communicate is to interact; to interact is to communicate. Interactions are not separate from the people involved and how they interpret experience. They are also behaviors that generate public information for observers. Researchers study interactions to understand the dynamics of groups and teams.

The most basic human interaction is dialogue. At a profound level, groups are conversational constructs.[17] Especially at management and executive levels, work life is a series of conversations larded with decisions and strategic direction. Conversation across boundaries is the great challenge of the virtual age.

At a more detailed level of work life, interactions are represented in the tasks that teams undertake and individuals execute. For large, complex organizations, interactions become formalized in work flows. Once the bureaucratic province of policies and procedures, work flow now belongs to software that tracks a work path among a distributed group of people. More generally, the need to easily map and track interactions is basic to virtual groups at any scale.

Trusting Relationships

Ultimately, it's all about trust. Relationships come from the learning and emotions retained from the intensity of direct experience and fed back into future interactions. They are the patterns that simplify the complex. Over time, relationships develop among people in a group because of their experience with one another, eventually enabling them to become a team.

Even the simplest relationship belongs to both people together, never to one person or the other. Although relationships exist between people, they do not occupy any physical space. They grow over time, may span years of inactivity, and yet may fracture in a moment. Our relationships are at once the most durable, the most fragile, and the most rewarding parts of our lives. Relationships among the members are the bonds that tie virtual teams and networks (see Chapter 3, "Trust").

In an age where relationships are the coin of the realm, riches come with a price. Relationships among all the people and organizations involved with a network can add up to a staggeringly large number of possible permutations. They comprise every combination of the people in the group plus innumerable linkages outside the team—the whole web of the team. Mapping detailed relationships inside and outside even a small group of people can become frightfully complex.

Managing relationships is a critical skill for now and the future, offering those natural networkers among us an increasingly important role in our organizations. Fortunately for those of us more relationally challenged, this is also an area where data gathering and processing power help reduce unimaginable complexity to practical daily simplicity.

CHAPTER 10

LAUNCH

Do It Yourself

This chapter focuses on how to launch your virtual team, increasing its speed, productivity, and "group intelligence."

A virtual team must be smarter than a colocated team—
just to survive.

Here we present the key ideas in this book as activities. Follow this journey and you will practice the virtual team principles described in the preceding chapters.

Traditional planning is a serial process: People start at the beginning, arrive at a fixed plan, and then go to work. Awash in the flux and chaos of change, the method by which a virtual team takes form is not linear. It cycles through a series of ever-better rapid prototypes of itself. The team does a mental self-mock-up as it starts, then refines it over time. Ironically, Internet speed requires more, not fewer, planning orbits. Short, effective planning sessions early in the life of a virtual team establish good habits, requiring discipline that many creative people naturally resist. But it pays off for virtual teams.

Your Journey

To get the most out of this chapter, stop right here and conjure up a real or imaginary virtual team. It can be any team that you're familiar with—the most successful team project you've ever been on, the team you're on right now, or a team you'd like to design.

We invite you and your imagined group to come along on a journey that will launch your team in a *turbo session* that kicks off your work together.

Apply your own experience as you read. Employ the steps to evaluate what worked in the past and/or as a checklist to start up and launch a new team. Ideas translate into real data that the team gathers about itself and its work, guiding it as it goes through its launch. Mentally enter information or check off items (for example, "We wrote down our purpose," or "Karl, Kee, and Keith are team members"). Use question marks where it's not clear how this applies to your example. Leave blanks for missing pieces.

As you accumulate a picture of your team and its work, you generate a database profile unique to your team. Your particular details of people, purpose, links, and time constitute a shared mental model that you can express in technology. Launch your team in seven steps:

1. Create identity.
2. Draft mission.
3. Determine milestones.
4. Set goals.
5. Identify members.
6. Establish relationships.
7. Choose media.

You can use these seven steps to meet differing launch needs:

- For a *simple team* with a short time frame, these steps may be all you need. A quick launch like this may be enough to create trust and a "back-of-the-envelope" plan.
- For a more *complex team*, the steps provide an early planning loop to generate scope, define frameworks, and make long-lead-time decisions. This early model makes later detailed planning more effective and faster.

- *Subteams* inside complex multilevel teams often can make do with this basic launch.

To succeed, the launch must involve the key people responsible for implementation and results, including sponsors. Participatory planning is a powerful way to achieve early virtual team alignment. This is the moment for a sponsor to make a lasting contribution and set up the team for success.

The creation of the first rough virtual team plan is a powerful, shared experience. Connect early and often. From your very first conversations, be conscious of how much the process is a mix of face-to-face, virtual real-time (synchronous, like phone), and non-real-time exchanges (asynchronous, like e-mail).

Remember, face-to-face is the fastest way to build trust, crucial in the early phases of virtual team life. If face-to-face meetings are too costly, do the next best thing and invest in telephone or videoconference (synchronous) meetings or same-time web-based interactive technologies. Use as many interactive media as the team can handle. And if you are too global to find same-time windows easily, learn how to hold asynchronous events using fast-cycle online discussion forums and conferences.

Go digital wherever possible and as soon as possible. As you head into the cycles of planning, use the technologies that will make your virtual team successful when it's up and running.

Now is the time to introduce new technologies and consider major changes! Encourage change and experimentation early and discourage it later.

Your virtual team is like an architectural sketch. Keep drawing it, cycling through, asking yourself questions until the model of your team meets these requirements: Is its purpose simple enough to recite in a sentence or two? Can you draw a picture of the organization for other people? Does it pass the gut test? Do you feel that the project is doable?

Seven Steps

Any successful virtual team must answer seven questions. As you move through this thought experiment and linear book format, remember that all these activities happen simultaneously even as the logic of the journey unfolds as a one-after-the-other series of steps.

Teams entwine social and task systems. In this launch scenario, task takes the lead, but the underlying social system is also being generated. While you focus on goals, you forge alignment through participatory processes where members seek shared understanding. When you map relationships at the intersection of people and purpose, you also establish the leadership structure.

Ultimately, it is a healthy social system that enables a task-oriented team's success in working across boundaries.

Step 1: Create Identity

How does a virtual team begin? People with an idea start talking, and soon a new virtual team is on its way to formation. Regardless of how it begins, a team grows as *people* with shared *purpose link* over *time.*

"We" marks the moment when a team becomes real. Sometimes an ineffable "click" is felt, or a satisfying "plunk"[1] is heard. This team consciousness usually dawns in the turbulent launch phase of its life cycle. The need to create team identity, however, begins with the first strands of relationships that emanate from a shared idea.

A team's name symbolizes its identity, its smallest mental model: Alpha, BagelNet, Calypso. Names may be wild creative expressions of mission or merely descriptive tags. A team often begins with a temporary nickname as an agreed-upon placeholder for a "real" name to come when the purpose is better understood.

Your name labels your team. Consider a formal name that clearly communicates what the team is about—for example, SunRevenues, Sun's web-available financial reporting system team. Then nickname the team or make it an acronym: SunREVs. (See Figure 10.1.)

Virtual teams often require an officially registered identity as well. While colocated teams get their reality by physical presence, virtual teams have to

---

Figure 10.1   Name

Team Name

---

stake out shared electronic space. Many organizations acknowledge the existence of a new virtual team with accounting codes, login lists, and web sites. At companies like Sun and GE where virtual teams are formal parts of the system, corporate support and electronic privileges require the filing of charter documents. For a start-up, incorporation is an early significant event, often marking the team's official beginning.

Step 2: Draft Mission

Rule number 1 of every team is to get the purpose right early and review it often. This exercise is at once more important and more difficult for virtual teams. Even when it receives its purpose as an explicit charter from above, a team must do the hard work of interpreting and expressing the mission in its own words. Functioning with far less oversight than is customary for a traditional team, everyone on a virtual team must understand and agree with the purpose.

Writing a vision or mission statement has become a joke to many. If the exercise stops there, chuckle on. However, when setting purpose becomes the basis for the group's work, it is a powerful source of energy.

We cannot overstate the value of a virtual team cycling through its purpose-setting exercise several times. Realize that even in the Internet Age missions coalesce over time and morph as needed in response to changes in the environment. What you are really doing here is initiating an ongoing mission-setting process.

In the end, your team must make its purpose explicit and concrete. For some, this means writing down the purpose in a formal mission statement; for some it is a list of outcomes; still others will embrace a diagram or picture that captures the essence of what the team is about. These, too, are icons of an emerging identity. (See Figure 10.2.)

Figure 10.2   Mission

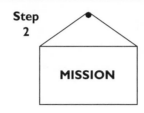

Ready to begin? Answer this question: "Why are we doing this?" Draft a statement of intent. Make your proposed mission—your topmost goal and essential motivation to action—explicit. Use verbs, action words. As time goes on, the revised and updated purpose statement becomes the formal instrument for stamping and evaluating the group's legitimacy.

Now answer: "What are we going to do?" Can you name the team's primary result? Use nouns to describe the real objectives, the bottom-line outcomes that are the team's reason for being. Mentally place yourself in time at the end of the project, then look back. Draw pictures that describe the final product of your team's work.

Decisions and deliverables—such as events, reports, presentations, prototypes, or anything else that represents the concrete consequences of joint effort—are all results. Some, like GE Six Sigma teams, express the ultimate products of their work in numbers. Market share, lower cost, and faster cycle times all are great metrics. Where criteria for success are clear, state them.

Every mission statement and its proposed result sit inside a broader vision, whether explicit or implicit. It's the vision that stirs the passion of purpose—or the ho-hum lack of it. Historically, the leader expresses and nurtures the vision with spoken words. Written down, the vision serves as the preamble to missions and goals. E-mails, memos, diagrams, presentations, white papers, and other symbols of shared motivation accumulate and help spark the emotional bonds that carry the chemistry of collaboration.

Step 3: Determine Milestones

For many teams, virtual or not, the period from the first quickening of vision to the stating of a clear purpose may take as long as the whole rest of the life of the team. Start-up can be frustratingly long or bewilderingly brief. Setting milestones signifies a quickening of the pace and advance preparation for implementation.

Teams live according to the calendar; they immerse themselves in time. They sputter into life as people talk, meet, argue, agree, and formalize. Early team history accumulates as people make contact and strengthen relationships, whereas it records later history in events, activities, and outcomes.

To establish its overall schedule, the team sets or accepts delivery dates for results, however imprecise the estimates may be. Key outside dates, such as budget cycles and major conferences that impact the team, help shape the calendar. One-time deadlines, milestones, or periods for performance evaluations all punctuate team life and help you rough out the phases and pace of activity.

New teams usually have a time frame in mind—whether fixed, firm, or flexible. This is the time container within which the team's life plays out. Use the "Stressed S" curve (Figure 6.2) as a guideline for marking expected milestones that segment the life cycle into big chunks. Time frames for start-ups are particularly opportunistic and situational; thus milestones are more difficult to discern and predict. (See Figure 10.3.)

Whether one date in the future or a time line of major milestones, this exercise creates a time frame for making estimates and setting goals. Of course, flexibility is the watchword for realistic schedules.

Step 4: Set Goals

The next step is to carve out the major pieces of work for the team, the internal structure that distributes leadership. To get from vague vision to concrete results, you need to organize the work and decide who's going to do what.

Figure 10.3   Milestones

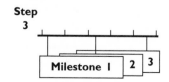

Do not leave your internal organization to chance.

Even the smallest groups form into subteams to get work done. Be conscious of your choices. Internal design is your key to collective intelligence.

Establish a set of goals that, when achieved, together accomplish the overall purpose. Well-conceived goals mark the major ingredients of the team's work and are the seeds around which subteams take shape to actually do the work. They are like the internal functions of a corporation—work units that productively organize clusters of people. For us as individuals, subteams mean we wear many hats in many small teams.

Make a first cut at naming the key goals of the team. (See Figure 10.4.) Keep these major categories to a handful or two (five to ten). Assess whether this set of goals covers the mission and the achievement of the overall result. Brainstorm this list as soon as you can and come back to it when you can. Keep the categories fluid as purpose, people, and links are initially itemized. Look ahead to nailing down the goal and subteam categories as the team positions for takeoff.

The right goals provide the magic of motivating energy.

After the first pass at goals, discuss a single concrete result for each goal. State multiple results as needed. Sometimes the result already resides in the goal statement, and you can simply pull it out and make it explicit so that you can track it. Other times, a perceived goal falls apart because the

Figure 10.4   Goals

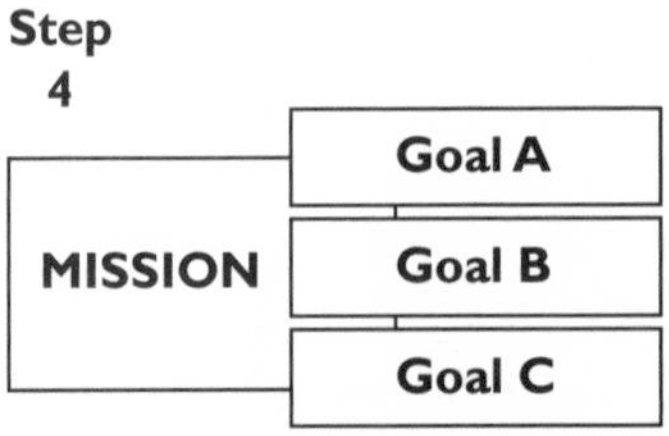

Step
4

	Goal A
MISSION	Goal B
	Goal C

group cannot see, or cannot agree upon, a concrete outcome or measure that represents it. Indeed, the discussion of results often uncovers real disagreements and viewpoints.

Collaboration depends on cooperation. Getting collaborative goals right is an art, not a science. Collaborative goals require interdependence, but dependencies are a feature of competition as well. Competitive conflicts develop from differences in people's personalities, motivations, fears, perceptions of the facts, opinions, interests, and how much power they wield.

The path to cooperative payoff often leads through the thickets of competitive conflict. Indeed, this is where truly excellent teams shine—in moments when they meet their greatest internal challenges. Virtual teams are particularly challenged and don't work well when internal competition is high. Trust breaks down, and face-to-face meetings or intervention by trained team professionals are sometimes the only ways to resolve the conflict.

Step 5: Identify Members

People or purpose, which comes first? Answer: Both. A team emerges from the goal-oriented activities of people. As a team crafts some detail around purpose, it concurrently identifies whom it needs to involve.

Make a first list of people and organizations in "bands" of membership from the team's point of view. At the top, write the names of the small core group, followed by the extended team of closely involved members. After that, record the external network of experts and support people whom you recruit on an as-needed basis (Figure 8.2).

Roles are important from the earliest moments of team formation. In many cases, roles become clear in response to the mission before people are identified to fill them in. Later, filling in roles next to people's names on the team roster helps clarify responsibilities. Role clarity must match role flexibility.

To track membership as explicitly as possible, generate a team table. Columns of name, role, organization, and workplace intersect with rows stacked in the order of core, extended, and external participants (Figure 10.5). By noting the home group of everyone involved and the location of their primary workplace, the team better understands who's involved and how virtual the group is.

Figure 10.5   Team Table

Step 5	Name	Role	Group	Place
Core				
Extended				
External				

The team table is a practical shared group model of the team's membership. Combined with filled-in profiles of individuals and organizations, the table turns into one of the most useful tools a team can create for itself—a group directory.

Early team lists are quite dynamic. The people who come up with the original idea may not be on the team, key people may require recruiting, and the team may identify empty roles for needed expertise, experience, or representation. Lists of members may start on the backs of envelopes, but they eventually become relatively formal.

A list of names offers an additional bit of basic information about the team: its size, even if membership boundaries are less than exact, particularly in the beginning. Thus, size is sometimes expressed as a range (for example, seven to nine people). Membership is often a moving target for virtual teams, becoming increasingly ambiguous at the fringes as the team grows.

To reach people in the virtual world, you need to know their addresses. Contact information is central to the team, cataloging its boundaries and the means of crossing them. Set up a template for personal profiles to collect the many addresses people have. Include everything you can think of: office locations, snail mail (traditional postal) addresses, phone numbers (office, home, car, cell, voice mail), fax numbers, e-mail accounts (perhaps several), and URLs. Make it easy for people to upload pictures and link to more information about themselves. In selecting categories for online profiles, consider the things you would naturally communicate in face-to-face settings.

Review and update your own contact information. Expand the list to include the new members as they appear. A virtual team has external contacts as well as internal interactions, so directories should include all the people in its larger network.

Step 6: Establish Relationships

To say that virtual team success is 90 percent people is not to say that those people are in isolation. The relationships among people are key: Who needs to connect with whom for what purpose?

For new teams with new objectives, relationships must emerge. Virtual teams can anticipate this by mapping the relationships needed to accomplish the purpose.

One hidden danger lurks on the sidelines of virtual teams: the idea that everyone needs to be involved in everything. You can avoid this recipe for disaster by clarifying just which goals and decisions need everyone's input and which do not. The rich conversation about who needs to be involved in which goals helps people sort through and reduce anxiety about what is attainable. The exercise inevitably flushes out additional needs for expertise and representation, leading to new recruitment and perhaps a larger team. At the same time, people often reevaluate, cluster, or break out goals further during this review.

Goals intersect with a team's membership in a simple relationship matrix.

Identify who needs to be involved in what through a dialogue that you can detail in a Relationship Matrix (Figure 10.6). This dialogue—whether

Figure 10.6   Relationship Matrix

Step 6	Name	Name	Name	Role	Name	Group	Role	Name	Group	Group
Goal A	X	⊗	X			X			X	X
Goal B	⊗		⊗	X		X	X	X		
Goal C	X	⊗		X	X			⊗		X

in person, on a conference call, or online—addresses each high-level goal and the subteam needed to achieve it. Whenever someone volunteers, is cajoled, or appointed (especially absent members) to a goal team, indicate involvement with an X in that member's column.

Each goal requires at minimum one person, and some goals call for everyone's involvement. For most collaborative goals, you need a subset of the whole team. Use the construction of this matrix as a way to explicitly distribute the work, obtain the right participation, identify leadership, and track commitments. (See Figure 11.1 for a more detailed view of this process-mapping technique.)

For each goal team, designate one or more members as leaders. These are the people responsible for specific results. Goals lead to results, so every result will have at least one person responsible for it. Leadership may be singular or multiple, determined in the course of the goal-by-goal dialogue.

Virtual teams increase their overall leadership capability as they divide the work. By identifying task-based leadership, a group distributes its management burden. A team may go into a relationship-mapping session with one appointed leader and come out with everyone feeling like a leader. Shared leadership creates trust in the team. The higher the level of trust, the less people will feel the need to be involved in everything.

Task leadership alone is not sufficient for virtual team success. The team needs people to provide process roles such as liaison, facilitator, knowledge developer, agenda designer, and communications support. It is relatively easy to make task leadership explicit. Not so with process leadership. Aside from overall team leadership, the social roles required to develop and maintain team processes are hard enough to recognize and acknowledge in colocated situations. Acknowledging and filling new roles expands a group's consciousness of itself as an entity.

Step 7: Choose Media

The relationship matrix and team roster indicate who needs to develop connections with whom to complete different aspects of the work. Many virtual teams need or may greatly benefit from face-to-face time, particularly at the beginning, to develop the plan and build trust. Physical separation is the most common plight of virtual teams, so it is important to evaluate the impact of distance in thinking about the team's communication.

Consider your options at this time of incomparable media choice. Review technologies in the media palette (Figure 9.1). Choose from all eras of communications to best fit the work process needs.

To simplify choice, we think about media in three basic ways: face-to-face, virtual same-time (synchronous), and virtual asynchronous. Face-to-face is in our genes and stands by itself as the reference point for direct team communication. Synchronous virtual meetings and other activities may be as simple as phone calls, as expensive as two-way video, and as productive as audio-enabled web meetings in virtual team rooms. Asynchronous connections can be made by mail, print, fax, and voice mail. It is, however, the digital media of e-mail, threaded discussions, interactive web sites, and knowledge management databases that provide a truly powerful anytime-anyplace foundation for successful virtual work.

Since the choice of team media is so often influenced by what people already use, it helps to have a way to choose media according to the nature of the work. Look at the goals in terms of the work they imply: generate, choose, negotiate, or execute.

- *Generate* is about creating plans and developing new ideas.
- *Choose* focuses on solving problems with correct answers and making decisions where there are no right answers.
- *Negotiate* is about resolving conflicts of clashing viewpoints and the more difficult mixed-motive conflicts of interest.
- *Execute* is about directly doing work.[2]

Now that you have a general feeling for the type of work required to accomplish the mission, consider how effective and efficient different media are. For generating ideas and executing activities, virtual media, both synchronous and asynchronous, can be as effective as face-to-face, and it is usually more efficient. Choosing and negotiating are often best done synchronously, and negotiating especially requires face-to-face sessions to be most effective.

The team's media plan grows out of the relationship matrix, conveying the means by which the team communicates the miracle of productive interactions (Figure 10.7).

A media plan may not amount to much if it simply mandates a face-to-face Monday morning meeting—a typical colocated team approach to staying connected. Virtual teams inevitably require multiple media in order to use the right specific medium at the right time.

Look for the most appropriate media to meet your unique needs, with obvious consideration of cost and availability. You may want a videoconferencing system but find it currently too expensive or impractical (e.g., there is virtually no synchronous time frame for a virtual team spread from California to Europe to Asia). Within your constraints, experiment to find what works best. Then stretch your sights, particularly to find ways to use more. Digital media provide the natural environment for virtual teams and will eventually become ubiquitous.

But new media is still new to most people. In determining the communication plan, have people indicate their relative preferences for different media or their willingness to gain access to and competency in a medium they do not currently use. Do not lose sight of the fact that people do not connect with media: They connect with other people.

It's important to agree to protocols for the use of your team's media. Agreements around protocols may flow proactively from best practices (which many of the stories in this book reflect), or they may be put in place retroactively when a team's pattern of communication is not working. An important part of the team's social skill is its stated communications norms and covenants.

Figure 10.7 Media Plan

Step 7

	Type	Media	Protocol
Goal A			
Goal B			
Goal C			

Play It Again, Sam

The seven steps of a turbo launch may be all you need. You ought not burden a relatively short and simple project of a few people. If you can settle the basics in a few meetings, face-to-face and/or virtual, and can summarize them in a couple of pages, you need go no further in designing your virtual team.

Or you may need to cycle through these essential elements several times, especially as new people join the team. This ensures that everyone thoroughly understands the shared mental models and that people work together to establish some basic trust.

Always invest in beginnings.

CHAPTER 11

NAVIGATE

Course Correction for Cyberspace

There's a story going around about how much of the time the U.S. Apollo space missions are on course. Three percent, the story goes. The rest of the time goes to course correction.

So it is with virtual teams. Cyberspace requires that, for the moment, 97 percent of our time is spent in course correction.

We need good tools to navigate. The first place to start is at home, creating virtual places to work that are good substitutes for physical places. This is a necessary early step.

Members gain more than information about tasks and behavior in traditional physical places. Very directly, people have a mental image of their colocated teams: sets of unique individuals assembled in their special places, who have a base, somewhere to operate from. Equally important is the team's work model, physically evident in its space. Materials, tools, partial products, and people at work all contribute to a concrete understanding of purpose and how the team pursues it. All of this together is the group's shared mental (cognitive) model. It's where a group makes course corrections on the spot.

As people construct new places, they embed in them their models—consciously or unconsciously. A virtual team does not just replicate the functions of an old physical place online. It also generates a new conceptual space that never has existed before.

New technologies are innovations that diffuse through society in well-recognized patterns. First, the new technology develops slowly against resistance, gaining a foothold by replicating and replacing functions of older technologies. Only after an innovation establishes itself as a good substitute will its truly innovative features and revolutionary effects come to full expression. Then its adoption rapidly expands through society.

> *The cognitive characteristics of groups are blossoming in the fertile soil of shared digital environments.*

When virtual teams explicitly share their models using common technology, their ideas go beyond the members themselves. The database of the online team room reflects many people's thinking, both in its overall information architecture and in the countless choices people make about their communications. Thus, a significant portion of the group's shared intelligence and its ongoing thinking is expressed and retained in bits online.

The Virtual Team Room

Rebecca Stillwater is a little nervous about her first meeting with the e-Experience Strategy Team on the Monday after New Year's. She joins just as the group kicks off its implementation phase.

The "e-Ex" Strategy Team (eXST) was set up six weeks earlier. The company has successfully met its e-commerce targets and now is into e-service development. This long-range thinking group is to look at how the company is going to get ahead of the web curve. Several vice presidents and one of the founders are members of a 17-person virtual team from all levels and regions within the company, as well as several outside consultants, a key vendor, and two customers who are codevelopment partners.

Like most people in the company, Rebecca already has stopped by the team's web site to look at its "outside" walls. The team's purpose, its members, and how to contact them (and its open positions) are visible to all. Rebecca sees the need for her skills, so she posts for the team and is accepted. Rebecca received the login keys to the online room a week earlier, as the team was wrapping up its launch activities. Ideally, she would have been there as the team formed and stormed its way to a clear set of goals. But the need for a systems architect emerges only as the team deepens its thinking about how to achieve concrete results quickly. In the few days she has before the holidays, Rebecca wants to get an inside view of the team's current status at year's end and how it got there.

Thinking Up to Speed

Clicking OK on her password brings her to the team's Portal Page, which seems to change hourly in these last frantic days before Christmas. The room is in rapid flux as the team concludes its launch. A new graphic of the team's envisioned result occupies a place of honor under its name and logo. Announcements and links to key documents straddle the central hot map that points to more detailed views. A navigation bar points her to the room's four walls, team discussions, the file library, a team directory, and the company's internal portal page.

She clicks on the top of the icon, and presto she's at the Time Wall. An agenda outlines the upcoming meeting, along with the expected prework for it and pointers to related information. A weekly schedule for the team is to the left side of the wall, and announcements for subteam events line the right side. Below, there is a Gantt chart that summarizes current tasks in little bars of time that chunk past, present, and future. Scrolling to the bottom of the wall brings up the big picture of the team's life cycle and its major milestones. Attached to this picture is a time line of the work process, meetings, and discussions that led to this moment in the team's life. Perusal of this material keeps Rebecca up very late one night, but she appreciates the insight into the group's thinking as well as getting a feel for some of the personalities.

Another click and she faces the Purpose Wall. On a "peg" at the top is the team mission, which someone has fancifully done up as a needle-stitch graphic. Already familiar with the vision and mission from the outside view of the Purpose Wall, she is intrigued with the internal goals developed by the team. These goals serve as the centers of agreement for the subteams now hard at work. She clicks on a goal and it unfolds into the next level. Detailed tasks, meetings, intermediate results, and decisions expected from the subteams all appear. Curious, she clicks on a task labeled "Explore database options" listed under the technology goal to see who is involved, the timing, budget estimate, and associated deliverables.

Looking for more detail on the technology subteam and its members, Rebecca clicks on the People Wall. Using the subteam button, she displays the names, roles, and locations of members in the central panel. A click on the name of one of the coleaders brings the smiling face of Brahm Rogers to the screen with some basic profile information alongside. He's included a link to his personal web site, where she learns that Brahm's been at the technical forefront of network developments—and that he loves to ski.

Returning to the People Wall with the navigation bar, Rebecca selects the outline icon and brings up an extended organization chart that is anchored in the middle by the strategy team. Subteams and members flow down from the team; other teams and related organizations reach out horizontally; and the sponsoring organizations fan out above the team. In a few minutes, Rebecca feels she has a clear view of the team's context, especially after reviewing the web sites of several unfamiliar sponsoring groups.

A ski fanatic herself, Rebecca is about to send a message to see if she can arrange a slopeside hello over the holidays with Brahm, the coleader she profiled, when she wonders what the team's protocols around e-mail might be. So she clicks over to the Links Wall and hits the e-mail button. This brings up access to team lists, an ability to send or forward e-mails to structured discussion topics, and the team's six rules of e-mail etiquette—including an open invitation to send personal notes. However, she sees on the electronic in/out indicator that her intended recipient is incommunicado for a week. Other buttons lead to information about using conference calls, setting up virtual meetings using a web-based real-time communications system, and an open item on setting up a regular videoconference with one of the customer-partners.

An especially valuable instrument on this wall is the map of conversations. Access to the flow of dialogue from the earliest online meetings gives her a real feeling for how the team talked its way to its current clarity. Here, too, is the source for much of her fledgling knowledge of the styles, experience, and expertise of her new team members. Below the map is a dense catalog of links, a team bookmark list to key resources in the company, applications central to the team's mission, and critical outside information sources.

She also chooses to generate and print out a complete high-level process flowchart that summarizes the team's planned work (Figure 11.1). It provides her with a map of the working relationships needed to accomplish the team's mission.

Figure 11.1 Virtual Team Process

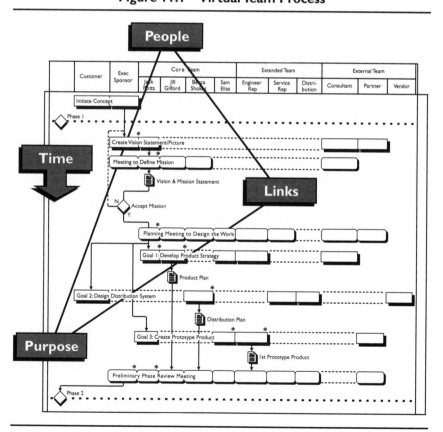

In his welcoming note with her login information, Brahm introduces the online room as the team's collective memory. A real-time memory, he says, of the group's thinking and interactions that has been recorded by, reported on, and tracked through the technology underlying the team room. A new member like Rebecca has access to a wealth of familiarizing information, organized in the natural context of the team's development and work. He also characterizes the online place as a "living status report," the current state and focus of the team. He says pointedly that team members are expected to spend time in the room prior to leadership meetings. Synchronous (real-time) sessions are precious and not to be used for round-robin informational briefings.

The Virtual Meeting

A few minutes before the appointed time, Rebecca logs in to the team room, and clicks on Attend Meeting. This milestone event is designated as a *shared-click* meeting, meaning that the team uses a web-based, real-time work environment that gives them shared whiteboards, click paths, applications, and polling facilities. *Self-click* meetings consist of a conference call with everyone on the web clicking themselves through the agenda as the team "walks around" the room.

Rebecca finds herself looking at a fresh and somewhat revised agenda posted on the Time Wall, a schedule sprinkled with links to relevant locations in the room. Alongside is an empty area entitled Meeting Notes, and at the bottom is an empty table for Issues and Actions. More interesting is the banter of voices as new people join the meeting and conversation flows through an "open mike." The tote board shows that almost everyone has gathered as the appointed time rolls around.

Brahm opens the meeting by reviewing the agenda and then suggests taking a few minutes to introduce their newest member. He moves the team with a click to the People Wall, where everyone sees Rebecca's picture centrally displayed. Her profile information (which Rebecca makes a mental note to complete) is to the right. On the left, a slice of the team's extended organization chart displays her home group in context. Rebecca has had time to think about what she wants to say about herself. She finishes with a quick review of the skills and experience that she thinks will be most relevant to the team's mission. Making a few notes in the team identity table as she speaks, Brahm posts his summary and asks Rebecca if it is accurate.

Brahm transfers attention now to the Purpose Wall. There's a major planning issue the team needs to address, the impact of the XML software standard on their partnering strategy. They review goals of the two subteams involved and vigorously debate the significance of the issue and how best to assess it. It's clear that most people need more information and time to think about it. The team agrees to set up a week-long conversation on the topic and to create an additional task for the technology team to track. Quickly setting up the task, Brahm then saves an empty XML Strategy Document that will contain the concrete results of this activity. He also creates an empty "decision" item for the team to fill in as the designated online conversation wraps up by week's end.

Bringing the team to the conversation outline on the Links Wall, Brahm asks where best to locate this new technology topic, and he immediately follows the suggestion to put it in the strategic dialogues. The group has made the real-time placement of key topics into an ongoing map of conversations almost a ritual. They acknowledge the dialogue's importance while providing a practical visual cue about where it is taking place. The group moves to the relationship map, which shows who is involved with each task. The new task is highlighted in anticipation of deciding who will take responsibility for this activity.

With a click, the group is in the Product Room, configured in a design that reflects the components of the group's output. The graphic of the team's product appears with richer detail about how the elements combine into a whole. Today's focus is on the service component, and three people speak about the significance of new documents posted here. They conclude with a request for help in reviewing several web sites that look competitive with their intended offering. Several subteam leaders then point to particular areas that are the subjects of meetings in the upcoming week, inviting anyone to join but calling attention to expected attendees.

With 15 minutes remaining until the end of the real-time web meeting, the group moves back to the Time Wall to review meeting notes and action items collected through the meeting. They use a technique based on the U.S. Army's After Action Review to assess what was supposed to happen, what did happen, what worked, and what didn't and to capture learning to add to their compendium of best practices.[1] The meeting ends with a brief appreciation and request for final comments.

Holding the Whole

We cannot tell a lie: Virtual teams are complex. They have all the complexity of any group—and then some, magnified by their distributed nature. To navigate intuitively through the team space, create online functions that support natural teams. In the preceding scenario of using a virtual room, we included functionality that supports three typical ways teams hold their information: in a place, a plan, and a handbook.

The Place

"We're witnessing the next change in communication style," says Bert Sutherland, who headed Sun Microsystems research and development for many years. "E-mail is a push model; I want to broadcast to someone. The web is a pull model; the information sits there until someone who wants it can pull it."

For millennia, new communications media have improved the ability to *push* information. With digital media, the historic trend to push is suddenly paralleled by dramatic new capability to *pull*—seeking and finding the information you need when you need it. In a pull model of information access, particularly one in which users are both readers and writers, it is vital that everyone share common views of what information goes where when. Hence the value of creating a common online place.

The World Wide Web stands out as the defining tool of the new world of virtual work. This vast new cyberterritory, which at the millennial dawn is still a global frontier, includes the Internet and the even vaster matrix of all interconnected computers inside and outside the planet's organizations and homes.

As an almost ideal medium for shared mental models, the web combines anytime-anywhere availability with an unrivaled flexibility of expression that embraces all other media. At the hub of the web is the *link*, not even a proper technology but a pure package of information, an address tag—the Uniform Resource Locator (URL).

On the web, you can link anything represented as information to any other information anywhere. Most remarkably, you naturally put these links into context, however consciously or unconsciously constructed. A team's web site is a place to clearly and explicitly grow its common information and shared perspective.

The web approach to team intelligence scales completely. Team places may entail the use of personal home pages (like those offered by many Internet service providers) or they may plug into internal enterprise networks where they leverage vast resources (as at Sun). Modeling tools can combine product and process views at any level of complexity.

- A virtual team web site can be as simple as it needs to be. A single home page with a name banner and clickable pointers to current events, purpose, people, and communications may be all you need.
- A typically complex virtual team can create a two-level site, a portal home page and four main pages for the walls, as in the preceding example.
- A very complex longer-life team can build out its basic process room to a multilevel structure. Subteams set up rooms using the navigation model of the main team room. Together they create a product room with walls for major components that act as common navigation for the team's specific work.
- Programs and enterprises use the web with all its interactive power to create visible dynamic models of teams in the larger context of many other teams. Sponsors, leaders, and members of multiple teams in particular appreciate the ability to navigate between and within team rooms using the same language for online work.

Remember that there are no rules for what you can and cannot do. Regardless of what information you share, just the fact that you keep it online is a tremendous source of common experience and pride for your team.

The Plan

The picture of progress in the Industrial Age was the sloped straight line of linear process. Progress in the Information Age is a spiral of iterations of widening scope stretching out along a life cycle. The combination of speed, complexity, and the change so emblematic of our time demands a different approach to the future than a one-time, fixed plan of action.

Iterating progressive refinements is a basic systems strategy for planning in the face of uncertainty. With skilled leadership and facilitation, planning events can serve to accomplish and mark iterations rapidly and cost-effectively. These iterations have both depth of detail and scope in time. Two rules of thumb govern these dimensions:

- Plan to the necessary level of detail, but no more.
- Detail the short term, sketch the long term, and fill in as you go.

The explicit, visible models that teams create are easier to access and depict than the models that people hold in their heads. As distributed work becomes more complex, digital media is the only way to make the team's shared models come alive.

Computer-based tools can help you display and update your team's work. We like a people-oriented process model of virtual teams (see Figure 11.1) based on a method called *deployment flowcharting*. This approach was pioneered by Dr. W. Edwards Deming and first employed extensively by Toyota in the 1960s. Myron Tribus is credited with developing the icons and elements for a general language of process design and representation. TeamFlow[2] is an artfully simple application for modeling and managing virtual team processes using this technique. At the heart of the deployment planning method is the relationship matrix (Chapter 10, step 6) that reflects agreements about who is doing what.

In the virtual team room, you in effect can walk inside your plan. Many of the displays and dashboards on the walls reflect an underlying planning framework that touches all the bases of being a team. By using people-purpose-links-time to organize the heart of the team space, you make the principles concrete and useful.

- **Purpose.** *Goals* serve as headings for groups of tasks and results. *Tasks* and meetings represent chunks of activity. *Results* and decisions appear as output elements and are stored as files.
- **People.** *Members,* individual and organizational, comprise the rings of team boundaries. Symbols on the tasks and other process elements designating roles indicate *leadership.* The hierarchy of the organizational chart and the levels of detail in the workflow reflect *levels.*
- **Links.** People access *media* through addresses in directories, pointers to attachments, and URLs everywhere to anywhere. *Interactions* happen over time, indicated by the workflows and conversations connecting people. The matrix of people and purpose represent *relationships* among members.
- **Time.** *Calendars* include team-specific result deadlines, task-completion milestones, and scheduled events, as well as holidays and other organizationally significant dates that impact timing. *Project* timing is associated with each process element and summarized in a Gantt chart. Phases through milestone decisions and events mark the *life cycles* of the maturing team.

The Handbook

As a team moves from launch to implementation, it accumulates considerable detail about its work. Within the room, the group compiles what traditionally would appear in a team handbook. The virtual team handbook functions as the basic shared-but-selective information place. It's a common resource for team members while serving as the guidebook for new members. You can generate a physical handbook from the information in the room, which can be packaged as a small document, a file folder, or a three-ring binder.

A carry-it-around handbook of key information is useful in conjunction with a more extensive web version. Put plan components like the relationship matrix, team directory, and other common information in the handbook. This can be a very low-tech and uncomplicated way to manage a simple team, or even a soon-to-be-complicated team in its early stages. The launch plan ideally contains enough detail for alignment without being so detailed that it unnecessarily constrains people.

Places, plans, and handbooks are ways to organize, simplify, and navigate shared information and intentions. As we become more adept at representing these functions online, we will only accelerate our already dizzying displays of information. Our ability to grasp the whole depends more on the integrity of the underlying frameworks and theory, aside from surface data, which changes more rapidly. Theory makes deep navigation possible.

CHAPTER 12

THEORY

A System Science of Virtual Teams

For the past 20 years, we've been researching and developing a science of networked organizations. Here we summarize the underlying theory of this science.

"General systems" provides the theoretical infrastructure for a network science. From that well-established base, particularly in the social sciences, we have developed a simple model with four dimensions: *people, purpose, links,* and *time* (review Figure 6.1).

With theory, the principles, practice, and place that a virtual team uses all can be threaded with consistency. Instead of virtual work being haphazard and sloppy, such an approach gives integrity and solidity to what can appear impromptu and random. The team structures its information and consciously manipulates it within a context that the team itself creates.

The four dimensions of the network model plug into the bedrock of general patterns of organization.

The Periodic Table

What is the basic data that a virtual team must acquire about itself? To account for all the essential characteristics that comprise virtual organizations, we need to go down a level, expanding each dimension into three elements. We array these 12 elements in the familiar systems model of inputs, processes, and outputs (Figure 12.1). This generates a "periodic table" of organizational elements, providing the conceptual infrastructure for practical approaches to creating and managing virtual groups on any scale.

This taxonomy (a theory-based framework of categories) provides the basic architecture for our four-wall design of an online virtual team room (Chapter 11, "Navigate"). We've talked about the elements in earlier chapters, and we'll review them here.

Purpose

- Cooperative goals   *Do*
- Interdependent tasks   *Doing*
- Concrete results   *Done*

In Chapter 7, "Purpose," we point out why a particular team works together. Purpose implies some minimal level of interdependence among the people involved. As we've said before, virtual teams are far more

Figure 12.1   Periodic Table of Organizational Elements

	Inputs	Processes	Outputs
Purpose	Goals	Tasks	Results
People	Members	Leadership	Levels
Links	Media	Interactions	Relationships
Time	Calendar	Projects	Life Cycles

System

reliant on their purposes than are face-to-face ones. Because they operate outside the bounds of traditional organizational life without bureaucratic rules and regulations to guide them, virtual teams require a common purpose to stay in tune.

Cooperative goals are what purpose looks like at the beginning of any successful teaming process. This is why so many books about teams begin by focusing on goals. A set of *interdependent tasks,* the signature feature of teams, connects desires at the beginning with outcomes at the end. When a team finishes, it has its *concrete results,* the final expression of its purpose, the measurable outputs of joint effort. These three elements—cooperative goals, interdependent tasks, and concrete results—enable virtual teams to stay focused and be productive.

People

- Independent members   *Parts*
- Shared leadership   *Parts as wholes*
- Integrated levels   *Wholes*

In Chapter 8, "People," we go into detail about the special challenges facing virtual team members. *Independent members,* the people and groups who make up the team, must act with a significant degree of autonomy and self-reliance. While virtual team leadership tends to be informal, it also is pervasive. The diversity of technical and management expertise required means that members share leadership at different points in the process. In cross-boundary work, *shared leadership* is the norm.

A team is a complex human system with at minimum two levels of organization—the level of the members and the level of the group as a whole. Teams also are parts of larger systems, growing out of and embedded in organizations. To be successful, virtual teams must *integrate levels* both internally (subteams and members) and externally (peers and supergroups).

Links

- Multiple media   *Channels*
- Boundary-crossing interactions   *Communicating*
- Trusting relationships   *Bonds*

To say it again, what gives *virtual* teams such distinction as a new form of organization is their *links* (see Chapter 9). Relatively suddenly, multiple, constantly enhanced modes of communication are widely available. Links provide access to vast amounts of information and unprecedented possibilities for interaction. Twenty years ago, we chose the term *links* for this defining feature of virtual teams because it bridges three key aspects of communication.

First, people need the actual physical connections—wires, phones, computers, and the like—that provide the potential for communication; they are the prerequisite for interaction. *Multiple media* are moving virtual teams from the extraordinary to the ordinary as the technology wave of Information Age change reaches the mainstream. Connections make *boundary-crossing interactions* possible. The back-and-forth communication among people—the activities and behaviors—constitutes the actual process of work. It is here at the boundaries of interaction that virtual teams are truly different.

Through interactions near and far, people develop *trusting relationships,* the invisible bonds (and baffles) of life (see Chapter 4, "Trust"). People's patterns of behavior mark the outlines of relationships that persist and feed back into subsequent interactions. As important as positive relationships and high trust are in all teams, they are even more important in virtual ones. The lack of daily face-to-face time, offering opportunities to quickly clear things up, can heighten misunderstandings. For many distributed teams, trust has to substitute for hierarchical and bureaucratic controls. Virtual teams with high trust return this valuable social asset to their sponsoring organizations for use in future opportunities to cooperate.

Times

- Coordinate calendars *Dates*
- Track projects *Durations*
- Follow life cycles *Phases*

Collaboration requires parallel work and mutually agreed-upon dates. In virtual practice, this means a need to *coordinate calendars* for having conversations and executing work. Virtual teams naturally *track projects* as they carry out their activities largely in cyberspace, which ensures collaborative feedback and learning. The most successful virtual teams consciously *follow life cycles* of team behavior. Forming, storming, norming, and performing all require extra effort, higher awareness, and greater participation by group members to manage the whole. Each team has its unique clock (see Chapter 6, "Time").

Practical Principles

The ability to adapt to the rapidly changing environment of virtual work is enormously enhanced by the use of theory. Experience meshed with theory offers principles for a coherent, testable, scientific approach to this new world of work.

You probably already practice many of these principles. By simply upgrading your knowledge and translating your experience into a concise language, you will enhance your own and your team's capabilities immediately. If you work with the principles long enough, you will gain the keys to better, faster, smarter virtual work.

These principles are not sacred, but since publication of our first book, *Networking* (1982), they have been reviewed, used, and practiced extensively by people in business, nonprofit, government, religions, and grassroots sectors. Together they constitute a tested theory of virtual work and distributed organization.

The great advantage of recognizing general principles is in their application. Principles allow you to take knowledge from one situation and transfer it to another.

Pattern Language for Virtual Teams

The word *network* is so common that some Internet search engines eliminate it from any search. The network idea is a general concept, like *system,* and applies to nearly everything: molecules, neurons, waterways, transportation, television stations, and computers.

Truly fundamental patterns of thinking reflect an underlying configuration for understanding the world around us—a "pattern language."[1] This shared language simplifies complexity. One such complexity-busting pattern is the systems principle of hierarchy.

This is hierarchy in the big picture, different from its conventional meaning in a social context. It's about organization generally—how the right design gives both cooperative and competitive advantage.

Nobel Prize–winning economist Herbert Simon tells the most famous parable of systems theory, a story of two Swiss watchmakers. Simon calls them Tempus (whom we call Linda), meaning "smooth time," and Hora (we call him Sam), meaning "serial time." Our adaptation of this story shows the power of hierarchy of the scientific sort. Simon names this pattern the "architecture of complexity."

The Innovators

Two young technologists, feeling the limits of their then-crude craft, begin to develop breakthrough products for their market. Soon, both develop splendid prototypes of awesome versatility and complexity. Indeed, Sam Serial, the prized protégé of the traditional masters in the field, finishes his model noticeably sooner than Linda Levels, the challenger of orthodoxy. Clearly, Sam has the edge in what could be a very big market. The business press eagerly look forward to the unfolding story.

News of the revolutionary demos spreads, and people start to call for information, interrupting the young entrepreneurs with questions. Within a few months, Linda is delivering product to delighted customers, while Sam struggles to complete the first production copy as orders pile up. Both decide to hire apprentices and to train new workers in their respective methodologies to meet the demand. Linda is able to train new people quickly and boost production enormously, while Sam sinks further into minutiae, as training crawls and products only occasionally appear.

After Sam Serial's bankruptcy, observers investigate to learn what they can from this epic story of success and failure. The key difference, they discover, is in how each entrepreneur designs the work of constructing the product—the organizational advantage.

Sam simply extends the old way of fitting pieces together into a whole by adding many more pieces. The effect is somewhat like a rich mosaic, a thousand parts put together intricately—a beautiful but fragile assembly.

Linda, however, borrows a method from nature and constructs a series of subassemblies, 10 pieces to a group, intermediate components of the product. The extra steps spent putting subassemblies together account for the initially longer time needed to build the prototype. Nevertheless, this integrated approach produces a design both elegant and resilient.

When assembly is interrupted, the partially completed unit is put down, and naturally it falls *a-part*. It *dis-assembles*. What works well in isolation does not always work well in the real world that is full of interruptions—otherwise known as *change*. For each thousand steps of process, Sam risks hundreds of steps at every interruption, while Linda loses only an average of five steps when she resumes the assembly process. Linda has designed stable structures between the elementary pieces and the product as a whole, specific points in the process that hold together without the next step.

The power of Linda's method of chunks within chunks becomes clear as volume increases and markets change. Linda Levels, with a probability of just one interruption per 100 steps, gains a 4,000-to-1 advantage over Sam Serial.

Complexity

Systems within systems within systems. Why is this design principle so universal and so powerful?

Simon says that complexity evolves much more rapidly from simplicity if there are "stable intermediate structures," subsystems sturdy enough not to pull apart. Hierarchies predominate in nature, he says, because "hierarchies are the ones that have the time to evolve."

This is a profound, basic, natural design principle: a hierarchy of levels.

In the scientific sense of levels, hierarchy is basic to astronomy: planets and satellites in solar systems in galaxies in galaxy clusters that are part of superclusters and even greater amalgamations. Hierarchy brings us molecules, atoms, particles, and quarks in physics. Biology has cells, tissues, organs, organisms, ecologies, and environments. Pennies make up dimes that make up dollars in the U.S. currency system. Time comes in subassemblies of minutes, hours, days, weeks, months, and years. Libraries shelve books according to the Dewey decimal system version of this theme. We even build our community communications systems this way with trunks, feeders, and drop lines to houses.

Levels within levels—hierarchies—permeate every aspect of the core technology of the Information Age. Computer hardware is built in levels—from binary switches to chips to logic boards to computers to systems with peripherals. We design software in levels of complexity from machine languages to assemblers to operating systems to applications; we structure files hierarchically in folders; and we connect PCs in local-area networks plugged into wide-area networks linked to virtual private networks on the global Internet.

We use the hierarchy principle every time we analyze a problem or break something complex into smaller parts. We also use it to put things together, for synthesis, to create new wholes out of parts. When we outline our thinking, we use hierarchy.

It is no surprise, then, that the same structure of levels permeates organizations. As individuals, we are parts of families who make up communities and neighborhoods, which in turn are included in local, state, and national jurisdictions. All of these are points of natural cleavage—stable intermediate structures, as Simon says—in the hierarchy of society.

> *All networks and virtual teams are hierarchical in the scientific sense. Even the simplest ones are made up of interacting parts that are themselves complex—people or groups.*

Interruption is a metaphor for change in the story of our inventors, Linda Levels and Sam Serial. The need to organize in stable clusters, modules, and levels increases as the pace of interruption picks up. Subassemblies—distinct components that can stand on their own—become more necessary, while rigid control structures become liabilities under the unrelenting push of ever increasing change.

Networks do not throw out the baby with the bath water. They directly incorporate the powerful principle of hierarchy in its timeless sense—the *force behind stable structures*—into the organizational form of networks, a key legacy of the agricultural era of hierarchy.

Hierarchy Ruler

To get a grip on size and scope, apply the "hierarchy ruler" (Figure 12.2), which is one of the most useful mental tools you can employ. On the hierarchy ruler, the anchor is in the middle instead of at one end. Set a point of reference and then look up, down, and across. Each boundary offers an opportunity for multiple perspectives, like that of Janus, the ancient Roman deity who could simultaneously see both inside and outside the walled city from his palace portal.

This mental ruler is a portable, general-purpose tool that can measure complexity in many kinds of things. Its anchor—its point of reference— is a movable one. Indeed, to tap this ruler's power, you *must* move the reference point.

Figure 12.2   Hierarchy Ruler

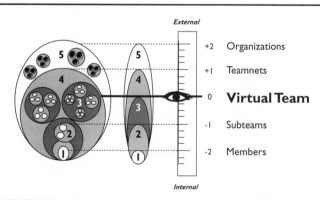

Place it at different boundaries to assess situations from other points of view. This is a critical cross-boundary networking skill that many people already use well intuitively.

> *The hierarchy ruler is a powerful tool for resolving conflict.*

The corporate boundary is a common point of reference. From the CEO view, the whole organization is your responsibility. From that boundary, you can see both the internal complexities (strategies, budgets, politics, love affairs) and the external ones (competitors, markets, global upheaval). While anchored at the reference point, do the following:

- *Look up.* Externally, ask what significant relationships the company engages—strategic alliances, associations, and coalitions; further out, see the enterprise in the context of whole industries and markets.
- *Look across.* At your level of organization, survey other enterprises, your peers as competitors, collaborators, customers, and vendors; see yourself as a center and view others from core to peripheral relationships.
- *Look down.* Internally, look for the major components, the departments or divisions that tell the broad story of what the enterprise does. Each internal division itself may be made up of groups within groups within groups.

Now move the reference point from the corporate boundary down to your own organization and drop it again to your team, then perhaps yet again to subgroups within the team. Or go up from the enterprise to alliances, coalitions, markets, industries and regions—ever wider circles of associations.

Rule of Two

Wholes and parts are gifts from the universe. They make it possible to simplify the complex.

> *The network itself embodies this valuable mental tool of*
> *levels within levels, a whole composed of people and*
> *small groups that are themselves complex.*

While whole-part pattern recognition enables a group to better cope with complexity, too much of a good thing will eventually lead again to information overload and breakdown. Too much focus on ever smaller parts leads to deadly, time-consuming micromanagement and planning inefficiency. Similarly, the meaning of myriad wholes that a team comprises can get lost in the global ever-after, in which boundaries abound.

In our experience, the hierarchy ruler works best when you observe the Rule of Two. This means that from a given point of reference, two levels up and two levels down usually provide about the right measure of scope and detail. The trick, of course, is to set points of reference at the most relevant levels of organization—those that reflect relatively stable structures and have internal coherence.

This prospective practical rule of thinking is akin to the experimentally established observation of the Rule of Seven—people can easily keep about seven categories (e.g., numbers, details, points, names) in mind at once.

Systems

Systems theory permeates advanced management techniques. When W. Edwards Deming, one of the founders of the quality movement, turns to science, he does not borrow from the traditional reductionism of Frederick Winslow Taylor. Rather, he views science holistically, as do other great first-generation systems scientists like Herbert Simon and Kenneth Boulding. Deming's business systems model is very straightforward:

> *Every value-producing organization receives inputs from*
> *suppliers and provides outputs to customers.*

Networks are systems, pure and simple. Anywhere a systems concept will work, so will a network concept. Indeed, for many systems, particularly social systems, networks are an easier sell.

In the social world, people do not much love the word *system*. It's easy—and often justified—to hate "the system." Some people hate it so much that they are blind to their aversion.

Little wonder. Most traditional systems are black boxes. Think of the tax system or the international monetary system or even the municipal garbage system. Most systems portray themselves as beyond the comprehension and control of ordinary mortals. Traditional systems science is much the same. It offers an obfuscating self-portrait of systems as black boxes, unfortunately too complicated for just anyone to understand.

With networks, you take the wraps off systems. Instead of black-box systems, you see "glass box" networks (Figure 12.3). The outer boundary of the network whole is transparent. See inside to the parts (the nodes) and to the relationships (the links) among the parts. The more clearly you lay out the network-system elements, the easier it is to understand.

Synergy

"The whole is more than the sum of its parts." This systems principle is so popular that it's a cliché. In networks, purpose is the "more than" that defines the whole, or synergy. Together, synergy is possible; in isolation, it is not.

Figure 12.3   "Glass Box" Network

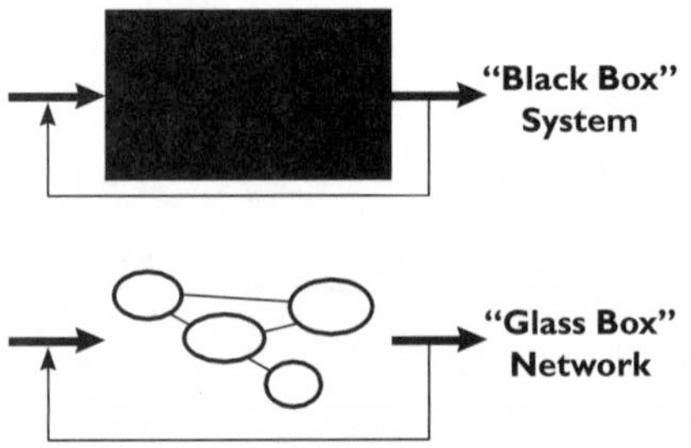

> *To function, your system—no matter how minimal—has to have some synergy or purpose.*

Purpose relates very practically to how people become legitimized in networks through contribution to the shared purpose. Develop purpose as a resource for your team, just as people develop procedures and policies using law as a resource. Encourage your members to participate in planning and decision making to internalize the purpose for themselves. Externalize the purpose through explicit plans, information access, and by creating symbols—logos, nicknames, acronyms. Instead of controlling one another through one-way orders or endlessly detailed policies, boundary-crossing virtual team members exercise control through their shared process—what we represent in the four-wall virtual team room.

Holons

Each of us is a *whole* person who plays a *part* in families, businesses, and communities. Arthur Koestler, author and systems thinker, coined the word *holon* to stand for this whole/part characteristic of everything.[2] And, as we saw in our parable of the innovators earlier in this chapter, complex boundary-crossing teams *are* systems of systems within systems. Every team is a hierarchy of wholes and parts. Complex team members are themselves systems of systems. The systems principles of segmentation and inclusion apply every time a group splits up into task teams or an alliance jells.

Nothing in groups is as complicated as leadership. One way to simplify complex wholes is to grasp a part that represents the rest. In the search for simple ways to "grasp a group," leaders come in handy. Leaders are people who stand for a group. All organizations have leaders, even self-directed groups, where leadership is assumed from within rather than appointed from without. Networks are rife with leaders.

Relationships

Relationships are elusive "things." For some people, relationships are real; for others, they are not. Some people literally cannot see relationships, even indirectly. These people do well in organizations with rules to govern behavior. They don't fare well in virtual teams and networks, where relationships are at reality's core.

There are so many relationships involved in life and so many different kinds of them everywhere you look. To simplify this vast interconnected mess, traditional organizations have many one-way signs. Hierarchies and bureaucracies take an extremely limited approach to how parts interconnect. Generally speaking, orders and information flow in a minimal number of formal channels. Information flows up and commands flow down. This traffic pattern gives rise to the walls, stovepipes, silos, and other hard-to-penetrate boundaries in organizations.

By contrast, in networks, connections are many rather than few. Information and influence flow both up and down the levels through links, as well as horizontally within levels. What is the situation with your boundary-crossing team? Do information and influence flow along a two-way highway, or are people stopped for going against the traffic?

Space-Time

The underlying framework for virtual time comes from physics and Albert Einstein's famous formulation of space and time as aspects of the same reality. While these dimensions seem so different in the physical world, their interrelationship is much more obvious in the cyber world.

Physical space is concrete and hard, whereas time is ephemeral. Cyberspace is more like time, largely conceptual and soft, albeit still rooted in physical realities of binary switching electronics. In cyber-space-time, more space (memory) generally means less processing time, and more bandwidth space means faster connections and less transmission time.

When place is virtual, time spent with other people is either sametime or asynchronous. On a practical level, it is the cybertime dimension that is most intransigent in the new world of work. Global teams are still bound by the revolution of the earth in 24-hour cycles and natural human sleep patterns. Synchronous time shrinks in global work requiring a correspondent increase in asynchronous capabilities. So we create collective online places that accrete information and change over time.

Process

The generic concept of process derives from a key pattern found in physical, biological, and social systems. The fabled S curve, the logistic growth curve, that we use to represent the change process (see Figure 6.2), appears in the original paper that Ludwig von Bertalanffy wrote establishing the field of general systems.[3] It was his first example of an "isomorphy," a general principle that holds across scientific disciplines. An isomorphy crosses boundaries.

Well understood in a wide variety of scientific disciplines, the S curve offers accumulated knowledge, available to those who want to deepen their understanding of process. Look to the points of turbulence in the "Stressed S" process and use them to your advantage.

Smart Teams

Smart virtual teams share ideas freely and creatively. People think through what they are doing. Brainstorming is one obvious way that a team thinks; planning is another. Every diagram a team makes, every memo written, agenda proposed, and idea exchanged—all of the team's shared interactions—naturally combine into mental (cognitive) models. As people share their mental models and test them in the team's environment, they collectively think up better ones. The better the shared understanding, the stronger the model. Better group models equal greater group intelligence.

All teams share mental models. In most situations, these models are fragmentary and unexpressed. In the conventional, well-structured, colocated team with its ever present boss and proverbial watercooler for informal interaction, it's all but unnecessary to develop a shared mental model. Lacking the traditional cues, virtual teams, by contrast, need new ones to stay aligned.

Virtual teams like those at Sun that follow clear processes, supported by technology that facilitates and captures their work as it unfolds, naturally develop ideas faster. They are smarter.

> *Virtual teams that create and display their mental models are smarter.*

Abstraction is sometimes difficult for people who prefer the concrete. Most of us feel comfortable with knock-on-wood, hard reality—the "I can see it, feel it, taste it" satisfaction of the material. Unfortunately, these signs of life are in short supply for virtual teams. The faster, more global, and more complex Internet Age demands greater abstraction. The trick is to learn how to use abstraction to advantage by applying it to your own situation.

In this way, abstraction increases your team's intelligence and capacity to produce concrete results.

CHAPTER 13

THINK

Reaching for Possibilities Together

> *Only a few generations of humans have had instantaneous electronic communications, and only now are we launching groups linked with the historically unique cognitive (digital) technology of computers.*

What does this make possible?

Humanity has progressed by substituting brain for brawn. We see the rise of smarter groups as new forms of human networks intertwine with the electronic world of technology networks.

Mind

In the Industrial Age, organizations were likened to machines. In the Information Age, both organization and computer networks feed off the same metaphor, the human brain/mind. Where once the extension of limbs and senses occupied center stage in the human development of tools, today digital technology amplifies gray matter.

The most distinctive feature of networks and virtual teams is the abundance and variety of links—of media, interactions, and relationships. For the initial analog phase of computer development, physical-brain analogies between corporate networks and human nervous systems are apt. As we rocket into web worlds interrelated through hypertext links, *mind metaphors* are coming to dominate descriptions of virtual organizations.

The characteristics of these emerging models reach back to roots in traditional hierarchy and bureaucracy as well as cast forward to the new capabilities in networks.

> *On the web, people express links and relationships in context.*

On intranets, extranets, and the Internet, a dynamic distributed human intelligence comes together and grows with the group. With hypertext links, the team's ability to create and use shared cognitive models crosses a fundamental threshold. The nature of the online space is no longer primarily an artifact of the hardware/software structure of the technology. It is a matter of choice, the human intellect creating a shared mental space.

Origins of the Search for Intelligent Life Online

George Boole struck the spark that ignited the conceptual soul of the now-maturing Information Age in 1853. His book, *An Investigation of the Laws of Thought*, established the binary logic that remains the essence of all computing today. Thus, at the very dawn of this epochal movement toward the digital era, Boole put forward the connection between human thought and its abstract representation in complementary 0s and 1s. He began his groundbreaking work thus:

> *"The design of the following treatise is to investigate the fundamental laws of those operations of the mind by which reasoning is performed . . ."*[1]

Portents of the vast change to come developed slowly and virtually imperceptibly through the next 100 years as Boole's engineering descendents, notably Charles Babbage and Ada Lovelace, created a mechanical means of configuring binary logic into a human cognitive helpmate. However, not until ENIAC was built in the mid-1940s did Boolean processing reach electronic speed and pure digital form.

Over the next decade, a few visionary thinkers began to see that computers not only reflect how individuals reason, but how groups of people connected by computers can reach new capabilities of reasoning together. One visionary was Joseph Licklider, the legendary founder of the ARPA office that spawned the Internet. In the 1950s, this original net wizard was "touting a radical and visionary notion: that computers weren't just adding machines. Computers have the potential to act as extensions of the whole human being, as tools that can amplify the range of human intelligence and expand the reach of our analytical powers."[2]

In 1962, after ARPA recruited Licklider, he personally connected the leading computer scientists of the day in the major research universities and a few companies. This human network was the embryonic beginning of the collaboration that in time stimulated development of the ARPANET, forerunner to the Internet. He called this group the "Intergalactic Computer Network," by which he came to mean "not just a group of people to whom he is sending memos but a universe of interconnected computers over which all might send their memos."[3] In Licklider's mind, networks of people and computers were conjoined.

The acknowledged hands-on pioneer in the area of large-scale cognitive computing is Douglas Engelbart. Engelbart's four-decade exploration and development first came to public view with publication of a 1963 article, "A Conceptual Framework for the Augmentation of Man's Intellect." Five years later, he demonstrated how to turn the technology part of his theory into practice with a stunning presentation to a conference of computer professionals. Twenty years before the industry considered them commonplace, Engelbart's system featured such innovations as a mouse, bitmapped graphics, multiple windows, and hypertext linking features—in 1968! Over the next two decades, Engelbart continued to develop the technology, initially known as the NLS system and later as Augment, while simultaneously bootstrapping organizational knowledge through the experience of the Augment development team.[4]

In contrast to artificial intelligence, which views the computer as an autonomous thinker, *augmented* intelligence views the computer as a tool to support and increase *human* intelligence. Moreover, human intelligence is extended to include our organized relations with others as well as the conventionally understood individual intelligence. Generalizing about intelligence, Engelbart (1963) writes:[5]

> *"Intelligence . . . seems primarily to be associated with organization. All of the social, biological, and physical phenomena we observe about us seem to derive from a supporting hierarchy of organized functions (or processes), in which the principle of synergism applies . . ."*

From the beginning, Engelbart emphasized the complementary nature of the "man-artifact" interface, the need to coevolve the human system (that includes elements like methods, skills, knowledge, language, training, and organization) along with the technology system.

When the history of group intelligence is written, Murray Turoff's name is also likely to be on the list of major contributors. Turoff created what was probably the first large-scale conferencing system in 1970 at the Office of Emergency Preparedness in the executive office of the president. He then designed and implemented, initially under National Science Foundation funding, the Electronic Information Exchange System (EIES), which continues today as the grandparent of online discussion platforms.

Turoff's conception of computerized conferencing grew out of his pioneering studies with Harold Linstone on the Delphi method. Delphi is an iterative paper-and-mail process "designed to structure group communication in such a way as to attempt to capitalize on the strengths and minimize the weaknesses of collective problem solving."

In *The Network Nation*, the 1978 classic of online conferencing, Turoff and his coauthor, sociologist Starr Roxanne Hiltz, raise the "philosophical or meta issue" involved in comprehending "the basic purpose of computerized conferencing systems"[6]:

> *Is it possible to conceive of a collective intelligence capability for a group of humans? Is it possible for a group of humans utilizing an appropriate communication structure to exhibit a collective decision capability at least as good as or better than any single member of the group?*

A largely untapped potential for computer-assisted communication lies in its cognitive contribution to the organization as a whole. As a virtual group's structure begins to appear online, it starts to develop a computer-enhanced intelligence.

Why Smarter Groups?

When we say, "That's a smart move," referring to a company or group announcement, we show respect for the organization's thinking.

Is there always a single smart person doing the thinking for every smart move by a group? Or are our metaphors of "brilliant" or "dumb" groups clues to a hidden reality of group cognition?

There *is something more* to the thinking of groups than is found in the thinking of individuals in the group. That *something more* is different from, not better than, personal thinking. Moreover, this reality is not hidden. Rather, it is very open, beneath our collective noses, awaiting only a shift in perspective to see the cognitive richness of our everyday lives.

> *The payoff for seeing how groups think is great:* smarter groups.

But we don't have to wait for tomorrow for smarter groups. Most people have at one time or another been a member of a group that really clicks—a family, work, political, religious, or volunteer effort. Most people intuitively know the tremendous personal satisfaction that is possible with high group performance. A small general improvement in people's ability to think and act collectively will have a great impact on solving the world's problems, large and small.

As the planet rapidly interconnects, sheer complexity puts an understanding of the whole beyond the reach of a single individual. Collective problems require collective solutions. Where success is a matter of agreement, as in a negotiation, it is the intelligence of the group that counts more than finding a correct answer, as in a spelling bee.

No single person is going to solve the problem of population or address environmental, viral, economic, genetic, or other really big issues that loom over the twenty-first century. They only can be tackled through collaborative action. If we do not understand how our groups think—or even that they do think—then we will be unable to meet the challenges of our rapidly changing world.

We need smarter, self-organizing groups to cope with complexity and claim our possibilities. To help get there, we begin with an abstract idea of how groups think and end with how to integrate cognitive capabilities into our four-wall virtual team room.

How Groups Think

Thinking is the functional ability to create, use, and adapt cognitive models.[7]

As individuals and as groups, we use models to understand the world. When data pours in, we sift it and sort it—by categories. We develop cognitive models from the pattern of relationships between categories.

Basic Categories

Thinking begins not with any old kind of category, but with a specific kind of category called a *basic-level category* in cognitive science.

Basic-level categories are simple ideas that everyone directly understands: cars, homes, jobs, and families. On the range of concepts from very general to very specific, people seem to understand ideas in the *middle*.

This is called the *basic level,* not meaning the lowest level, as the word *basic* might suggest, but the most common, most widely understood middle level.

According to research, people grasp the idea of "dog" (an intermediate concept) more directly and easily than "animal" (a more general idea) or "golden retriever" (a more specific concept).

People categorize from the most accessible part of their experiences. Categories begin in the middle. This *basic level* anchors our gestalt sense of whole things and allows us to extend concepts upward to more *general levels* and downward to more *particular levels.* Chairs are a basic-level category; furniture is more general (up, or superordinate) than chairs, whereas rockers are more specific (down, or subordinate).

Groups also categorize from the middle. For example, a planning group tries to define yearly goals at the appropriate level of generality—where the idea is easy to grasp and easy to sell. Basic-level goals then anchor very specific (subordinate) tasks that spell out how to achieve the goals. Looking up, the goals relate to broad (superordinate) organizational strategies, mission, and vision.

Basic Patterns

To basic categories we add the idea of basic patterns. Patterns are the configuration of connections among categories.

The *container* is perhaps the most basic pattern of our daily experience. We are ourselves containers. Our bodies are, quite literally, vessels. Things go in and out of ourselves. Our physical body is a container—like a can, cup, or box. We are also contained. With our bodies, we constantly move in and out of other containers—like rooms, houses, and cars.

Our everyday human experience as both containers and contained gives us a typical way to think about containers in general, an abstract *schema.* The container pattern consists of just three elements: inside, outside, and boundary. Schematically, it looks like a circle with a point of reference inside or outside.

We use the container schema all the time as we move through the concrete and abstract categories of life. Imagine the typical morning of Rebecca Stillwater, who lives in the Boston suburbs and works in the city. She goes *out* of her house, *enters* her garage and gets *into* her car. She pulls *out* of the garage and the driveway, eases *into* a flow of traffic and drives *into* the city. She pulls *into* her parking space, gets *out* of her car, and goes *into* her building. She shows her badge and signs *in.*

When Rebecca signs in, she enters a very different kind of container than her home or car, but it is no less real. She enters an organization—a social structure, with an abstract inside, an outside, and a boundary. Her badge shows that she belongs inside the social box.

Containers represent a level of human experience common to everyone. This pattern allows us to build mental bridges from physical activities to abstract ones. We metaphorically extend physical vessels, for example, to social ones via the *container* pattern.

Containers help us structure our daily lives. They also provide structure for some of our most sophisticated philosophical ideas, including the idea of categories itself. Categories are containers: They hold related instances.

From biology to economics to engineering to business, the container schema underlies the concept of "system." Indeed, the recurring container pattern in human experience is what makes a systems theory possible. Anatol Rapoport sees system science as rooted in classification, which he considers "perhaps more fundamental (because it is more elementary) than measurement."[8]

Whole-part is another basic pattern, which inherently structures the whole-part principle. It provides one of the primary means to extend categories, the use of one part or member to stand for the whole, called *metonymy* (the categorical representation of leadership). And, just as the container schema underlies the concept of system, the whole-part schema underlies the systems idea of "hierarchy," the sets-within-sets structure of complexity.

Basic Models

In this view of human thought, cognitive models tie categories and patterns together.

Concepts—which are in fact categories—are meaningful in the context of an encompassing model. "Tuesdays," "weekends," "workweek," and "day," for example, are concepts in a culturally and astronomically defined cognitive model of "a week" that makes sense only in context. Given the model, everyone understands what it means when we say a meeting is scheduled for next week; and everyone understands when we say, "It takes a week to get anything done around here."

A cognitive model is a system of categories related through recurring patterns.

Containers and whole-part patterns are common to both personal and group cognitive models. All cognitive models represent information by chunking experience into labeled containers, or categories. And all models have at least three levels of structure: the model as a whole, its categories (parts), and the content items populating the categories.

While categories may differ, both groups and individuals connect categories in similar ways.

The notion of category itself reflects these two aspects of cognitive models: the common framework and the differences of content. For while the content of a category varies, the container structure of the category does not. Categories are simply containers. Categories are vessels that can hold an infinite array of ideas and experience.

An organization chart represents a group cognitive model, a system of linked categories (work groups) structured by the whole-part pattern, which gives meaning to the enterprise as a whole. A group also has other cognitive models, such as those based on purpose, plans, and conversations.

Group Cognitive Model

Picture an organization chart. What the chart represents is a default view of how the group sees itself: its categories of roles, job descriptions, and titles. A complex group forms and names subgroups, divisions, departments, and task teams. Each box is a category that shows a part of how the group divides up its inner world.

Both people and subgroups of people represent categories in the membership model of a group. A vice president of marketing is a role category that is "filled" by a person. A marketing department identifies a major subgroup category; it denotes a specific function within a larger architecture of functions that together constitute the whole organization. The title, VP of marketing, for example, is meaningless by itself; it acquires meaning as a node in a network of groups and titles that together constitute the configuration of an organized whole.

Reporting categories, invariably connected through whole-part, hierarchical relationships, comprise a cognitive model. How is the configuration of subgroups and roles a default model for a group? Consider the processing of incoming information, a basic function of our personal thinking apparatus.

When a group receives information, say an e-mail or a letter with a request, it is routed to the most relevant person (role) or subgroup for assessment, or meaning. The group's cognitive model functions effectively when people in a group easily and quickly pass information, problems, and possibilities along to "the right place." If, however, new information arrives and no one knows what to do with it, the shared cognitive model does not function well. Because there are no established roles or subgroups to handle the input, the group experiences frustration.

An organization chart is a literal picture of a group's membership model. Each box in the chart is a category, a container representing specific responsibilities and information. These boxes are connected by whole-part relations often shown in a tree configuration, a single cognitive model.

The importance of how a group chooses to divide itself up, to create its cognitive model, becomes apparent when a group consciously goes about changing this model. Reorganization, a frequent activity in rapidly changing environments, is a collective cognitive process.

When a group reorganizes, it usually does so to improve performance, to be more effective, to be, in a word, *smarter.* How a group differentiates itself, how it names its parts, is a critical determinant of how smart it will be. During reorganization, a group creates new categories, new organizational positions and subgroups (perhaps hiring people), deletes some existing categories, abolishes some subgroups (perhaps laying people off), and rearranges existing relationships (e.g., changing reporting structures). At the end, there is a new cognitive model, represented by a new organization chart.

Group Reality

So where do human categories come from?

There are two major schools of thought about this. The view that reaches back to Aristotle is that categories are abstract, independently meaningful concepts, unrelated to human vagaries. The new view is that human categories are concrete; they emerge from being human and having bodies. We draw on the concrete view of categories and apply it to groups.[9]

The Body

As *Homo sapiens,* all people share fundamental similarities, a common pool of categories connected to activities like eating, drinking, and sleeping. The most basic and common categories emerge from our earliest childhood experiences, and they transcend cultural differences. Basic categories are surrounded by a vast penumbra of other categories that spring from differing environments and histories.

> *If individual human thought is based on the human body, then what is the thought of a group based upon? Group thought is based on group realities.*

Communication that is external to individuals is internal to groups. The stuff of group cognition is what people say, write, and do, particularly communication that lasts. Memories with emotional impact, written words, rules agreed to, and symbols rallied around carry the traces of people's interactions with one another and part of what it means for a group to be embodied—to have concrete experience.

Group entities are concretely real. Not concrete like individuals, but concrete like groups. While human bodies are distinctly singular and centralized in nature, group bodies are essentially multiple and distributed.

Immense variations in size, longevity, and purpose suggest that group categories are different from individual categories and that the range of differences among groups is much greater and content is much less common than it is among individuals.

The distributed nature of groups makes them difficult to see from a single perspective. For our conceptual lens, we use four views, each representing a different dimension of group reality, a different facet of the "quality without a name" of a living group.

Typically, we see groups through the people dimension, because human groups are quite obviously made up of people. Common sense tells us to know a group through the people that make it up—its members. Thus, the group includes (the two or more) people that comprise the group. Since this dimension is more generally about the nodes that comprise the network, it also includes things that a group owns or uses. Property, resources, and technologies are very material, very concrete, parts of group reality, particularly for long-lasting and/or large groups.

Groups have purposes. People *group* for a reason. It takes work to form and maintain a group. Purposes may be implicit, such as those of friendship networks, or explicit, such as those expressed in company charters and annual plans. In teams, purpose and the achievement of goals motivate the group. Without its tasks, a work group has no coherence, no integral reason for being. For every human organization, large and small, there is a pattern of activities, reflecting its certain set of purposes.

In groups, people communicate. They establish relationships. No relationships, no group. Communication—talking, writing, physical cues, digital connections—weaves another dimension of group reality. Groups may also have rules, communications, and interactions that have been formalized and habitualized. Norms, rules, policies, and laws are conceptual models based on communications that become independent artifacts within a group.

Groups exist *in time*. They are organic human entities that reflect change and adaptation over time. Groups also have life cycles, which can be very short—hours or days—to months, years, centuries, and, in the case of some religious organizations, millennia. Calendars, agendas, schedules, and milestones provide various ways in which groups develop time-oriented cognitive models.

People, purpose, links, time—four dimensions of group reality. While these certainly are not the only ways to see groups, they are basic and broad enough to shed insight into how groups think.

Cognitive "Stuff" Online

"Computers are to mind what machines are to muscle." As the cliché reflects, computers are natural cognitive media. It is not surprising, then, to find the same general cognitive patterns infused throughout the hardware and software interfaces that people use on a daily basis.

Most cognitive scientists believe we think by using language. Many believe we also use images to think, and some believe in even more forms of cognitive representation. On the face of it, the online contents of e-mail and threaded discussions are sets of natural language statements, a list of propositions—public mental representations. While text predominated online for decades, the newer technologies and economics of imagery on the web make all forms of expression, including audio and video, common to the group memory in the new millennium.

Categories, levels, and networks infuse the online environment. The online database memory has a thoroughly hierarchical architecture. Online communities create mailing lists, conferences, meetings, topics, and the like—intermediate group structures. These groups have an autonomous online life, yet are interconnected as a network whole. Static databases, too, have their own integrity and special purpose, and yet are often linked together in networks. Most significantly, the physical substrate of online groups is a computer network, itself built upon a telecommunications network.

An online group memory that includes "live" participants has recall ability not available to individual thinking entities: the ability to ask questions.

Asking and answering are the essence of human networking. As in personal memory, where recollection can prompt a chain of thoughts leading to insight, so asking a question online may prompt a series of responses that take all participants beyond the understanding they started with. More generally, conversations that flow in digital space are naturally captured and capable of recall, summarization, categorization, and connection.

A Place to Think

A virtual room, a cyberplace, is a team's basic container. A place to be enables a vital human system to develop, which in turn configures and transforms the place that it lives in.

An application's user interface is software that helps people leverage computing power. The interface usually draws from the craft of the capability being enhanced: Spreadsheets are natural to accountants, documents to writers, and graphics to artists. Most software assumes an individual is the user, but in the networked world, teams are also users of software: E-mail is meaningless if only one person has it.

How can we devise a team interface in digital technology? By creating and using shared cognitive models in an online place, a room where people generate their own customized "Group GUI" (Graphical User Interface).

People filter incoming information through cognitive models, recall old memories through models, and create new models to predict the future. So do teams. They can explicitly create and manipulate these models in a computer-mediated environment. For the globally distributed groups made possible by technology, there is an especially urgent need for visible, explicit, shared models to give meaning to the online world.

Behind the four-wall virtual team room is an interactive environment that naturally enhances the team's intelligence. People are able to use the tools and displays of their shared information in practical but intelligent ways without regard for the abstract underpinnings. Cognitive capabilities lie deep in the conceptual architecture of the room and its technological substrate, an invisible electronic infrastructure that supports human relationships.

Portals

The virtual team room *portal* page provides entry to a place that holds the identity of a virtual group. This expresses both the basic container pattern and the central idea of hierarchy, a point of reference.

The virtual team and its portal page are the locus for a mission and the focus of internal leadership. The portal also identifies the top level for planning and managing a task-based project. In the language of the Internet, the portal represents the home page of the team web site. It bespeaks the central focus of the team and offers selected links to the things most relevant to that focus. Also associated with setting up a new group home is a new database for the group's growing profile, plan, and process information.

Whole Parts

Organizations and individuals are themselves complex containers. Underlying the freewheeling ad hoc ability to profile members and construct groups on the *people wall* is the immensely powerful whole-part functionality of a hierarchical tool.

With the extended-organization chart, you can see up and down the levels of the organization from a given point of reference. This capability underlies the team's ability to differentiate itself as its purpose unfolds. As a team works, it subdivides and reorganizes itself to best fit the configuration of tasks. An even moderately complex team will soon form subteams, a natural step that is all too often taken unconsciously, with little thought and allowance for the review and feedback process required to get any set of basic categories right.

Hierarchical clustering infuses throughout the architecture of any web site and, of course, any online room. Navigation schemes set the handful of high-level categories that best span the range of information contained in the site. These "getting-around" schemes typically are available in frames at the top and/or sides of web pages, and clicks on a major head often reveal a subhead level of outline detail.

The team table also has center-periphery pattern features. Core, extended, and external team members are arrayed in three rings of involvement. The central membership of the team exists inside the penumbra of people participating less intensely.

Pursuit

The *purpose wall* contains the "goal-path-result,"[10] the pursuit of objectives through time. This design is the same as the "input-throughput-output" model that we use to organize the taxonomy of virtual team elements (Figure 12.1). It is the simple human idea of starting somewhere with an idea, an intent, and proceeding through a series of steps to reach some end—a goal, an outcome, or a result.

The very human process of aligning around vision and goals can be messy, particularly for virtual teams. The map of organizational purposes (Figure 7.4) provides a common framework for constructive conversations on collaboration.

The project management system and the electronics behind the purpose wall support planning and tracking goals, tasks, meetings, decisions, and concrete outcomes.

Meshing Links

Links, the mental construction tool for the ephemeral fabric of the *links wall*, represent a very basic pattern, the connection of point A to point B. The essential meaning of the web is "to link." Links provide the extraordinary ability to move instantly from anywhere to anywhere on the planet—both literally and figuratively. Links connect us to others in networks, and links connect technologies together as networks.

Different media offer people pathways with different connecting characteristics. Depending on the medium, different senses and brain structures engage, which translates to a need to employ multiple media to fully enable group cognition.

Patterns of enablement, removal of restraint, compulsion, diversion, counterforce, attraction, and blockage bespeak the range of relationship configurations people use to shape their social world.[11] These rule-driven processes are at the heart of replicable workflow models that use technology to move work from person to person.

By linking categories together into cognitive models, a team creates its mental reality. While individual relationships are the spice of our moment-by-moment experience, it is the pattern of relationships that creates a social whole over time.

Learning

Since digital reality ultimately expresses itself as data, we stand on the threshold of a new era of social self-knowledge. More and more of group life will occur online and be captured in a data model underlying its team room. There, at the data level, the basis for true social science emerges.

The fundamental problem with the human sciences is often characterized by analogy with the Heisenberg uncertainty principle, which says that at the level of quanta in physics, the interference of observers dependent on light or other electromagnetic means to measure subatomic phenomena means they can know a particle's whereabouts or its speed, but not both at the same time. What is applicable in the physical domain of quantum mechanics far from the levels of sensible experience is an in-your-face limitation on the human sciences. You cannot bring natural groups into a lab, and scientist-observers always affect the behavior of people in a group being observed.

But when a group naturally gathers data on itself online, it creates the potential to learn through feedback loops. How are we doing against our plan? What tools do we use to address conflicts? How long does it take to reach decisions using different media? What's the inflow and outflow of members? Answers to myriad questions like these gradually will build a base for collective self-knowledge.

Popping up a level, we see knowledge harvested across many teams that are learning from their own processes. Many teams within a common culture, such as a global enterprise, as well as many teams coming from many cultures, will provide a vast new scientific territory to explore and mine for deep knowledge as well as immediate application. Because this new scientific gold mine is embedded in the practical everyday use of collaboration technology, knowledge gleaned from this environment is highly likely to be relevant to boosting the performance of digitally endowed human entities.

Our vision is of an emergent level of group thinking that in turn stimulates the evolution of individual human consciousness.

Do groups think? Can we imagine they do and make it real by creating thinking groups? These are big questions to hold in our individually small hands.

CHAPTER 14

FUTURE

We are two people among 6 billion.
With you, dear reader, we are three.
What does that mean?
Can a person grasp a planet?
Can a planet know a person?

Star Maker

Stand with us here, in a field on a mountaintop in the Adirondacks, a spot where we feel particularly in tune with the universe. Watch the weather boil over purple peaks. Close your eyes and step out. Change your scale of perception with us, so that we may find a comfortable perspective in which to place our planet and ourselves.

Step out to the Milky Way, the shimmering necklace of stars that rings the clear night sky. Quickly swing by the sun, pass the giant planets and the outer extremities of our solar system, pass Alpha Centauri and Sirius a few light-years away, and speed 30,000 light-years to our galactic center. Grow and adopt the perspective of Olaf Stapledon's *Star Maker*,[1] become the brilliant spiraling association of 400 billion suns in a disk 100,000 light-years across that is the Milky Way.

See, close by, the minigalaxies making up the Magallanic Clouds, and our neighboring galaxies Sculptor and Fornax, part of our little local group, which extends out about 2 million light-years to include the beautiful Andromeda. Play, then, as part of our local group, with other super-galaxies, such as nearby Virgo, Perseus, Coma, and Hydra.

Raise your gaze yet farther, and look to the rims of the universe. Stretch your galactic mind to encompass your 100 billion brothers and sisters, each a bright being averaging 100 billion stars.

Ancient Hindu scripture says that our universe may be but an atom in another universe, a mote in another god's eye. But we have gone far enough to recognize our Milky Way as an individual among other galaxies that together form groups in a larger environment of cosmic groups.

So now, returning to the dense core of our own galactic perspective, look outward across your gracefully spinning body, past the Sagittarius Arm, farther out to a back eddy nestled in the Carina-Cygnus Arm, and focus on the small, second-generation star that humans call the Sun.

As we turn our perspective and sense of scale back toward the human home, passing Altair and Procyon and finally Alpha Centauri once again, notice that the solar system as a whole looms in the distance and takes on the appearance of individuality against the relative emptiness of intragalactic space. The whole system of stars, planets, satellites, comets, and encompassing energies is an entity in the galactic association of solar systems.

Parked outside Pluto's orbit, the Star Maker might wonder about the complexity of this integrated solar animal, 5 *billion* years old. A glance at the solar subsystems confirms the suspicion of intelligence indicated by the profusion of nonrandom radio signals that fill the inner solar space and that even now leak into galactic space. As our perspective narrows to the source of these signals, we approach the third planet.

Although still young, the brain of the solar system, the earth, already has 6 billion neurons and is rapidly growing more. Remarkably, as we zoom in on the pulsing marbled orb that constitutes the seat of solar intelligence and examine one of the billions of elements of this emergent planetary brain, we enter yet another cosmos. Each planetary neuron—

a person, a human being—has a brain with something like 10 billion neurons, each neuron capable of perhaps 50,000 connections.

You are home.

Right now the natural limits, smallest to largest, of human networking are at minimum one of us alone and at maximum all of us together— a range from one person to six going on seven billion people at the turn of the twenty-first century.

Certain large numbers are sometimes breathlessly advanced to illustrate unimaginable complexity: neurons in the brain, people on the planet, stars in the galaxies, galaxies in the universe—individuals and billions all. Using a third-grade-arithmetic trick, cancel out all the billions and review the cosmic journey:

> Our universe has 100 galaxies.
> Our galaxy has 400 stars.
> Our star system has a brain with 6 people.
> Our body has a brain with 10 neurons.
> Can you hold it in your hand? Universe, sun, and self?

Searching for Intelligence

A single e-mail captures the spirit of projects previously unthinkable that are now under way:

```
Date: Sun, 26 Dec 1999 02:32:53 -0800 (PST)
From: "SETI@home" <setiathome@ssl.berkeley.edu>
Subject: SETI@home newsletter

Dear SETI@home user:

Thanks for your interest and participation in
SETI@home. This is our first e-mail newsletter.

With your assistance, SETI@home has been amazingly
successful. 1,500,000 people in 224 countries have
```

> downloaded the SETI@home screensaver and together
> they have contributed 125,000 years of computer
> time, with the common goal of finding the first
> sign of intelligent extraterrestrial life.
>
> We've been recording data at the Arecibo radio
> telescope since December 1998, and most of the
> data through May 1999 has now been analyzed. 100
> million signals have been detected and stored in
> our database. The second-phase processing, which
> rejects [hu]man-made interference and looks for
> "repeat" signals, will start soon. This is when
> we hope to actually detect an ET signal!
>
> Furthermore, thanks to the abundance of computing
> power, we'll be augmenting SETI@home to look for
> new types of signals...

We are two of those who have downloaded the SETI (Search for Extra Terrestrial Intelligence) screen saver. In the idle time between typing these words that you read now and having a bite to eat, our computers process signals for SETI. While essentially effortless on our part, SETI could not happen without the cooperation of our 1.5 million "colleagues": a dozen companies, including Sun, Intel, IBM, and Paramount Pictures; nonprofits like University of California's Digital Media Innovation Program and the SETI Institute[2] itself; and, naturally given the times, Space.com.

The SETI screen saver is a project of the Search for Extraterrestrial Life Institute, physically located in Berkeley, California, where most of the research scientists and their teams are situated. But their phenomenal computing power, on which they depend, is global. By distributing packets of signals to a vast network of PCs around the world—basically to anyone willing to download a simple little processing program—SETI is able to do with its network what is simply undoable without it. SETI's purpose? It's recursive: to process signals sampled from everywhere in the universe to discover intelligent life, a potential finding made possible by distributing processing among a sampling of the universe of intelligent machines.

At the Frontier

Cyber frontier: We and other writers have perhaps too often used the frontier analogy with respect to cyberspace. Thus, it is worth listening to someone who has been to "the end of the earth" for a reminder of just how really appropriate it is.

John Lawrence,[3] who organized the first UN site at the 1995 United Nations Fourth World Conference on Women in Beijing, is a fascinating character among those involved in the creation of electronic places. At one time a geological explorer for the New Zealand Antarctic Research Programme (Lawrence Peaks, part of the Transantarctic Range in Victoria Land, Antarctica, is named for him), he says today: "One simply trades one form of frontier for another. I know the feeling of stepping out onto land that no human in recorded history has stepped on. It was a feeling very similar to what cyber people are feeling now as they go out into this peculiar virtual world."

Lawrence continues, "There's an adrenaline rush as one goes over new surfaces, seeing completely new vistas that have never before been seen by the human eye. It's incredibly exciting and each person has his and her own way of coding all that. But this is different and more intriguing because explorers have gone out into new territory in physical space for hundreds of years. That particular adrenaline rush has been described for generations. But this new one has barely been described for a generation, and that's a rush in itself."

Of course, cyber explorers can be anywhere.

Protecting Prairies

Sitting in Fergus Falls, Minnesota, population 12,000, Peter Buesseler is a pioneer in the use of virtual teams who served as a key node and webmaster for the Great Plains Partnership (GPP), the initiative of 13 western states, three Canadian provinces, two Mexican states, numerous federal and local agencies, American Indian tribes, environmental and agricultural organizations, businesses, and landowners concerned with the viability of the Great Plains.[4]

"How am I protecting prairies while I'm going around with a screwdriver in my pocket?" asks Buesseler, who is also Minnesota's State Prairie Biologist. Buesseler is friend to many Minnesotans who are trying to get online. "We're in a rural part of the country here and e-mail is not much available. I'm often involved in helping people I need to work with find out what kind of access is available to them. I talk to the telephone companies for them, and then take my screwdriver with me to their offices or homes to attach their modems."

In the mid-1980s, Buesseler could not even type. Since then he has turned himself into "a little techie," he says, in order to be able to reach the people he needs to work with. "It's a lot easier for me to do it than for them to wait three months if they made the same request from their data centers. It builds a relationship that is not as structured. We can ask each other for things that we might not think to ask each other. It's a barn-building type of arrangement, which gets at the core of my work."

We conduct our interview with Buesseler, along with two of his colleagues, Brian Stenquist, a strategic facilitator, and Susen Fagrelius (who has consulted to Minnesota's Department of Natural Resources), via conference call, naturally, as the three of them are 300 miles apart and we are in Boston. At one point Buesseler says, "I am sitting here mentally doodling spiderwebs which are held together and anchored at key strategic points all the way around. But the material that it takes to hold them together is pretty minor. It's both very delicate and incredibly strong at the same time. A spider can walk across it but other insects that try to walk across get entangled."

Buesseler clearly draws the analogy to the network that each virtual team spins—at once fragile but strong, unique yet constantly changing, interacting with its environment that it reconfigures to its best advantage.

"You can tell the species of a spider by the pattern of its web. Each is different, and no spider will ever make the same web twice. It's always dependent on the environment. Is it using a twig or a doorway? In the morning, it is beautiful and glistening, but it is in constant need of repair and demands a lot of upkeep. Its design is always contextual, always aware of its environment and drawing its elements together." The same is true for virtual teams.

Islands of Trust

There are islands of trust at every scale. Couples, partners, families, groups, neighborhoods, departments, communities, enterprises, regions, industries, and nations all have stocks of social capital. Company cultures are storage vaults of social capital based on their history and current dynamics. This investment is available to capitalize (or not) new relationships. Each time a new group comes together, it plants the seed for a new island of trust.

Accelerating Trust

Social capital consists of relationships among people. It doesn't behave in quite the same way as physical capital. Matter, when used, degrades. Information, when used, accumulates. Unused, information loses value or becomes a weapon in the struggle to compete and control, thus increasing mistrust. Like communication, trust is very personal and yet cannot be possessed by a single individual. It takes two to create social capital.

Trust, or its lack, is an all-pervasive cross-cultural reality. All people in all cultures in all ages have depended on trust, but its value has greatly expanded in the Network Age.

- *People* fundamentally trust others—or not. A presumption of trust enables a successful strategy of collaboration to be better innovators, competitors, and survivors.
- If *purpose* is the glue, trust is the grease. Purposes operate through trust—the source of legitimacy for and the vital spark of networks. Trust enables people to establish purposes that they articulate in detail and maintain over time.
- Trust enables people to construct *links*. It undergirds high-performing organizations with the profuse voluntary communications of fast, flexible, integrated responses.
- Trust usually takes *time* to develop, and it also happens in an instant and ruptures just as fast.

The greater the trust, the lower the cost of communication and relationship building. The more extensive the network, the greater the opportunities arising from commonly held goals.

Conversely, mistrust creates difficulties at each step in developing and executing a purpose. It takes longer to arrive at common goals since suspicion demands greater specificity. Enforcement is costly in terms of legal, accounting, and inspection fees, and close monitoring is burdensome, sometimes proving fatally inflexible.

Among the ebbs and flows of turbulence and quiet come some defining moments—usually unexpected and often unwelcome. Crises often precipitate positive feedback loops in social capital—either viciously or virtuously. The vast Mississippi River floods of 1993, for example, drew upon and reinforced the hard-won prairie values of neighborly help. Awful as the rising water was, the flood also washed in a new wealth of social capital formed by countless helping hands as some compensation for the damage. Recovery from natural disasters, increasingly (and sadly) more prevalent, requires social capital.

Social capital is continuously accumulating or degrading. It increases and decreases through dynamics of history, circumstance, crisis, and creativity.

> *In the Network Age, horizontal connections explode. Winners in the twenty-first century—companies, countries, and people—will be those with the greatest social capital.*

All islands of trust, large or small, are embedded in larger environments of relationships that themselves represent stocks of social capital. Social fabrics can be rent by disasters—natural and otherwise, from an oil spill (Valdez) to a nuclear meltdown (Chernobyl) to hurricanes (Hugo)— that threaten the health of communities and families; by migrations and refugees; and by rippling layoffs that destroy economic and personal stability. Relationships are difficult to maintain as physical infrastructures deteriorate, inhibiting travel and communication. Poverty creates isolation, violence and fear, dependence, and lack of access to connections.

Most corrosively, poverty reaches into all communities and undermines and attacks social wealth.

The key to a society's ability to generate social capital lies in its practice of equality—political, social, and economic. Equality is under siege by the powerful global trend of an evolving two-class society, 20 percent wealthy and 80 percent poor, both within and among nations.

We have to reverse this widening disparity to reap the benefits of cooperation on a global scale. To do so, John Evans, chairman of Torstar, the parent company of Canada's largest newspaper, *The Toronto Star,* says we need "a new investment of social capital in community [and] new networks of civic engagements, involvements and commitments from individuals, private groups, corporations. . . . 'A society that relies on generalized reciprocity and mutual assistance is more effective than a competitive, distrustful society.' "[5]

Access to the net initially has created a digital divide of haves and have-nots. A social choice, not a technological imperative, rules here. The real cost of the divide is in computers and local connections, not in available information. Technology costs are plummeting, as they have for decades, while new technologies are rapidly increasing the ways people can connect to the net. The fundamentals of this new platform for human interaction support the possibility of access for all without regard to physical location, appearance, or class.

A Matter of Survival

Ross Ashby's "Law of Requisite Variety"[6] is one of the most famous systems principles. In essence, the law says that for a system to survive, it needs to be at least as complex as its environment. As the environment becomes more complex, the system—whether an organism or an organization—learns and adapts, handling more complexity. Otherwise, sooner or later, it dies.

As our world becomes more complex, faster paced, and more global, we need to smarten up. Growing smarter means incorporating more variety, gaining access to what's happening, and intelligently connecting bits of knowledge to anticipate the future. Organizations must incorporate even greater diversity to survive and thrive as the pace speeds up. More complexity compels more organizations to develop networks to increase their social capital.

Networks incorporate diversity and carry reciprocity across boundaries and borders of every scale and scope. Wide-ranging webs provide the amplifying effect that social network analyst Mark Granovetter calls "the strength of weak ties."[7] He shows how connections at the edges of people's networks, rather than conversations in their core cliques, boost the effects of innovations, ideas, and opportunities.[8]

> *Boundary-crossing networks and virtual teams decrease the cost of transactions, open new channels of cooperation, and expand social capital, allowing new patterns of trust to develop.*

Virtual teams provide extra value beyond accomplishing specific goals like developing a new chip. By bringing people together to pursue shared aims, they add to the stock of social capital. Even when people participate in networks that fail, they frame new relationships and bank trust that they can draw upon in the future.

The Biological Internet

"Trust is really essential," says Frank Starmer who for many years has led a global scientific team, with labs in more than 30 countries, comprising people who rarely if ever meet face-to-face.[9] "For a group to be creative, it must have trust. Islands of trust do not have to be vast to be vital.

"It's essential to develop a level of trust where you can say anything and not regret it or feel that it will come back to haunt you," Starmer says. "Only then are all the communication paths open. No one is wasting time trying to decide whether to say this or that. Complete openness and freedom lead to unconstrained thinking, which leads to good science or good art or good whatever you're doing.

"Collectively, we feel stronger as a team than we do as individuals. Otherwise, we'd drop out of the group. There'd be nothing to gain.

Together, we are more competitive in the science world. Each person contributes some special talent or insight into our overlapping interests."

> *"We speak of a biological Internet. Each person has a nervous system that coordinates and controls. But there is also absolute trust between every part of the body. It's essential for coordinated behavior. And our lab without walls is just a big collective organism with a common goal."*

Imagine your organization with that level of trust. Common goals, coordinated effort, unconstrained thinking, each person contributing, more competitive, all-channel open communication—and the creative juices are really flowing.

> *Trust is the key to virtual teams.*

NOTES

Introduction

1. *New Shorter Oxford English Dictionary,* 1993, p. 371.
2. We are grateful to Shell Oil Company for its pioneering work on "networked communities."
3. This is our sixth book. Previous books: *Networking* (Doubleday, 1982); *The Networking Book* (Viking Penguin, 1986); *The TeamNet Factor* (Oliver Wight/John Wiley & Sons, 1993); *The Age of the Network* (John Wiley & Sons, 1996); and *Virtual Teams* (John Wiley & Sons, 1997).
4. Over the years, we've worked with Apple, AT&T Universal Card Services, BankBoston, Calvert Group, Digital Equipment Corporation, GE, Hewlett-Packard, Hyatt Hotels, Pfizer, and Shell Oil Company.
5. In 1972, we bought and used a Wang 600 Programmable Calculator to run calculations for our cable viability model. In the mid-1970s, a Wang 2200 powered our fire-prevention education work with the U.S. Department of Commerce, which later helped us manage our original research based on material from 1,600 networks. Even earlier, in 1959, at age 15, Jeff started building digital devices, culminating in a 1961 prize-winning piano-sized computer that programmed a high-school master schedule built of IBM electromagnetic relays, switches, and lights and nicknamed the "Don-omatic."
6. *Cable in Boston,* Whitewood Stamps, Inc., 1974.
7. Jeffrey Stamps, *Holonomy: A Human Systems Theory* (Seaside, CA: Intersystems Publications, 1980).
8. We've been influenced by the work of Ned Hermann (*The Whole Brain Business Book,* McGraw-Hill, 1996), especially through its application

by Manny Elkind of Mindtech, 35 Williams Road, Sharon, MA 02067, 781-784-2315, melkind@ziplink.net.

Chapter 1

1. We found this quote on the Context Institute site, http://www.context.org. We sent e-mail to Jaime Snyder, Fuller's grandson, asking to use the quote and inquiring when and where Bucky said this. Jaime's reply: "It is certainly fine to use quote: but I do not know its source. It certainly sounds like Bucky and the idea is consistent with his thinking but I do not know where it might be from. If you have access to a Synergetics Dictionary (a wonderful out of print four-volume research book) at a library you might be able to determine its source." (E-mail from Snyder, "Subject: quote," January 11, 2000.)

2. From an interview with Jim Lynch, vice president of Sun's Corporate Quality Office, February 9, 2000.

3. Andy Campbell, now senior vice president at Applied Knowledge Group, Inc., first said this to us in a telephone conversation in 1993 while he and we were working on the National Performance Review (see Chapter 8, "People").

4. "As of July 1999, 205 countries or territories had at least one connection to the Internet. Thus only four new countries joined the Internet in the first six months of 1999. This is a diminished Internet spread rate, because there aren't many new countries to join." Source: "State of the Internet," Matrix.Net, Inc., http://www.matrix.net.

5. "10 Employees. No Headquarters. $45 Million Payoff. Why Lycos Bought a Virtual Company," *The New York Times*, February 27, 2000, Business section, p. 4.

6. See the book *www.newbusinessdimensions.com* by Bart Piepers and Marcel Storms (Amsterdam, BIS Publishers: 2000), and their web site, http://www.newbusinessdimensions.com.

7. E-mail from Bart Piepers, "Subject: Good luck with your book," January 28, 2000.

8. Interview with John Whyte, CIO, Ernst & Young International, January 24, 2000.

9. See Nua Internet Surveys at http://www.nua.ie/surveys/how_many_online/index.html.

10. See *Weaving the Web* by Tim Berners-Lee (San Francisco, CA: HarperSanFrancisco, 199).

11. "Poll: On-line population soars to 56% of US adults," *The Boston Globe,* December 22, 1999.

12. "Wide Web: Survey finds number of sites at 1 billion," *The Boston Globe,* January 23, 2000.

13. "Computer Industry Almanac Says Over 364 Million PCs-in-Use Worldwide Year-End," March 23, 1999, http://www.techmall.com/techdocs/ TS990323-7.html.

14. "For close to a decade the size of the Internet has doubled every year. In MMQ 601 we noted that. . . . [i]t now appears that this growth rate is slowing somewhat. Careful statistical analysis reveals the beginnings of an 'elbow' over the 1997–1999 period. At that time, growth had reached a factor of 2.1 prior to ebbing to 1.46. Incorporating the July 1999 data puts this factor at 1.5. The growth rate of the Internet is, indeed, slowing." Source: "State of the Internet," Matrix.Net, Inc., http://www.matrix.net.

15. Ibid.

16. This is the subtitle of Ray Grenier and George Metes's book, *Enterprise Networking: Working Together Apart* (Bedford, MA: Digital Press, 1992).

17. GM, Ford, and DaimlerChrysler announced their joint venture on February 25, 2000.

18. See Lycos at http://www.lycos.com/info/.

19. Frances Cairncross, *The Death of Distance: How the Communications Revolution Will Change Our Lives,* Harvard Business School Press, 1997.

20. Interview with Dr. Henry McKinnell, president and chief operating officer, Pfizer Inc., president, Pfizer Pharmaceuticals, January 19, 2000.

21. Interview with Russ Baird, quality training leader, GE's Leadership and Development Facility at Crotonville, New York, January 28, 2000.

22. Ray Grenier and George Metes, *Going Virtual: Moving Your Organization into the 21st Century* (Upper Saddle River, NJ: Prentice Hall, 1995).

23. Sun's first machine shipped with Transmission Control Protocol/Internet Protocol (TCP/IP).

24. Interview with Al Ormiston, vice president and general manager, eSun, February 23, 2000.

25. See http://www.ventro.com.

26. E-mail from Rear Admiral Tom Steffens, director of the Center for Intelligence and Information Operations at the U.S. Special Operations Command, Tampa, Florida, "Subject: Re: Interview," February 13, 2000.

27. Norbert Wiener, *Cybernetics or Control and Communication in the Animal,* (MIT Press, 1948).

28. For more on CERN, see its World Wide Web site: www.cern.ch.

29. E. T. Hall, *The Hidden Dimension* (Garden City, NY: Doubleday, 1966).

30. For more on the relationship between proximity and collaboration, see Thomas J. Allen, *Managing the Flow of Technology: Technology Transfer and the Dissemination of Technological Information within the R&D Organization* (Cambridge, MA: MIT Press, 1977). Data are given in *The Age of the Network,* p. 47.

31. From a slide developed by Shell's Network Learning & Support Center, 1999.

32. *Virtuous* is the term for positive feedback popularized by Peter Senge. See his book, *The Fifth Discipline: The Art and Practice of the Learning Organization* (New York: Doubleday/Currency, 1990).

Chapter 2

1. See Landmark Graphics at http://www.lgc.com/about/about.asp.

2. Interview with David Sibbet, January 24, 2000. See Grove Consultants, http://www.grove.com, David Sibbet's company's site.

3. *Networked Community Fieldbook,* Shell Oil Company, March, 1998.

4. McQuillen now heads Shell's Learning Center.

5. Ibid.

6. See Etienne Wenger, *Communities of Practice: Learning, Meaning, and Identity,* Cambridge University Press, 1999, and "Communities of Practice: The Organizational Frontier," by Wenger and William M. Snyder, Harvard Business Review, January 1, 2000, http://www.hbsp.harvard.edu/hbsp/prod_detail.asp?R00110.

7. Shell Services International had made this move the prior year.

8. The phrase, "Think globally, act locally," first was used by Rene Dubos, the two-time Nobel Laureate.

9. Economically Viable Alternative Green, an Australian environmental group, estimates that there were about 270,000 people on earth about 10,000 years ago (http://www.altgreen.com.au/population/How_many .html).

10. In regard to the structure of fire departments, for three years in the 1970s, we helped the U.S. Department of Commerce set up America's first national fire-prevention education program.

11. See "Australia to Share in 'Heavenly Twins,'" 18 February 1998, http:// www.science.org.au/academy/media/astro3.htm.

12. See "New ABB shows strong '99 earnings, cash generation," February 3, 2000, Press Information, http://www.abb.com.

13. Interview with Harry Brown, CEO, EBC Industries, Inc., January 10, 2000. For more on EBC, see *The TeamNet Factor,* pp. 137–139, and *The Age of the Network,* pp. 79–85.

14. See Wit Capital at http://www.witcapital.com/company.management.jsp; Ameritrade Holding Company at http://www.amtd.com/html/about5 .html; and Sony at http://www.world.sony.com/IR/Financial/AR/1999/ Management.html.

15. Interview with Mike Howland and Carol Willett, January 20, 2000, http://www.akgroup.com. For contact information, see Chapter 4, note 19.

Chapter 3

1. Buckman Labs was founded in 1945, the year we date the birth of the Information Age (see Chapter 2).

2. "The Power of Collaborative Knowledge," speech by Robert H. Buckman, delivered at "Lessons from the Front: Putting Knowledge Sharing to Work" seminar, U.S. Department of Defense, General Pershing Room, July 28, 1999.

3. Reuben Harris is now chair of Department of Systems Management, Naval Postgraduate School, Monterey, California.

4. Buckman Laboratories (A), ©Harvard Business School, N9-899-175, Rev. September 17, 1999, p. 5.

5. Interview with Sheldon Ellis, director, Bulab Learning Center, Memphis, TN, October 7, 1999.

6. Interview with Edson Peredo, president, Buckman Laboratories International, Inc., and chairman and CEO, Buckman Laboratories, Inc., Memphis, TN, October 8, 1999.

7. For more on the importance of the span of influence, see Reuben T. Harris, "Think Spans of Influence, Not Spans of Control," *The Tom Peters Group Update 1*, no. 2 (1991).

8. As recently as the mid-1980s, the standard model of small groups required a hunt through research in anthropology, sociology, organizational psychology, and management. At that time, there was a building consensus that a small group was a coherent system that one could study independently at the crossroads of several disciplines, but it was not a well-developed field. A decade later, a search of the literature on groups and teams turns up a coherent field of research.

9. A 1996 summary of current research quotes a respected researcher's 1984 review of the literature with approval.

10. An oft-quoted research definition of teams offers the three small-group characteristics together with a task-oriented purpose: "Teams are distinguishable sets of two or more individuals who interact interdependently and adaptively to achieve specified, shared, and valued objectives." Guzzo et al., *Team Effectiveness and Decision Making in Organizations* (San Francisco: Jossey-Bass, 1995), pp. 13, 115.

11. E. F. Schumacher, *Small Is Beautiful: Economics As If People Mattered,* (HarperCollins, 1989).

12. For more on the relationship between proximity and collaboration, see Thomas J. Allen, *Managing the Flow of Technology: Technology Transfer and the Dissemination of Technological Information within the R&D Organization* (Cambridge, MA: MIT Press, 1977). Data are given in *The Age of the Network,* p. 47.

Chapter 4

1. Interview with David Sibbet, January 24, 2000. See Grove Consultants, http://www.grove.com, his company's site.

2. This quote from historian Frederic Lane, which we found in *Making Democracy Work: Civic Traditions in Modern Italy,* by Robert D. Putnam (Princeton, NJ: Princeton University Press, 1993), p. 124, originally appeared in *Venice and History,* by Frederic C. Lane (Baltimore: Johns Hopkins University Press, 1966), p. 535. We are indebted to Putnam for much of the information on which this section is based.

3. This quote from *Making Democracy Work,* p. 129, is originally from *Before the Industrial Revolution: European Society and Economy, 1000–1700,* 2d ed., by Carlo M. Cippola (London: Methuen, 1980), pp. 198–199.

4. See *The TeamNet Factor,* pp. 157–159.

5. The rise of small business networks was the "hot news" that many business writers and reviewers picked out of *The TeamNet Factor.*

6. There was enormous disparity in social services between the north and the south. For example, Emilia-Romagna had one child-care center per 400 children; Campania, in the south, had one center per 12,560 children, or 300 percent fewer.

7. For the detailed analysis of Emilia-Romagna's "good government," reporting the study's composite index of institutional performance, see *Making Democracy Work,* p. 76.

8. Social capital has been a research topic and a concept under development for more than a decade, especially in sociology. See Ronald S. Burt, *Structural Holes: The Social Structure of Competition* (Cambridge, MA: Harvard University Press, 1992), for an excellent treatment. We use Putnam's formulation here.

9. The quote on reciprocity is from *Making Democracy Work,* p. 139 (see note 3).

10. For a superb three-part series on problems in the fishing industry, see "Troubled Waters: Fishing in Crisis," by Cohn Nickerson, whose first article, "Stripping the Sea's Life" (*The Boston Sunday Globe,* April 17, 1994), jumped from p. 1 to p. 24, where it had the headline "Greed, Mismanagement Ravage Fisheries."

11. The observation that cooperation becomes increasingly rational and practical is from *The Evolution of Cooperation,* by Robert Axelrod (New York: Basic Books, 1984).

12. The quote on defection is from Robert Sugden, as quoted in *Making Democracy Work,* p. 178 (see note 1).

13. James S. Coleman, "Social Capital in the Creation of Human Capital," *American Journal of Sociology* (1988 supplement), S98.

14. See Centra at http://www.centra.com.

15. Ibid.

16. Robert D. Putnam's new book: *Bowling Alone: The Collapse and Revival of American Community* (New York: Simon & Schuster, 2000).

17. Robert D. Putnam, "Bowling Alone: America's Declining Social Capital," *Journal of Democracy 6,* no. 1 (January 1995), pp. 65–78, and "Bowling Alone, Revisited," *The Responsive Community* (spring 1995), pp. 13–33.

18. Interview with Keoki Andrus, The Launch Group (see http://www .launchgroup.com), January 14, 2000.

19. Interview with Michael H. Howland, president and CEO, Applied Knowledge Group, 11921 Freedom Drive, Suite 550, Reston, VA 20190; 703/904-0304, http://www.akgroup.com, January 20, 2000.

20. Lipnack and Stamps, *The Age of the Network,* pp. 16–17, and *The TeamNet Factor,* p. 11; Adam M. Brandenberger and Barry J. Nalebuff, *Competition: A Revolutionary Mindset That Combines Competition and Cooperation: A Game Theory Strategy That's Changing the Game of Business* (New York: Doubleday, 1996).

21. For a superb treatment of this topic, see *Regional Advantage: Culture and Competition in Silicon Valley and Route 128,* by AnnaLee Saxenian (Cambridge, MA: Harvard University Press, 1994).

22. Ibid.

23. For an extended study of Harry Brown and EBC Industries, see Lipnack and Stamps, *The TeamNet Factor,* pp. 137–139, and *The Age of the Network,* pp. 79–85.

24. See *Grassroots Leaders in the New Economy: How Civic Entrepreneurs Are Building Prosperous Communities* by Douglas Henton, John Melville, and Kimberly Walesh (San Francisco: Jossey-Bass, 1997). Henton and his colleagues did the original research that led to the formation of Joint Venture Silicon Valley Network and have served as its principal consultants since its inception. For more information, contact them at: Collaborative Economics, 350 Cambridge Avenue, Suite 200, Palo Alto, CA 94306 (phone: 650/614-0230; fax: 650/614-0240; e-mail: CoEcon@aol.com).

Chapter 5

1. Joshua Meyrowitz, *No Sense of Place: The Impact of Electronic Media on Social Behavior* (New York: Oxford University Press, 1985).
2. For information about Sun's achievements, see http://www.sun.com/dotcom/whatis/index.html.
3. Motorola was the first recipient of the Malcolm Baldrige Award, the U.S. government's quality award (see Chapter 9, "Links").
4. The definition of Java is from http://java.sun.com/nav/whatis.
5. Sun Microsystems Inc.'s groups include System Products, Enterprise Services, Storage Products, Network Service Providers, Software Products & Platforms, iPlanet, Global Sales Operations, and Customer Advocacy.
6. E-mail from Suzie Grace, communications manager, Sun Microsystems Corporate Quality, "Subject: SunTeams details & key information," January 24, 2000.
7. From an interview with Jim Lynch, vice president of Sun's Corporate Quality Office, February 9, 2000.
8. *Ping* is an acronym for "Packet Internet or Inter-Network Groper." Loosely, ping means "to get the attention of" (http://www.whatis.com/ping.htm).
9. Interview with W. R. "Bert" Sutherland, director of SunLabs, Sun Microsystems, June 17, 1996.
10. Op. cit., Meyrowitz.
11. Interview with Meta Greenberg, January 2, 2000.
12. See Etienne Wenger, *Communities of Practice: Learning, Meaning, and Identity,* Cambridge University Press, 1999, and "Communities of Practice: The Organizational Frontier," by Wenger and William M. Snyder, Harvard Business Review, January 1, 2000 (http://www.hbsp.harvard.edu/hbsp/prod_detail.asp?R00110).
13. Interview with Loree Goffigon, director, Gensler Consulting, February 14, 2000.
14. The Education Development Center was founded in 1958 by a group of MIT scientists to develop a new curriculum for high school physics. Today it is an international research and development organization "dedicated to building talent and know-how for human advancement." See http://www.edc.org.

15. Ray Grenier and George Metes, *Going Virtual: Moving Your Organization into the 21st Century* (Upper Saddle River, NJ: Prentice Hall, 1995).
16. Lipnack and Stamps, *The TeamNet Factor,* pp. 31–34.
17. See *Virtual Teams,* 1st ed. (John Wiley & Sons, 1997), pp. 176–177.
18. Kathleen K. Mall and Sirkka L. Jarvenpaa, "Learning to Work in Distributed Global Teams." This paper is available online at http://www.bus.utexas.edu/~jarvenpaa/gvt/hicss.html.

Chapter 6

1. For more on "Stressed S," see *Virtual Teams,* pp. 142–144.
2. Ludwig von Bertalauffy, *General Systems Theory: Foundations, Development, Applications* (rev. ed.) (New York: George Braziller, 1968).
3. Lipnack and Stamps, *The TeamNet Factor,* pp. 221–223.
4. Senge, *The Fifth Discipline.*
5. Technically, *slowing* is negative feedback, *growing* is positive feedback.
6. Data on number of knowledge workers is from Steelcase-sponsored research conducted by The Futures Group in 1995.
7. Interview with Earnest Deavenport, former CEO, Eastman Chemical Company, 1996.
8. Jessica Lipnack and Jeffrey Stamps, "The Virtual Water Cooler: Solving the Distance Problem in Networks," *Firm Connections 1,* no. 2, May–June 1993.

Chapter 7

1. Lipnack and Stamps, *The Age of the Network,* pp. 52–58.
2. Peter F. Drucker, "The Age of Social Transformation," *Atlantic Monthly* (November 1994), pp. 36–41.
3. Peter F. Drucker, *Management Challenges for the 21st Century,* (New York, NY: HarperBusiness, 1999), see http://www.amazon.com/exec/obidos/ASIN/0887309984/o/qid=948109643/sr=2-1/104-9714499-1728465.
4. Dean W. Tjosvold and Mary M. Tjosvold, *Leading the Team Organization: How to Create an Enduring Competitive Advantage* (New York: Macmillan, 1991); Dean W. Tjosvold, *Working Together to Get Things Done: Managing for Organizational Productivity* (Lexington, MA: D.C. Heath, 1986).

Chapter 8

1. Interview with Dr. Henry McKinnell, president and chief operating officer, Pfizer Inc., president, Pfizer Pharmaceuticals, January 19, 2000.
2. See http://www.pfizer.com/pfizerinc/about/inside/mff.html.
3. E-mail from Stewart Brand, http://www.longnow.com, "Subject: Re: Is this you?" February 27, 2000: "In fall 1984, at the first Hackers' Conference, I said in one discussion session: 'On the one hand information wants to be expensive, because it's so valuable. The right information in the right place just changes your life. On the other hand, information wants to be free, because the cost of getting it out is getting lower and lower all the time. So you have these two fighting against each other.' That was printed in a report/transcript from the conference in the May 1985, *Whole Earth Review*, p. 49." Brand also mentions this idea in *The Media Lab* (Viking-Penguin, 1987), p. 202. "Since then," he writes, "I've added nothing to the meme, and it's been living high wide and handsome on its own. I saw in a *Wired*, April '97, that Jon Katz opined on p. 186: 'The single dominant ethic in this [digital] community is that information wants to be free.' "
4. See *Reinventing Government: How the Entrepreneurial Spirit Is Transforming the Public Sector* by David Osborne and Ted Gaebler (New York: Plume/Penguin, 1993). Osborne served as a key contributor to the National Performance Review.
5. Interview with Marion Metcalf, September 1993.
6. See http://www.context.org.
7. Marion Metcalf was active in various choral groups in the Washington D.C. area and served as president of the Board of Directors of the Capitol Hill Choral Society at the time of her death.
8. Interview with Bob Stone, January 27, 2000.
9. Andy Campbell, who served on the National Performance Review, came up with the name in a brainstorming session at the meeting.
10. To obtain a list of National Performance Review materials, send a one-line e-mail message via the Internet to almanac@esusda.gov with the following text: "send npr catalog," or send a letter via U.S. mail to National Performance Review, 750 17th Street NW, Washington, DC 20006 (phone: 202/632-0150).

11. In addition to the contacts listed in note 2, NetResults information is available on MetaNet (phone: 703/243-6622); CAPACCESS, an electronic service provided by George Washington University (phone: 202/986-2065); and Fed World, a U.S. Department of Commerce service (phone: 703/487-4608).

12. Interview with Bob Stone, January 27, 2000.

13. "INS: Integrated Card Production System," in "It Pioneers: The 21 winners of the Government Technology Leadership Awards forge into the IT frontier," by Joshua Dean, GovExec.com, December 1999, http://www .govexec.com/features/1299/1299s6.htm.

14. E-mail from Al Gilman, "Subject: Why you want to tell the story of Marion's award," January 21, 2000. See http://www.w3.org/WAI/PF.

15. "What Are We Going to Do with(out) Marion?" Eulogy by Larry Metcalf at her memorial service, December 17, 1999.

16. See Caucus at http://www.caucus.com.

17. E-mail from Jennifer Sutton, "Subject: Re: How are you and Al's e-mail," January 11, 2000. Sutton read poems at Marion Metcalf's memorial service.

18. Arthur Koestler, *The Ghost in the Machine* (London: Hutchinson & Co., 1967). The holon has been part of our conceptual family for three decades now. Jeff found the hierarchy concept so pervasive in the systems literature, and the word *holon* so elegant in capturing the essence of the idea, that he titled his doctoral dissertation (and his 1980 book by the same name) *Holonomy,* which means "the study of holons." The holon "wholepart" was first among the 10 principles of our first two books. Although we had sharpened the principles to five in *The TeamNet Factor* and *The Age of the Network,* in both books we reintroduced the holon idea at the very end as part of the underlying systems framework supporting the network principles.

19. Herbert Simon, "The Architecture of Complexity," *Proceedings of the American Philosophical Society,* 1962.

20. Luther P. Gerlach and Virginia Hine, *People, Power, Change: Movements of Social Transformation* (New York: Bobbs-Merrill, 1970).

21. Allen W. Johnson and Timothy Earle, *The Evolution of Human Societies: From Foraging Group to Agrarian State* (Palo Alto, CA: Stanford University Press, 1987), p. 52.

22. This is known as *metonomy* in that branch of cognitive science that looks at thinking through the categories (mental models) we use.

23. Lipnack and Stamps, *The Age of the Network,* p. 84, and *The TeamNet Factor,* pp. 47–49.

24. Glenn M. Parker, *Team Players and Teamwork: The New Competitive Business Strategy* (San Francisco: Jossey-Bass, 1991), p. 53.

25. See *Virtual Leadership.*

26. Johnson and Earle, *The Evolution of Human Societies,* p. 320.

27. Lipnack and Stamps, *The TeamNet Factor,* p. 13.

28. Research has repeatedly demonstrated the inverted U–shaped relationship between size and performance. Paul S. Goodman and Associates, *Designing Effective Work Groups* (San Francisco: Jossey-Bass, 1986), p. 16.

29. Robert Reich, "Entrepreneurship Reconsidered: The Team as Hero," *Harvard Business Review* (May–June 1987).

Chapter 9

1. The "only connect" quote is from *Howards End,* by E. M. Forster (London: Edward Arnold, 1910).

2. See http://www.icimod.org.sg/general/brochure1.htm.

3. E-mail from Mohan Kumar, via Dennis Roberson at Motorola, "Subject: Re: Geo? Again," January 31, 2000.

4. A T1 line is a high-speed digital connection capable of transmitting data at 1.5 million bits per second.

5. See ICIMOD site, note 2 above.

6. See *Tools for Thought* by Howard Rheingold (MIT Press, 2000) at http://www.rheingold.com/texts/tft/1.html.

7. Interview with Howard Rheingold, January 21, 2000.

8. *New Rules for the New Economy: 10 Radical Strategies for a Connected World* by Kevin Kelly (Penguin USA, October 1999).

9. We first met Roberson face-to-face at NCR's "Great Performers" recognition event in Barcelona, Spain, in April 1997.

10. Technically, this high-speed, high-bandwidth connection is called a *switched T1 line.*

11. From Groupe Speciale Mobile (French) that came up with the global digital standard (Global System for Mobile Communications), now adopted in more than 200 countries in Europe, Asia, and Africa. See GSM http://www.tmtouch.com.my/corporate/gsm.html.

12. Marshall McLuhan, *Understanding Media: The Extensions of Man* (New York: McGraw-Hill, 1964).

13. Interview with Terry Heng, Global Software, Motorola, January 28, 2000.

14. Nicholas Negroponte, *Being Digital* (New York: Knopf, 1995).

15. In 1989, Digital, bought by Compaq in 1997, had 150,000 employees, $13 billion in revenues, and the largest private computer network in the world.

16. For more information on the use of the word *matrix*, see Matrix Information and Directory Services at http://www.matrix.org.

17. William Issacs, *Dialogue and the Art of Thinking Together: A Pioneering Approach to Communicating in Business and Life* (Doubleday, 1999).

Chapter 10

1. Interview with Carol Willett, executive vice president, Innovation and Learning, Applied Knowledge Group, January 20, 2000.

2. Guzzo, Salas, and Associates, *Team Effectiveness and Decision Making in Organizations.*

Chapter 11

1. See *Learning After Doing, Another New Way of Working from The Network Learning & Support Center,* copyright © 1999, Shell Oil Company.

2. See http://www.teamflow.com for an example of deployment flowcharting.

Chapter 12

1. See *A Pattern Language,* by Christopher Alexander et al. (Oxford, England: Oxford University Press, 1977).

2. Arthur Koestler, *The Ghost in the Machine* (London: Hutchinson & Co., 1967). The holon has been part of our conceptual family for three

decades now. Jeff found the hierarchy concept so pervasive in the systems literature, and the word *holon* so elegant in capturing the essence of the idea, that he titled his doctoral dissertation (and his 1980 book by the same name) *Holonomy,* which means "the study of holons." The holon "wholepart" was first among the 10 principles of our first two books. Although we had sharpened the principles to five in *The Team-Net Factor* and *The Age of the Network,* in both books we reintroduced the holon idea at the very end as part of the underlying systems framework supporting the network principles.

3. Ludwig von Bertalauffy, *General Systems Theory: Foundations, Development, Applications* (rev. ed.) (New York: George Braziller, 1968).

Chapter 13

1. George Boole, *The Laws of Thought* (New York: Dover Publications, Inc., 1958).
2. *When Wizards Stay Up Late,* by Katie Hafner and Matthew Lyon (Touchstone, 1998), p. 27.
3. Ibid., 38.
4. For more information on Doug Engelbart's work, contact the Bootstrap Institute, 6505 Kaiser Drive, Fremont, CA 94555 (phone: 510-713-3550; e-mail: info@bootstrap.org; and see the Bootstrap Institute at http://www .bootstrap.org).
5. "A Conceptual Framework for the Augmentation of Man's Intellect," by Douglas Engelbart. See http://bootstrap.org/biblio.htm#04.
6. See *The Network Nation: Human Connection via Computer,* by Starr Roxanne Hiltz, Murray Turoff and Suzanne Keller.
7. George Lakoff, *Women, Fire, and Dangerous Things: What Categories Reveal about the Mind* (Chicago: University of Chicago Press, 1987).
8. See *Holonomy,* p. 13, for Rapoport reference.
9. See *Metaphors We Live By,* by George Lakoff and Mark Johnson (University of Chicago Press, 1983).
10. In the literature, this is called "source-path-goal."
11. Mark Johnson, *The Body in the Mind: The Bodily Basis of Meaning, Imagination, and Reason* (Chicago: University of Chicago Press).

Chapter 14

1. Olaf Stapledon, *Star Maker* (New York: Dover Publications, Inc., 1937).
2. For more information on the SETI project, see http://www.seti.org.
3. See John Lawrence at http://www.manageforresults.com and http://home.att.net/~jeslawrence/jeslawrencehomepage.html.
4. The Great Plains Partnership (GPP) was initiated by then-governor Mike Hayden of Kansas under the auspices of the Western Governors' Association, which maintains an active role in the group. For more information about GPP, see its home page: http://rrbin.cfa.org/rrbin/gpp/gpphome.html.
5. We thank David Williams of High Point, North Carolina, for sending us the article, "A Timely Warning to the Developed World" by Michael Valpy, *The Globe and Mail,* December 17, 1993, p. A2, from which the quote on social capital was taken.
6. Ashby's seminal article "Variety, Constraint, and the Law of Requisite Variety," drawn from his book, *An Introduction to Cybernetics* (London: Chapman and Hall, 1956), appears in *Modern Systems Research for the Behavioral Scientist: A Sourcebook,* edited by Walter Buckley (Chicago: Aldine, 1968), p. 129.
7. For the basis of this important concept, see "The Strength of Weak Ties," by Mark S. Granovetter, *American Journal of Sociology,* vol. 78, no. 6, pp. 1360–1380.
8. See *Structural Holes* (see note 13) for a similar idea that helps to maximize the efficiency and effectiveness of networks.
9. For more on Frank Starmer's global "lab without walls," see *The Age of the Network,* pp. 21–24.

ABOUT THE AUTHORS

Jessica Lipnack and **Jeffrey Stamps, Ph.D.,** are the world's leading experts in virtual teams and networked organizations. For over 20 years, they have consulted, lectured, conducted seminars, and have been widely published. They have launched virtual organizations (teams) for Fortune 100 companies, small and medium-sized businesses, nonprofit organizations, government agencies, major religious denominations, and educational institutions.

Lipnack and Stamps are cofounders and directors of NetAge Inc., developers of virtualteams.com®. The company was founded in 1998 to bring their "peopleware" methodologies to virtual teams and organizations of all sizes.

Virtual Teams: People Working Across Boundaries with Technology is their sixth book. For more information:

NetAge Inc.
505 Waltham Street
West Newton, MA 02465
Voice: 617.965.3340
Fax: 617.965.2341
E-mail: info@virtualteams.com
Web: www.virtualteams.com

INDEX